D0940345

How To Have It All!

IMPORTANT NOTICE

This publication is designed to provide valuable information. It is sold with the understanding that the publisher or author is not engaged in rendering legal, accounting, or other professional service. If legal advise or other assistance is required, the service of a competent professional should be sought.

The author and publishers disclaim any personal loss or liability caused by utilization of any information presented in this book. Claims of liability, if any, shall be limited to the amount paid for the book less the amount paid for postage and handling.

Printed in the United States of America
0 9 8 7 6 5 4 3 2 1

-TABLE OF CONTENTS-

CHAPTER 4 - PAY LESS TAXES

CHAPTER 5 - INVESTMENT SECRETS

CHAPTER 6 - TRAVEL SECRETS

CHAPTER 10 - YOUR FAMILY

CHAPTER 11 - INNER STRENGTH

CHAPTER 12 - HEALTHFUL HEALING

CHAPTER 15 - TRIM HEALTH-CARE COSTS

CHAPTER 16 - MORE INVESTMENT SECRETS

CHAPTER 17 - LEGAL AND ESTATE-PLANNING

CHAPTER 23 - CONSUMER SAVINGS

CHAPTER 24 - CHEAP AND FREE!

CHAPTER 25 - HOLIDAY AND TRAVEL

Introduction

So you want to have it all? Well here's your chance! What you hold in your hands is a wide variety of extremely helpful, little-known and highly credible information.

Whatever you seek, chances are you'll find an answer in this book. It took months and months to dig for the right answers. If it's financial help you need, you got it. Marriage giving you trouble, just check inside. Need some job advice, no problem. You are guaranteed to find so much "hot stuff" you'll be amazed. You'll be a walking reference book for your family and friends.

You'll learn to shop like never before. You'll find out how to have prices slashed no matter what it's for from a college education to home repairs. Much of this information is likely to upset a lot of people. Because it's information many companies and industries hope you never find out. Doctors will miss you because you'll be taking care of yourself. The repair man will not get rich from you. And you'll be all the wiser.

How To Have It All!

Where else will you find so much good information in one place? In this book you'll find information for living life effectively. It's a struggle for everyone to get over life's obstacles. This book is designed to carry you over them like never before.

You'll be healthier, more successful, smarter, a better spouse, parent and friend, and richer. It's all true if you pay close attention to the gold mine of secrets inside. Good luck!

Chapter

Building Your Future   ①

How investment advisors can steal your money:

I t's no secret, investment advisors are salesmen at heart. They make a living from your investment. You invest, they make money. So how do you avoid letting them steal your money? Easy.

You can start by following these 3 guidelines:

1) Ask to see the paper work: Never purchase anything without having your advisor show you the prospectus. Many times advisors will try to push you to buy a "hot" stock, bond etc. However, if there is no paper work out on it consider it no good.

2) Be careful of broker fees: If your advisor recommends something that will be successful only if it is invested and reinvested many times -- be careful. What you don't see is the fee he is paid every time he does that. If he often tells you your stock is falling and to sell, and at the same time tells you to buy another stock, this is called churning. There is no guarantee for you, but your broker makes a lot of money.

3) Shop around: An investment firm's main source of income is money that accumulates from you and others that they hold and invest again. They make billions on the interest. When you invest in Ginnie Maes and other low interest securities, they pay you a small rate, but make money on your interest. Always shop around to get the highest interest on your money within your risk tolerance.

Always remember an advisor/broker is helping you because it's to his advantage so he can collect a commission. Stay away from advisors who try to push you into certain investments. Do your own homework first and ask his advice, but never let him make the final decision. Plenty of people have gone belly up because they took bad advice from an advisor who had only his best interest in mind.

The truth about treasury bills:

If you're going to buy a government bill you can save 3-5% by doing it yourself instead of going through a broker. Treasury bills are sold at auctions on Mondays. To buy, you must have the full $10,000 purchase price up front. To buy one call or send a letter to the nearest Federal Reserve Bank branch. You will be sent a letter of receipt. You will also receive a refund for the government discount. You also can borrow up to 90% of a treasury bill's value from the bank which you deposit it in. Which is good if you need the money in a hurry.

However ...

If you have $10,000 dollars of disposable income to invest you can often find CDs that will offer the same risk and can earn more than a treasury bond in the same amount of time.

Insider tip: You can buy the T- bill, borrow up to 90% of it's value -- and use this extra money to invest in a higher risk, potential reward investment. That way all the risk is not on the T-bill alone.

Contact your nearest Federal Reserve Branch for details.

Atlanta
104 Marietta Street,
NW Atlanta, GA 30303
(404) 521-8653

Boston
P.O. Box 2076
Boston, MA 02106
(617) 973-3800

Cleveland
P.O. Box 6387
Cleveland, OH
(216) 579-2000

Houston
1701 San Jacinto Street
Houston, TX 78346
(713) 659-4433

Los Angeles
P.O. Box 2077
Terminal Annex
Los Angeles, CA 90051
(213) 624-7398

Miami
P.O. Box 520847
Miami, FL 33152
(305) 471-6257

New York
Federal Reserve
P.O. Station
New York, NY 10045
(212) 720-5823

Salt Lake City
P.O. Box 30780
Salt Lake City, UT 84130
(801) 322-7882

Seattle
P.O. Box 3567
Seattle, WA 98124
(206) 343-3615

Make $50,000 a year part-time with real estate:

Fortunes can be made ... and fortunes can be lost just as easily! Real estate is historically the only constantly stable investment. Chances are if you buy real estate, you will be able to sell it for a profit 10 years later or even 1 year later. My wife and I bought a home in Salt Lake City for $67,000 and sold it 3 months later for $77,000! It can be done. Chances are the real estate market will never be dead as some experts predict. Real estate is still the most sound investment for your money. Perhaps the real income comes from owning property and renting it out for a profit. Or buying low and investing some money into fixing it up for a profit.

You've probably heard the 3 rules of real estate; location, location, location. If you're buying to use as a rental, make sure it's close enough that you can always keep on top of it. When buying any piece of real estate always consider it's location. If it's been for sale for a long time and it's priced right, it's probably not selling because of where it is. Important: Houses on busy roads or in bad areas may present a problem when you try to sell them.

A great place to buy real estate dirt cheap is from government auctions. They seize property and unload it for a fraction of its value. Which you could immediately turn around and sell for a profit.

You can contact the GSA for details on obtaining discount U.S. seized property by calling (800) 472-1313. Or write to

Consumer Information Center
Department 514A
Pueblo, CO 81009

Ask for a free copy of their sales list. Also, you can contact one of these regional offices:

Office of Real Estate Sales, U.S. GSA
10 Causeway Street
Boston, MA 02222
(617) 556-5700

Office of Real Estate Sales, U.S. GSA
Peachtree Summit Building
401 West Peachtree Street
Atlanta, GA 30365
(404) 331-5133

Office of Real Estate Sales, U.S. GSA
819 Taylor Street
Ft. Worth, TX 76102
(817) 334-2331

Office of Real Estate Sales, U.S. GSA
525 Market Street
San Francisco, CA 94105
(415) 744-5952

Making money in real estate is as simple as this: Buy low, sell high. And doing this isn't hard.

The two ways to make the most money with the least work are:

1) Do some homework. Select an area that has a rising market. Preferably one that has been down for a long time that is experiencing a boom.

Insider Tip: Don't ever choose what appears to be the best property in the neighborhood. Because when you go to sell it, it will be appraised at the market value of the ones surrounding it and may bring the value down.

2) Buying to rent. This allows you the freedom of paying off the mortgage while the house appreciates with no money from your pocket. And if the rent is higher than the payment, you have a steady profit.

The key here is in choosing renters. Renters often have a bad reputation of damaging property. Because they don't own, they don't care about it. Offer some sort of incentive (like extra money) even beyond a security deposit to keep it in good shape when they move out. It pays off to be in close proximity to the property so you can act quickly in case of emergency repairs or other problems.

This is the easiest way to make extra money on the side. Depending on the housing market in the area, your equity will continue to increase with little work or money from you.

How to protect your assets from a lawsuit:

These days people will do anything for a buck. Including suing you for everything you've got. Assuming you are not at fault, or not at as much fault as the plaintiff claims, there are things you can do to protect yourself and preserve your assets.

From just about any insurance company for only 100 to 200 dollars a year, you can get an umbrella policy for 1-2 million dollars in coverage for any type of lawsuit. This is the cheapest and best protection around.

Over 50% of couples will get divorced. Even those who are least likely to get divorced -- get divorced. If a divorce ends in a messy fight over property a business, homes, cars, etc. it could all be split 50-50 no matter who owned them previously. If you have a large estate that could be lost in a divorce, your best defense is a prenuptial agreement that you both sign before you get married. This essentially says in the event of a divorce, the two parties will retain possession of what was theirs before marriage. Most lawyers can assist you with this.

It is always a good idea to put things involving property in writing. This way if someone tries to sue you, you can produce a written agreement on the terms.

How to avoid credit counseling
and debt consolidation ripoff:

The very last thing you need when debt is hampering your life is a bad credit counselor to rip you off. Credit counselors can be a big help. For a small -- or no -- fee they will help you and your creditors work out a payment plan. They will keep creditors off your back, and help you consolidate to pay off your debt. This can be a fantastic service that will take some stress out of your life.

But Beware! While there are those services that truly want to and will help -- there are plenty that will only make things worse.

Many of them advertise on TV and display a 900 number. Stay away! When you call you'll be charged $3-$5 dollars a minute which could cost you $40-$50 dollars just to get some initial information. Then they will charge you an additional $250-$500 fee to do work for you. And all you'll find out is what you just learned.

To find a reputable and helpful credit counselor you can write:

National Foundation for Consumer Credit
8611 Second Ave., Suite 100
Silver Springs, MD 20910

Also, if you need help with debt consolidation and structuring payment reduction plans the company below offers FREE help.

Budget Acceptance Co.
P.O. Box 970
Bozeman, MT 59771
1-800-735-0443

Secrets for getting a loan or credit:

Today getting a loan or credit is painless and easy unless you have black marks on your credit report. This will cause bank and credit card companies to turn you away immediately. Why? They fear that you won't be able to pay them back and would rather not hassle with trying to collect the money from you. They want to be sure you are ready, willing and able to make payments. So you have 2 courses of action:

1) Work to develop an A+ credit rating.

These are things banks are looking for:
1. A positive and current credit rating.
2. Home ownership.
3. An American Express or Diners Club card.
4. More than a year at your current job.
5. At least one fully paid or current bank loan.
6. A Visa or Mastercard.
7. Current department store accounts.
8. A telephone in your name.

The more things you can check off on the list, the better your chances are of getting the money you want.

It also helps to always do all your banking at the same bank. Use it for your checking and savings account, safe deposit box and any other loans you may have. This will establish a relationship with the bank and its employees. When you go to ask for a loan dress your best and ask to work with the bank manager. If you have been a good customer they will give you what you need even if you've had problems in the past.

There are always credit cards available, but with a price. Most credit companies are willing to give you a card if you have a less than perfect credit history, but will do so at a higher than normal rate. So shop around and see what's available.

Do everything you can to clean up your credit report. Anytime you ask for a loan or credit, that's what is going to be looked at. Check it for mistakes, errors or old accounts with wrong information. You can obtain a credit report for free. TRW offers one free credit report a year. Write to:

TRW Consumer Assistance
P.O. Box 2350
Chatsworth, CA 91313.

Be sure to include your full name (with middle initial), your spouse's name, Social Security numbers, birth dates, current address, copy of your driver's license.

The #2 company will charge you $8 dollars for your credit report. Call 1-800- 685-1111.

2) Some other things you can try are:

    1. Use a co-signer. Ask a friend or family member.
    2. Ask the lender what you need to do to qualify. They will never volunteer their flexibility.
    3. Keep trying. Each lender is different. Some want your business, some don't.

How to borrow $20,000 in 24 hours:

You're a lot closer to having $20,000 or more than you think! And the secret is timing. Getting it is easy, but you are best off if you have a plan for paying it back.

Here's how to do it. Get a list of 20 banks in your area. And be prepared to spend a day "collecting." Unless you are well-off and have a spotless credit record, no one bank is going to lend you $20,000. But several banks will lend you $2-3,000 without much problem. If you go to 20 banks and collect $2,000 from 10 of them -- there's $20,000. And here's the trick.

It takes 2-3 days to process a loan and have it show up on a credit report. So when every bank you go to checks your credit, nothing will show up. You can go to as many bank as you like, but none of them will have record of your previous loans.

Now you must realize, just as your available credit is immediate, so is the payment. Your reason for doing this should be to use the available money to somehow turn a profit. In which case you can pay off all your debts and keep the rest.

One true story is of a man who did this to buy discount house siding from a wholesaler to mark up and resell for a profit. He took his $20,000 dollar loan and turned it into $60,000 in a matter of days. He had done his homework and lined up buyers before he ever borrowed the money. So beware! What is borrowed must be returned. But getting it is simple.

How to cosign a loan and still not be liable:

It's not always the best idea to be a co-signer. And if you really have to, the better you know the person and his ability to be responsible, the more likely you are to never be involved beyond just signing your name. Here are 3 ways to keep yourself from getting stuck with someone else's debt.

1) Retain something of value: Have the person give you something that has value. This way even if they default you'll have something as collateral. It could be coins, jewelry antiques, etc.

2) Co-sign assets not cash: If you co-sign on a house, boat, car etc., there is property to give back and you come out O.K. However if it's just a cash loan, the person could spend every nickel of it and default. Then you're in trouble because there is nothing to return.

3) Instead of co-signing, just buy the property outright or get the loan yourself and "rent" it to the person. Now you are in control and everybody gets what they want. And if the person doesn't pay you, make it clear that you'll sell it. There may even be reason to mark it up and make a small profit to make up for depreciation.

How to avoid lump sum retirement distribution mistakes:

When the time comes to retire there is the possibility of taking it all in a lump sum. This way it's yours to do as you wish. However there are rules. And the biggest one is that once you declare yourself retired and receive your cash, you cannot work full or part time and receive a salary or pay from the company you were working for. If you do, your lump sum is fully taxable and you will watch much of it disappear. If you need to still be affiliated, resign and have them hire you back as an independent consultant.

Secrets for successful retirement planning:

The best thing you can do for a successful retirement is to start today. No matter what it is. If the very least you can do is put $5 dollars a month away, then do it. If you're young, even that will provide something since you're starting early. And hopefully that amount will grow as you increase your income.

Unless you want to be destitute and working until you're 80 you should consider the following.

If you are 30 years old and put away $300 dollars a month in a mutual fund or other interest bearing investment, by the time you retire you'll have a whopping $1.5 million! Sounds good huh? The problem for most people is putting it away, and using it before retirement. It takes lots of planning and some willpower to make it successful. Also, to see the effects of waiting, if you start at 40 years old, and put away the same $300 dollars a month, by age 65 you'll only have $400,000. It pays to start early.

Here are 5 tips to help you retire in comfort:

1) Make plans now: Many successful people are so because they had a dream or a vision that they kept in their heads. Its hard to fail when you have a determination to reach a goal. Think about the kind of lifestyle you want to live and where you want to live. What do you want to do? And what do you think it will cost? Always keep these thoughts in mind and convince yourself of how it will be. Soon you'll find yourself working towards that goal and successfully achieving it.

2) Start saving now: Everyday you wait, you lose more money you could be earning in interest. The good thing about retirement is that you have years and years to plan and save. No matter how small a monthly contribution to a retirement fund, it will still earn interest. And interest adds up to make a worry-free retirement.

3) Invest wisely: Don't sell yourself short by just sticking money in a savings account. Because you have a long time to save, you should put your money in something that will grow over time. Be sure it's something safe, yet growing substantially. Most financial planning businesses will sit down with you for free and help you decide the best place for your money.

4) Pick a target date: Do you really want to retire at 65? Many are waiting longer these days. Or maybe you think you'll be well off and can retire sooner. Set a realistic date and start planing for it. It may even help to pick a date sooner. Say 5 years earlier. This way when the time comes maybe you'll be ready. If not you have a 5 year cushion to work with.

5) Playing catch-up: Are you in your 40's or 50's and haven't started yet? Well don't worry. Just get on with it. You're not alone. Most people are cash poor with only about $11,000 in assets when they retire. If you fall into this group of people who have a dismal outlook for retirement, here's what you can do.

1) Drop your life insurance: This may be taking up a large part of your money. Replace it with an inexpensive term policy. This should free up more money to put away and reinvest.

2) Start a tax deferred savings plan: Such as an IRA or 401(k). This comes out before taxes and will grow at a faster rate.

You can also check on the status of your social security. To forecast how much you will have at retirement call 1-800-772-1213.

NOTES

_____

_____

_____

_____

_____

_____

_____

_____

_____

_____

_____

_____

_____

Chapter
_____

On-The-Job-Advice

2

The best careers for 1996-2005:

Today's work force is drastically different than it was 10 years ago. Terms like corporate downsizing, buy-outs, mergers and trimming are commonly heard on the evening news. And it ultimately spells out-of-a-job for millions of people. There is no more job security, no corporate careers. The good ones are hard to find. With the way the world is changing there are careers that will be hot and in demand.

So here are your 11 best career moves for today and beyond.

1) Electronic Engineering: By the year 2000 it is estimated the U.S. will need 40% more electrical engineers. With the rapid advancement in technology, more trained people are needed to develop and test new products. Starting salary - $30-$35,000, top level $75-$90,000.

2) Nursing: America's nursing ranks are dwindling. Especially private care nurses. With the Baby boomers advancing in age, the senior citizens population will explode in the next ten years, putting a huge demand on health care professionals. Starting salary - $25-$30,000, top level $50-$65,000.

3) Systems Analyst: With all the computers in business today, it takes a lot of work to maintain them and keep them running properly. With some businesses so reliant on their computers, it can be a stressful job. Because down-time is lost profits. Starting salary - $25-$30,000, top level $60-$65,000.

4) Environmental Engineering: This is a new field cropping up because of the deteriorating condition of the earth. These engineers research the effects industry has on the earth and how to control pollution and ensure a safe, clean environment. Starting salary - $25-$30,000, top level $70-$85,000.

5) Industrial Hygiene: New legislation demands higher standards for pollution and waste treatment. There is a need for people to keep industrial manufacturing clean and healthy. Starting salary - $28-$33,000, top level $125-$130,000.

6) Loan Workout Specialists: Believe it or not the savings and loan disaster of the 80's is still having an effect today. With so many accounts going into default, people are needed to restructure and reschedule delinquent loans. Jobs are available with banks and other financial institutions. Starting salary - $31-$40,000, top level $75-$80,000.

7) Compliance Officers: This high-growth industry keeps track of all the new laws and new federal regulations. They are hired to make sure businesses are keeping to the laws and following the government instructions. Starting salary - $35-$40,000, top level $90-$100,000.

8) Food Distribution Managers: Food sales to nursing homes alone were in excess of $2 billion dollars last year and expected to increase. People are hired to move food to where it's needed quickly. Plus, determine how much is needed by any one buyer. Which could be the military, hospital, schools etc. Starting salary - $22-$25,000, top level $40-$45,000.

9) Forensic Accountants: Money cops. These people dig around the paperwork of bankrupt companies to look for fraud, unpaid taxes, insider trading and overvalued assets. Starting salary - $30-$35,000, top level $125,000 and up.

10) Health Designers: These professionals redesign homes and offices to meet the people's needs who occupy them. Especially with the large number of elderly who choose to stay home instead of be in a nursing home. Starting salary - $25-$30,000, top level $75,000 and up.

11) Computer Security Specialists: There is much to be lost when sensitive data is stored on a company's computer system. These people reduce the risk of theft and tampering of the systems. Starting salary - $30-$35,000 top level $80,000 and up for real geniuses.

Any of these require a college degree. But not always. I know a man who has made millions in direct marketing with a high school degree and a self developed talent. Any college will provide valuable resources for you to see where you really shine.

Careers to avoid:

Many factories aren't filled with people any more. They've been replaced by robots and computers. These are some careers you may want to think twice about before entering.

Manufacturing: Like you're read, technology is replacing jobs that people once had on assembly lines and so forth. And if a company could, they would replace all the people with machines because they work for free, don't require health insurance and never complain.

Auto mechanic: Most new cars being produced today are running for 100,000 miles before the manufacturer suggests a tuneup. As materials get better, cars are lasting longer with fewer breakdowns. It could put a damper on the auto mechanic trade in the future.

Person-to-person sales: It costs an average of $212 to send a sales man out on a sales call. With direct marketing, phones, faxes and the Internet, the market place is coming closer and person-to-person sales is becoming too expensive to maintain.

The main thing to keep in mind is that to make a decent living in the world you need to have a higher education. Employers are looking for a degree that says you are smart enough and determined enough to stick with something and succeed.

How to push your resume to the top of the stack:

When job hunting, you can't afford not have your resume be a shining portrayal of yourself. Or else it will immediately be filed in the round file. You must use your resume as a tool to convince an employer -- sight unseen -- that you are the very best person for the job.

There are several important tips when preparing a resume.

1) Keep it short: 1 page is the best. If you have a lot of work experience to include, 2 pages will do. Remember, the people looking at resumes are busy. They don't want to read a novel when the next one on the stack is short and concise.

2) Use lots of white space: No long paragraphs. Indent, use bullets and space between everything. Don't make it too wordy. Be sharp and clear with your words. This is a bare bones account of your working life only. Not a detailed history.

3) Use quality paper: Use 20-24 pound stock. You can almost count on every other resume being on white or cream paper. Put yours on a light blue or green with a similar envelope. This way you can reference the "resume on blue paper" when speaking with your potential employer. Don't use loud, gaudy paper, it will have the opposite effect.

4) Never lie: Don't even embellish too much. Of course, you want to look good. But executives who've read hundreds of resumes can see right through the fluff. If you flipped hamburgers at Mcdonalds, don't put "chef in popular restaurant." Be honest.

5) Be positive: Don't put bad experiences or other tragic events. Only those which helped put you in a position to be better qualified for this job.

6) Make it perfect: Never, ever, leave a typo or error in your resume. It indicates sloppy work and that you're too lazy to check your work. Give it to someone to look at for you and make it error-free.

7) Be detailed and specific: Include previous job locations, times of employment, and what you did. List your responsibilities.

Other tips to remember:

Make sure your name, address and phone number are at the top.

Always list work experience first and education second. List education from highest to lowest. Do not go lower than a high school education.

Always be prepared to provide references. But on the resume put "references available on request."

If you have room, list special skills, hobbies and interests. Also, these days, being computer literate is important. If you are, list what programs you are proficient in.

If you're applying for more than one position, make different versions of your resume for each position.

Always put an objective statement at the very top under your name and address.

Always include a cover letter telling in clear language what qualifies you for this job and more importantly, what you will do for the company that hires you.

How to make $500 just for reading:

Sounds too good to be true doesn't it? Well it's not at all. This is a virtually work-free way to make some extra cash. Reader's Digest will pay $500 dollars to anyone who submits a story that is used in their magazine. Anecdotes are their favorite. Stories from school, funny military stories, stories from work. Anything that is amusing. You can also scan newspapers for things. And also misspelled classifieds that are funny. Keep your eyes open and see what you can find. There's no limit to how many you can submit.

Send your type written story to:

Reader's Digest
Box LL, Pleasantville, NY 10570

How to get a raise:

The first thing you must do is ask yourself some questions.

1) Do I deserve a raise?
2) Have I been there for a long period of time without getting a raise?
3) Was I promised one upon hiring and not gotten it?

If you answer "yes" to one or more of these questions then it's time to get to work and get the raise you deserve.

Timing is very important. Rushing into a boss's office and demanding a raise is never the way to approach it. Instead, ask if you can talk to him. Set an appointment if necessary. Make it for a time when he or she will be calm. Perhaps in the morning before the stress of the day builds up.

State your reasons for deserving a raise. If it was promised, point that out. Point out other accomplishments or contributions you have made. Point out your diligence and dedication and what you've done to help the company succeed.

If you are getting a new job, the best time to talk about a raise is your first day. Set a goal. Decide with your boss when a performance review will be done to get a raise.

Take into consideration the company's cash flow and the health of your industry. Is there money for a raise? Be aware of how the company is doing.

If you're told no, don't quit (unless that seems the best alternative). Instead ask when you can come and talk about it again. Perhaps after the next review. Whatever you do don't get mad or damage a good boss-employee relationship.

How to overcome office politics:

Climbing the corporate ladder can lead many people to lay their ethics aside and do whatever it takes. It can be very frustrating for those who have chosen to be the best employee they can be and hope for the best. Use these 12 guidelines to stay on top.

1) Don't get to involved with any one clique in the office. Keep in touch with all of them.

2) Listen to office gossip. But avoid spreading it. It is a good source of information but not always credible.

3) Look for a mentor. Someone who has some seniority but is still among the working ranks. Try do what that person is doing successfully.

4) Don't try to be the boss's favorite. This will only get you resentment from your peers. Instead, do all you can to help your boss succeed. But don't make it your goal to be there every time he turns around.

5) Going over the boss's head. Proceed with caution! Whether you're right or wrong, this could quickly put you out of a job, or at the very least get you black listed. If you feel you should, make absolutely sure you have sufficient reason to so it. And carefully weigh the consequences.

6) Moving up: To move up the corporate ladder you must be aware of who could move and leave a spot for you to fill. Once you get wind of those opportunities, let your superior know that you would like to be considered and why.

7) Be willing to help: Learn a little about everyone's job. This will enable you to help out in a pinch. And it will make you more flexible and "job-smart." That's what employers like to see in a person. It will get you noticed without coming off as an aggressive job stealer.

8) Learn the unwritten company polices and rules. All companies have them and are sometimes more important than the written ones. It's your job to learn them and don't count on anyone to teach you. Learn them and adhere to them. It will save you from making costly mistakes.

9) Ask a top executive in the company how to get ahead. This is the best person to ask because they've already done it.

10) Be thick skinned. It's not worth it to take personally what fellow workers say or do to you. Just let it go. It's about them not you.

11) Make sure you get credit for what you do. You must speak up sometimes because there are always those who are more than willing to take credit for your good work. And that could cost you a promotion.

12) Be ethical. You must decide beforehand what you will and won't do, and stick to it. You may be put in a situation that you don't feel right about. It's easier to decide if you already have thought about how far you'll go for your company or boss.

NOTES

_____

_____

_____

_____

_____

_____

_____

_____

_____

_____

_____

_____

_____

_____

Chapter

Money Savers

3

How to collect
from Social Security at any age:

You don't have to be 65 to collect Social Security. You can be any age -- even a child. But you have to know the secrets of collecting. Here are the ways you can collect from Social Security at any age.

1) If you have a parent that died before collecting. If they paid in and earned 40 points, you are eligible to collect their benefits. The same is true if you have a spouse that dies.

2) If at any age you become disabled, you can collect Social Security. If you make more that $500 dollars a month, you will not qualify. You must be examined to make sure you qualify. If your spouse becomes disabled and you are over 65 or have children under 16 you can collect Social Security.

How to get the most
from your insurance policy and pay the least:

There's only one thing that hurts more than shelling out thousands of dollars a year to insure you, your family, your car, house and everything else -- that's not having insurance when you need it. That can cost you a fortune and put you in financial trouble for the rest of your life. We all hate to pay the premiums year after year, especially if we never collect on them. But it's a necessary part of life.

Here's some tips to getting the most bang for your insurance buck:

Before we go into specifics on insurances you must know these fundamental rules of thumb. Always shop around. This is the best way to get the most for your money. Call 10 companies no matter what you're looking for. Keep track of their rates and compare. You'll find that one company may be just as good and have much lower rates. Never settle for the first rate you're quoted.

And one more thing, remember that an insurance company is only a business. They want to keep their money as much as you do. So make sure they spell out the policy and make sure it has everything you want. Or else when it comes time to make a claim, they'll do everything they can to fight it.

Auto insurance: Auto insurance tends to higher in proportion to other insurances. That's why as stated earlier, shop around. You are guaranteed to have it pay off. The best way to save money is to be a "low risk driver."

Plus, ask for these discounts:
Female, 30 to 64 (25%)
Senior citizen (5% to 15%)
Farmer (10% to 30%)
Good student (25%)

Student away at school (10% to 15%)
Have an anti-theft alarm (5% to 15%)
Have seat belts(10% to 30%)
Car pool to work (15% to 20%)

Raise your deductible. This can save you a lot on your premium. Up to 30%.

Don't pay for medical coverage if it's covered on your health insurance.

If your car is old, get liability only. The insurance company will only replace it's blue book value. And if it's 10 years or older, chances are you'll pay much more in premiums than you will receive from the insurance company .

Drive safely, slow down, wear a seat belt. If you get in an accident your rates will increase. Slowing down and being attentive will pay off. Also if you get caught speeding you will have "points" put on your record that could also raise your rates up to 10%.

Homeowners insurance: If you feel like taking a risk, here's another option. Arrange to insure your home for 80% of it's value instead of 100%. This is banking on the idea that very few houses are total looses. There will most likely be something salvageable. This can save you as much as 10% on your premiums. Also shop around because some companies will penalize you for doing this, some will not.

Life insurance: Life insurance can be the most confusing and have the most options. Basically there are 3, term insurance, whole life and universal life, which is also an investment.

The best rate you will find is on term insurance. It is pure insurance. They average 70% less than the other 2 options. It is best to change every 5 years because most companies offer low rates to new subscribers but only for 5 years. The other 2 types of life insurance will cost much more. And because it's an investment there is an element of risk involved.

If you want to shop for insurance at home, these companies will help you find a low rate insurance option.

> Selectquote (800) 343-1985
> Insurance Information, Inc. (800) 472-5800
> InsuranceQuote Services (800) 972-1104

How to gain up to $30,000 from your mortgage:

If you already have a mortgage, this simple trick will save thousands of dollars over the years of your mortgage. For example if you have a 30 year mortgage at 10% you will pay about $746 a month. However, if you pay just an additional $50 dollars a month you will save a whopping $57,283 in interest charges and shorten your payoff time to 22 1/2 years. That means you'll have an extra 8 years worth of payments you can stick in your pocket. Pay an extra $150 and you'll shorten your payoff time by 15 years. And save $96,966! Remember, you must still make your monthly payment, but adding a little extra will relieve you of it much sooner!

How to get credit cards
with bad credit or no credit history:

In today's world not having a credit card can bring you economic despair. It's become a credit card world. And without one you can't make a lot of purchases. Like shopping by phone or renting a car or buying tickets. You are shut off from a whole world of convenience. Well don't worry there is hope. Fortunately for you many banks want to give you credit because it means money for them. That's why they invented a secured credit card.

Basically you are giving yourself credit. The bank requires you give them from $500 to $5,000 to deposit in an account. Then they will issue you a credit card with a limited credit line. If after 6 months you have demonstrated that you can make prompt payments, you can switch over to a regular credit card. They also will return your deposit.

Here are 5 banks that offer secured credit cards.

American National Bank,
890 Palmer Ave., Suite 403,
Larchmont, NY 10538.
1-800-533-3295.
Fee: $69.

American Pacific Bank,
P.O. Box 193605,
Portland, OR 97280.
1-800-879-8745.
Fee $30.

Star Bank.
P.O. Box 956,
Cincinnati, OH 45273.
1-800-999-0619.
Fee $20.

Suburban National Bank,
34 Reads Way,
New Castle, DE 19720.
303-322-4305.
Fee $20.

Community Bank of Parker,
19590 East Main,
Parker, CO 80134.
1-800-779-8472.
Fee $20.

For information on other secured credit card programs, you can call 1-800-326-3311.

Use 50% less of your laundry detergent with the same clean results:

The recommended usage on most any kind of detergent is going to be more than you really need. Why? More sales for the company. They are not interested in saving you money. Using a half a scoop instead of a whole scoop is more than enough. Even if you used no soap at all, washing with hot water would get your clothes 90% clean. Try using half the amount and see if you can tell any difference. Bottom line is -- you won't. And you'll spend half as much every year. That sure adds up.

How to avoid late charges on an overdue bill:

If the bill was late because you received it late, simply send the envelope with the late postage date on it in with your payment. You are required to receive your bills at least 14 days in advance.

You can also try calling and explaining why the payment was late. If it is a valid excuse and you have an otherwise good payment record, they will probably drop the charge. You can also try talking to the manger or a higher up and explain that you've been a good customer and you shouldn't be penalized.

How to save hundreds on car repair bills:

This is a very touchy and sensitive topic for most people. Who hasn't been ripped off or deceived by a mechanic? Well, here are weapons you can use to fight back and pay less to fix your car.

1) Find a reliable mechanic. Sounds impossible huh? If you wait until you need one you'll end up going anywhere. Find one before you need one so you won't make a rushed and costly decision. Ask for recommendations from family and friends. You can also check out a repair shops complaint record with the Better Business Bureau. Also make sure they have certified mechanics. Look for certificates especially an ASE (Automotive Service Excellence Certification). Then you'll know you are getting trained professionals.

2) Find out the shop's policies. Before they lay a hand on your car, find out their rates, guarantees on all work done and methods of payment accepted. If it's not clearly posted or you get shaky answers, go somewhere else.

3) Clearly explain all symptoms. Don't tell him what's wrong, instead tell him every sound, movement and detail so he can diagnose it quicker. Otherwise you pay for his time to find out.

4) No matter how big or small the job, never let a mechanic do work until you have given authorization. Many will do the work without telling you first and you will be stuck with a bill that's more than you expected.

5) Find out if the repair is under warranty. If so make sure you follow the instructions exactly. This will ensure that you are reimbursed. If you're not sure if it's covered or how to fix it if it is, call the manufacturer directly or the nearest dealer.

6) Before you pay, take your car for a test drive. Make sure the problem has been fixed.

7) Read the repair bill completely. Make sure you've only been charged for repairs you've received. And get copies of all paperwork.

8) If you don't know much about cars , bring along someone who does.

9) Be up front with the mechanic. It also helps to let the mechanic know that you don't trust mechanics and that you'd like to be a long time customer if he does a good job. If he knows you're skeptical and wary, he may be more honest to get your business.

10) Pay hourly - not flat rate charge. Mechanics will often do it in much less time and charge you extra. Tell them you don't want a flat rate charge, but a per hour charge.

11) For maintenance or minor repairs, go to auto shops at K-mart, Sears or other places that are less likely to pad your bill.

12) Double up on car repairs. If you need new brakes and a new alignment, it will be cheaper to have them done together.

13) Use rebuilt or used parts. Often you can go to a junk yard and buy them yourself. They can cost 60-75% less than new ones. Especially if your car is 8-10 years old. New parts may last longer than your car and would be wasted money.

14) Take your car to a vocational school. Many of these take in cars to let students work on them. Often they only charge for parts and you'll have 4-5 people working on your car plus an instructor.

15) Learn to do basic repairs yourself. You'd be surprised at what you can do. I personally have changed a battery, battery cable, an alternator, a thermostat and a headlight. And I don't consider my self real knowledgeable about cars. One time my wife got a book from the library and we worked on the car together an saved about $100!

16) Get more than one estimate. If it's a big job costing hundreds or thousands of dollars, get more than one estimate. There is no set industry fee. One shop may do it for much less than the one across the street. Get estimates from at least 3 including labor and parts.

Biggest care repair scams.

Transmission repair. Because most people know little about a transmission, mechanics will try to point out the metal shavings in the transmission pan and tell you it needs to be replaced. Don't believe it. This is normal.

Oil leak. Sometimes they'll spray oil on the engine to simulate a leak.

Be skeptical if he tells you more than one part needs to be replaced. Make sure you find out exactly why and ask to see the damaged parts.

How to get free money
from the government for your good idea:

Did you know the government hands out $2.5 BILLION dollars a year. And there's no reason why you can't claim some of it. Your chances of getting some money is far greater than you think. If you have a great idea that you think will make you a ton of money or will improve people's lives, then the government may have up to $100,000 dollars with your name on it. And this money is in the form of a grant which means it's yours and never has to be paid back. However you do have to a bit of homework to make sure you're in the guidelines of receiving the cash. Here are several sources than will assist you in finding your cash windfall.

To locate federal money:

See the "Cataloge of Federal Domestic Assistance" in the reference section of your library.

Or you can order a subscription to the catalog by contacting the Superintendent of Documents, U.S. Government Printing Office, Washington, D.C. 20402. Or call (202) 783-3238.

Also at your library you'll find "The Action Guide to Government Grants, Loans, and Giveaways" (George Chelekis, Perigree Books, New York, NY.)

You can also get a Federal Assistance Programs Retrieval System (FAPRS) by contacting: Federal Domestic Assistance Catalog Staff, General Services Administration, Room 101 Reporters Building, 300 7th Street, SW, Washington, DC. (202) 708-5126.

How to save up to 80% on appliance repair bills:

Have you ever been sold on an appliance repair contract when you made a purchase. Chances are you'll never get your money's worth from it. You only have a 1 in 5 chance of ever needing a repair. And if you do, it will be less than what you've paid for the service contract. It's a very big money making operation for the company.

Instead, skip the service contact and if you ever need a repair, have an independent repairman come do it. Most service contacts expire before the appliance is old enough to need it.

When making the decision to repair or replace a dishwasher, T.V., air conditioner, dryer or VCR, it pays to weigh carefully your options. Many times if the appliance if 8-10 years old the problems with them will be big ones. Ones that are costly and are only a band aid. They will go downhill from there. You will save money if you just replace it with a new one. If you find yourself facing a repair bill that is half the value of the appliance, it's time to buy a new one.

- Get 2 or more free estimates.
- Look for a moonlighter who charges less.
- Do it yourself by getting a book from the library.
- Ask a friend or neighbor that's handy.

The best time of year
to buy a house and save 10%:

The best time is during the dead of winter. Why? Because these are the people that are desperate to sell their house. You will get a good price because they are in dire need to unload their house.

The second best time to buy is Spring. Watch around your town, city or neighborhood around springtime and many people will have their house for sale. Why? People are anticipating a summer move or job transfer when school lets out. This is a good opportunity because of the competition.

How to get Medicare to cover anything:

To get the coverage you want, you must know how to play the game. It's not easy, but it is possible.

Medicare has 2 parts:

Part A, Which covers hospital expenses, is free and is overall pretty good.

Part B, Covers doctor bills and other medical costs and is optional. You are expected to have other insurance to cover what they won't.

You must know these things about Medicare.

1) What is the maximum per dime that they will pay? Will it pay the hospital's semi-private rate?

2) How do they define a "new benefit period?" Usually you have to be out of the hospital for 60 days to begin coverage on a new illness.

3) Will Medicare pick up the difference between "reasonable costs" and the actual cost?

4) Can you upgrade the benefits scale by paying a higher premium?

5) Does the policy have a siding scale depending on age? If you are young, you will probably get a lower rate.

If you pay close attention to the details of your policy you will not get stuck with any hefty bills.

How to comfortably save hundreds on your utilities:

Everybody wants to save money on utilities. And the good news is there are so many simple things you can do to save hundreds, maybe even thousands during the year. Here are some simple, energy-saving tips that will put cash in your pocket.

1) Reduce your water heater costs by reducing the temperature from 145 to 120 degrees. Your family will never know the difference.

2) You'll save 7% on heating costs if you plug up all your holes with caulking, insulating, draft guards under your doors and weather stripping. Plus, cover your widows with plastic film.

3) Install a low flow shower head and save up to 50% on your water usage.

4) Install storm windows to cut costs by 30%. If you can't afford them, covering them with plastic film will work also.

5) Remove or cover well your air conditioner in the winter. All your warm air escapes and the cool air comes in. Cover all holes around it as well as covering the inside and outside of it.

6) Use flow detectors and heat reflectors to direct air from the walls into the center of the room.

7) Fix all leaky faucets. One drop per second uses 8 gallons of water a week.

8) Save 20 cents a load by using cold water instead of hot.

9) Turn off your air conditioner when you leave home and save 40 cents an hour.

10) Close the damper on your fire place when not in use.

11) Change your furnace filter monthly. It will operate better and be more fuel efficient.

12) Save $40 dollars on your electric bill by replacing your light bulbs with fluorescent bulbs. They last 10 to 14 times longer, and use 75% less electricity.

13) Hang dry your clothes and save $10 to $20 dollars a month on your electric bill.

14) Buy appliances with energy saving stickers on them.

15) Contact your utility company about enrolling in cost-saving programs. You may save up to $100 dollars a year.

16) Close off heating and air conditioning vents in rooms that aren't used regularly.

17) Install light dimmers. They can cut lighting costs up to 50% during the year.

18) Adjust your toilet to use less water. Do it by lifting the lid on the back and adjusting the bulb level. Or use a brick or other object to take up space.

19) Water your lawn only when you need to. Most people water their lawn way too much.

20) Do you light up your whole house and stay in one room? If so, be more diligent in turning off lights and unwatched T.V.'s.

21) Use fans instead of an air conditioner. They are much less costly and often do just as good a job.

22) Wash only full loads of dishes and clothes. Use buckets of water to wash your car and a broom to sweep your driveway instead of the hose.

These tips, if used properly, will save you lots. They're very simple to do and well worth it!

Home businesses you can do part time and earn $40-$60,000 a year:

Turning your home computer into a healthy, profitable business.

Just about everyone these days owns a computer. If you do, or are planning on getting one, then here's 3 hot ides that could easily earn you thousands of dollars a year just by working in your spare time.

1) Typing, writing and editing service: If you live near high schools, colleges or businesses, this may be a great income generator. Place an ad in the classifieds or put up flyers on bulletin boards in grocery stores and on school campuses. You can charge by the hour or the page.

2) Resume service: People are constantly looking for a job. Even if you know nothing about a resumes yourself, it's not hard to learn. An ad in the classifieds should bring people running. You'd be surprised how many people don't know where to begin. You can help present the person objectively, design it and print it out for a flat fee or charge by the hour. Go to your local library for books on resume writing.

3) Be a computer teacher: Everybody needs to know how to use a computer. And there are a lot of people who are willing to pay to have someone teach them. You can teach the basics or teach more complex software programs. Charge a fair hourly rate. A little advertising in the classifieds or around town should drum up some good business.

How to win with adjustable rate mortgages:

Adjustable rate mortgages can be a great break for the buyer these days. It helps you get into a house at a low interest rate initially. But beware! Some banks are out to get you. They sweet talk you in by offering a low rate, and then it increases and increases until you are stuck and can't afford your payment anymore. But there is a simple way to avoid this from happening. A good ARM will fluctuate but it should have a cap. Meaning whatever the rate is initially, there is usually a 2-3 year fixed rate with a 2% cap. So after 3 years is up, the rate may go up or down but not by more than 2%. So if you start out at 7.25% after 3 years it could go up to 9.25% or down to 5.25%. Make absolutely sure this is how it works with your lender. If not, go somewhere else. You should also get the terms under which you may refinance. So if the rate goes down, you can lock it in for the remainder of your 30 year mortgage. Make your lender spell it out to you. If it sounds strange or confusing, leave.

ARM's are really good if you only plan to be in the house for a short period of time (3-5 years). And if the forecast is for interest rates to go down in he future, using an ARM will be in your favor when rates go down and you can lock in an even lower rate without refinancing.

How to pay 80% less for your life insurance:

Americans spend a startling $7 billion dollars a year for life insurance. And guess what? Most of it is not needed experts claim. So how do you make sure you're not contributing to the excess? I'll tell you.

1) Don't buy more than you need. Who is dependent on you if you die right now? If you're single, then you don't need any. So don't let someone talk you into buying it. Take the time to figure out what your dependents need if you die. You only need enough coverage to provide them with adequate financial resources. Your goal should not be to make them wealthy beyond belief. Realize you have a very small chance of ever collecting on it while your dependents need the money to live on.

2) Shop around. That should go without saying. Never buy from the first person you talk to. Keep shopping until you find the company that offers the highest amount of coverage for the lowest amount of money.

For a quote by phone call, TermQuote (800) 444-8376 or SelectQuote (800) 343-1985 or InsuranceQuote (800) 972-1104.

3) Buy direct from the insurance company. There are several companies that will sell direct to you "no-load" polices. In effect you cut out the middle man and his commission. These are companies that will do this. USAA Life (800) 531-8000, Amertis (800) 552-3553, Geico (800) 824-1247, Amica Mutual (800) 242-6422.

4) Don't insure your children. You could spend up to $200 dollars a year for each child. Life insurance is to provide for dependents left after a death. There is no reason to cover your children. But a salesman will tell you otherwise.

5) Don't buy credit life insurance. This is insurance that will pay off a car loan or other in case of death. It is usually overpriced. You can get the same coverage from basic life insurance and disability.

6) Ask about discounts. You may be eligible to get a discount if you exercise regularly, do not smoke and don't engage in high risk activities.

Other buying tips:

> - To keep costs down, buy term, not whole life.
> - Buy only 5-7 times the primary earner's income
> - As you get older and your assets grow, you may begin to need less and should make an adjustment.

How to avoid supermarket scanner ripoff:

I guarantee you that you have already been the victim of a supermarket scanner. They overcharge, forget sale prices and read the bar code wrong. Plus the cashier makes mistakes. And some stores do nothing about it. It's a way of stealing your money without you ever noticing.

Fortunately, you can stop it all together. Always make a note of the price for each item if it's not marked on the item itself. Either in your head or write it down on your list. Watch as each item is scanned and make sure it's the correct price.

A second line of defense is to go over your receipt when you get home. If you've been overcharged, bring it back with the receipt and have it corrected. They may even give you the item free to apologize for making a mistake. If you find this happening on a regular basis, contact your local Better Business Bureau and alert them.

How to get coverage with a doctor
not approved by your insurance or HMO:

Sometimes you just have to see another doctor. If you're on vacation or just not around your regular doctor or HMO, you have little choice. This is when you'll run into trouble when trying to collect. You do have some recourse.

Don't think that it will be a cakewalk because the insurance company or HMO's method of operation is to pay as little as possible. You may have to fight to get them to pay. You'll need to have a good reason for going to an unapproved doctor. Was it because yours was not around? Were you out of town? Was it an emergency? Was it a special case where you knew it would be cheaper somewhere else and were only trying to save money? Whatever the reason you need to have documentation and a doctor's statement of why you needed treatment from him. Continue to call and write and submit the claim until they pay. It will work, but expect them to be stubborn about it.

Common homeowners insurance mistakes and how to avoid them:

If you're a homeowner then you must insure your home. Many mistakes are made when people go scrambling for insurance because the bank requires it before you close on a house. If you know you're going to buy a house, get started on your policy early so you have time to understand it fully -- and avoid traps that will cost you.

Here are some cost-saving tips for buying homeowners insurance.

1) Have your home and personal property appraised. Get an independent appraiser, not one a bank supplies, to give you a real market value. Also videotape all your belongings. With these two things you will have visual proof of what you had and what the condition and value is. Keep this documentation in a safe deposit box or other place outside your home for safe keeping.

2) Insure your home for its true replacement value. Don't go under that amount. It may be a bit cheaper, but if you have to rebuild you'll only get the 80% you were insured for.

3) Raise your deductible. Most people have $250 cash. Many even have $500 or $1,000. The higher your deductible, the lower your premium. This will save 10% to 25% a year.

4) Buy your policy direct from the insurance company. This will save you from paying a commission to a salesman, and lower your cost.

5) Buy from an "A" or "A+" company. Buy anything less and you'll get what you pay for. Also be sure to shop around for the best deal.

6) Keep your policy current. Make sure you update it every year to reflect any changes you have made or an increase in market value.

7) Buy all your insurance from one company. Often when you buy your auto insurance, renter's insurance, etc. from the same company they will give you a discount.

8) Ask for other discounts. There are several discounts you may qualify for.

- Having smoke detectors
- Burglar alarm
- In-house sprinkler system
- Being a non-smoker
- Having fire-resistant materials your home
- Being 50 or older and retired

Remember you must ask. An agent won't offer them freely.

How to make sure your insurance company is safe before you buy:

The last thing you ever want to hear is that your insurance company failed and you're out of luck. It happens all the time. There are ways for you to check your insurance company to make sure it's safe.

The A.M. Best Company publishes an annual report that rates a company's liabilities and overall health. This report is available at almost all local libraries. Or you can call and get a verbal report at (900) 420-1400. It will cost $2.50 per minute. Or you can call Standard and Poor's (212) 208-1527 and get a free report or Duff & Phelps (312) 368-3157 for a free report.

Also be aware that the rating system has been changed and "A+" is now second best instead of the best. And since "A" companies still go bad, you're best off to stick to the big names.

How to get medical insurance even when you are uninsurable:

People with serious medical conditions or who fail insurance physicals have a hard time finding insurance. Because the insurance company knows they will lose money. But there are ways around it.

Here's what you can do:

1) You can buy insurance that will cover everything but whatever it is you suffer from. For example, if you have cancer, it will cover everything but cancer costs. It may not sound all that great, but it's better than nothing.

2) Find an independent agent who knows all the standards of each company. You'll find that they vary from one to another. An independent agent has no bias for or against certain companies, so he will be your best help. Also a good agent will know how to word your health problems to make them sound less serious.

3) If all else fails, your final attempt would be to get coverage under a group policy. Such groups are, social clubs, fraternal orders, professional organizations and churches. Those groups will charge a fee, but getting coverage when you need it will be worth it.

How to save 40% off sale prices at any store:

The key here is timing. This is not about wholesalers or discount stores. This is about saving 40% or more at any store you go to! There's a strategy involved. But it's easy to follow.

Every month of every year has bargains that will mean great savings for you. You can easily save 40%, if not much more. This is when merchants are most likely to have a sale. The stores need to unload to make way for new products. And you can make out like a bandit.

January: Everything that didn't sell at Christmas, cards, decorations, clothes, candy, toys, etc. Plus winter coats, accessories, linens, books, appliances, furniture, carpets and rugs.

February: Used cars, lamps, furniture, silverware, dishes, kitchenware, air conditioners, sportswear, sporting goods, TV's, stereos, toys.

March: Winter sports equipment, housewares, garden supplies, children's shoes, and infant clothing.

April: Women's shoes, lingerie, fabrics and paint.

May: TV's, luggage, jewelry, outdoor furniture, tires and auto accessories, Mother's Day specials.

June: Men's clothing, floor coverings, bedding, Father's Day specials.

July: Men's shirts and shoes, children's clothing, lingerie, sleepwear, furniture, summer sports equipment.

August: Curtains and drapes, men's and women's coats, linens, tires, bathing suits, fans and air conditioners.

September: Fall fashions, fishing equipment, school supplies, major appliances.

November: Winter clothing, blankets and quilts, shoes, men's suits and coats.

December: Men's and children's clothing, resort wear, men's fashion accessories.

How to get your credit card interest lowered:

Why pay 18%-19%-even 20% when you can pay 6% or 7%? It's easy. It's just as simple as calling the credit card company and telling them you want your interest rate lowered. And they do it. Why? Because if they don't they may lose your business to a credit card company with a lower rate. The competition is fierce out there for your credit business. And often credit card companies will offer a low teaser rate for 6 months or a year. When the year is up, simply call them and ask them to extend it and they will if they want your business. If they won't, cancel the card and switch over to another one. You can save a lot of money this way.

How to spot insurance companies
that won't pay when you make a claim:

Any insurance company, big or small, wants to take your money and hopes that they will never have to give any back. But there are some that are dishonest and corrupt and you may never see a dime when you make a claim. Here are some ways to check the credibility of your insurance company before you buy.

1) Ask to see the company financial record. If the company is doing well it will have on hand about 6-7% of its life insurance policies in a cash reserve.

2) If a surviving beneficiary is offered installments instead of a lump sum, be careful. They may hold your money in a very low interest bearing account. You could reinvest the money yourself for a greater yield.

3) New York has the toughest insurance regulations in the country. If your company is not qualified to operate there, find another company.

4) How long must you wait before money is paid out to you? Read the fine print. Some may hold it for up to 6 months before you get paid.

5) How are the company's investments doing? Ask for a prospectus to see how they have been doing. If they haven't been doing well, they may shut down on you.

How to get a nearly free college education without income qualifications:

Have you got the $50,000 to $100,000 you're going to need to send just one child to college? (Multiply that by the number of children you have). So how do you do it? The good news is that about $130 million in scholarship money went unclaimed last year. Plus the government gives away billions in federal grants and loans. There is definitely a piece of it for you if you know where to look. And unless you feel confident you can come up with then money yourself, you should start looking soon.

Just because you make a lot of money doesn't mean you won't qualify for federal money. Here are some things you need to know.

The government takes into account family size, age of older parents, number of children in school, and large medical payments, when they do their qualifying formulas. You could be making over $100,000 a year and still qualify. Make sure you list funds you don't have access to. When they review your overall financial picture, they count these funds. If you show they're not accessible, they will not count them.

Make sure you get all your applications in on time. And make sure you fill everything out correctly. Also remember government aid is issued on a first come, first serve basis. So apply early.

Bills you can pay late without a late fee:

Sometimes the money just isn't there to pay bills. Some will accept a late bill with no charge, some will not. Never pay a mortgage or car payment late. They have a direct line to the credit bureaus and it will go on your record. For other bills, call and ask what their "grace period" is. It can be 5-15 days and some are even as long as 30 days. Doctors also are willing to extend more time in paying bills. Explain the situation to your doctor or even the receptionist and they will most often give you more time.

How to get your dream house now with poor cash flow:

Affording any house is always a financial equation that's hard to solve. But the rewards are well worth it. Struggling to get a down payment together plus closing cost and millions of other costly details that always emerge can be stressful. Here are some ways to come up with the money you need to finally buy your dream house.

1) Lower your debt load. Pay off all the debts you can. Consolidate everything you can. Pay off credit cards and dump all your balances onto one low interest credit card. Whatever you can do to pay off debt will improve your chances of getting a loan.

2) Don't try to buy more than you can afford. The rule is 2 1/2 times your annual gross earnings. Add up all your debt including your house payment with insurance, interest and PMI insurance and see if it works. This should give you an idea of what you can afford.

3) Start off with a townhouse or condo. They tend to be more affordable. Plus, it eliminates a lot of costs that come with a house. You just pay an association fee. Often it includes water, sewage and insurance. If you can do this, you can build up equity to buy a house in the future.

4) Ask your boss if there's a program available for home buyers. They may help pay insurance or closing costs. I once asked my boss for money to buy a house and I got it. It can't hurt to ask.

5) Check local public housing agencies. Sometimes they will loan money for a down payment.

6) Save on fees. Ask the current owner if they have the appraisal, title, and survey information. If you deal with the same companies they may give you a price break.

7) Go to a state or federal auction where houses are put up for sale with huge discounts.

8) Borrow money from friends or relatives.

9) Sell things to raise money.

10) Get a part time job to save money for a down payment.

How to avoid buying a "lemon":

Using some common sense and a little detective work, there's no reason to ever be stuck with lemon.

1) If buying from a classified, and the price is below blue book value, be careful. It's possible that it's a desperate seller who just wants to unload it quickly. Or the seller knows it may fall apart on you soon but will swear it's in good shape.

2) Inspect the car thoroughly. Look at the inside. Are there any leaks? Is the brake, clutch or gas pedal worn, but has low miles? If so, perhaps the odometer has been turned back. Leave. Check the sides by looking across the car from either end. Any bulge or crease may be the result of an accident. Make sure the tires are not worn. If they are, it could also be because of an accident that threw the frame off.

3) Take it for a test drive, a long test drive. Go up and down hills to check the brakes and acceleration. Try out every control. Stop and get out to make sure all lights including turn signals are working. Make sure the stereo is off so you can listen carefully to all noise. Do the gears grind? Does it shift smoothly?

4) Take it to a mechanic you trust. Have it checked out by a mechanic. He may or may not charge you to look at it. See what he can find wrong with it. Ask if it looks like it's been in an accident.

5) Check the paint job. If it's been painted it may have been in an accident.

6) Make sure it has a VIN number. Write it down and check it with the police station to make sure it's not stolen.

7) Write an agreement with the seller that you want 30 days in which you can bring it back. If he disagrees, he may be hiding something. Just asking to do that is a good indication of how the seller feels about the car.

How to drive a top quality car and travel for free:

If you're ready to take a long, enjoyable road trip then you'll love this. Rental car agencies often need cars driven back and forth across the country. And they'll pick up the tab. It's a great way to go. Especially since most rental cars are luxury cars or close to it. To get more information call any local rental car outlet.

Another way to travel for free is to work for a "drive-away company." You'll see ads in the personal section of the classifieds that are looking for drivers. When people move and don't want to drive 2 cars or want to fly, but need to get their car there, too, they hire these companies to find drivers and pay all expenses.

Here are some numbers you can call for information.

A-1 Auto Movers - 216- 226- 2886.
Auto driveaway Co. - 216-331-1495.

How to save $1,000 or more when you lease a car:

Depending on who you talk to, leasing can be good or bad. What's good is the lower payment, no maintenance cost and getting a new car every few years. What's bad is that you'll probably pay more over the long run for it, and you don't own it. Despite the downside, more and more people are leasing every year because it is more afford-able. Here's some tips to get a lower lease price.

1) Shop around: Leases are arbitrary. One dealership may want $3,000 down, one may want nothing. You may have a slightly higher payment if you put less down. But if you have no cash to put down, then it will work great for you. Also, if the car is advertised with money down, ask to waive the down payment and they may.

2) Ask about leasing a used car: Many times if a car is in good shape and has retained its value, a dealer will lease it. The price will be much less than buying or leasing it new.

3) Waive the maintenance fee: They are usually not worth the cost if it's a brand new car.

4) Negotiate for more miles. Just before the price is settled on, if you are only are allowed 40,000 ask for 50,000. If they really want your business they'll do it. Because if you go over the allotted miles you will be charged 10-15 cents per mile you're over.

5) Negotiate a price. Negotiate the price (the monthly payment) just like you would a car. Remember this is a dealer run show, they decide what the lease price is, not the car company. Keep bargaining until you get what you want.

6) Shop around again. Once you have your absolute lowest price, tell them you'd like to think about. Go to another dealer with the same car and show them the deal. Ask them if they can do any better. Repeat this until you find who really has the best deal.

Using these tips you'll easily save more than $1,000. Good luck!

How to make sure you donate to the best charity:

When you donate to a charity, you'd like to know the money is really going to help those in need. Sadly, many times it's not. It only goes to support a lifestyle of luxury for charity scam leaders.

Use these guidelines to make sure you are donating to a worthwhile charity.

1) Stick with large charities. You will be safe if you donate to the biggest like United Way, UNICEF, etc. They tend to be monitored more closely because of the large sums of money they collect each year.

2) Give to older, more established organizations. They will give more of your money to the needy. Newer ones have higher start-up costs and your money will be used for administrative purposes.

3) Check the financial records. Request a copy of the group's IRS Form 990. This will tell you where their money has been used most. Good charities spend 75% of the money to help people. If they spend 50% or less on the cause, give somewhere else.

4) Check salaries. If you see that the top executive receives more than .25% of total funds raised, this charity is making money for the executive, not needy people.

5) Make sure you know exactly who you're helping. Some will call it one thing and do another. Make sure you ask where the money is really going.

6) If a solicitor comes to your door, ask to see a copy of his local permit. A legitimate charity will have one that you can have and keep.

7) Never donate over the phone. Instead make a pledge and ask to be billed. Also, ask for some literature to be sent along with the bill.

8) Watch out for sales tactics. If they offer to send someone to pick it up or really pressure to to make a donation, they are probably out to steal your money.

Follow these guidelines to avoid fueling a scam artist. These days there is lots of it going on. And while charities need money to help the less fortunate, it's to everyone's advantage for you to be very cautious.

How to dress your best on a limited budget:

Whatever your "best" is, it's still going to cost you money. And if you have champagne taste and a beer budget, not to worry. There are so many low cost clothes available, you can dress as you wish. You'll find some great bargains that will save you hundreds. You'll learn to never pay full price for clothes again.

Some buying tips:

1) Before you shop, look at the clothes you have and think about what you can buy that would go with what you have. Instead of buying whole outfits, buy clothes that match your existing wardrobe.

2) Always try clothes on. It may look like it will fit, but it also may not. And it's better to find out before than after you've bought it. Also remember most clothes will shrink, so measure accordingly.

3) Take a friend who is honest and can serve as a clothing guide.

4) Don't buy something unless you love it. We all have new clothes in our closets that have never been worn because we decided we didn't like them once we got home. Don't waste your money on stuff that will go unused.

5) Stock up. If you see a great buy on socks and underwear, buy a lot. You'll always need them. You may even get a discount if you buy a lot at once.

6) Buy shoes early in the day. You'll get a better fit than if you wait until afternoon or evening when your feet are swollen.

7) Never pay full price for an expensive clothing item. It will go on sale eventually. And if it doesn't, it can probably be found at a discount store somewhere.

Where to save big on brand-name clothes.

Outlet shopping centers: The number of outlet shopping centers around the county has skyrocketed in the last few years. Your savings at these stores will range from 25 to 70 percent. These stores have great discounts because they buy direct from the manufacturer instead of through a distributor. They are usually located in out-of-the-way places where rent and land is cheaper. They typically carry brand-name, high-quality clothes. So if you like nice clothes, this is a good buying option. To locate an outlet in your area call (800) 555-1212.

Off-price chain-stores: Filene's Basement, T.J. Maxx, Syms, Burlington Coat factory, Ross Dress For Less and Marshall's are all these types of stores. This is where you'll find factory overruns, closeouts, and out-of-season clothes. They carry quality clothes at an up to a 60% discount. These are not seconds or rejects.

Thrift shops: Here you'll find a lot of used clothes. It's especially good for children's clothes. A lot of children's clothes are outgrown before they are worn through. And keep in mind, many donated clothes are in great shape because they were hardly worn. So don't think it's all just junk. You'll be pleasantly surprised.

Consignment shops: This is a good place for you to buy and even sell some clothes. Consignment shops will not accept clothes unless they are in good shape and marketable. People bring clothes in and the store sells them and shares the profits 50-50 with the person. You will get a good deal on nice clothes. And if you have some clothes that you're not using, bring them in and make some money.

Warehouse clubs: Big warehouse clubs like BJ's, Wholesale Club and Sam's Club offer merchandise with deep discounts. The only snag is you have to get a membership. You can get one if your employer has one, from a credit union or other organization. A membership will cost from $10 to $35 dollars a year. The clothing selection will be limited, but they are high-quality and low priced.

Discount department stores: Wal-Mart, Kmart, Ames and Target have large clothing selections and everything from high to low quality. The one thing you'll always find is savings. It may not be a big fancy department store, but if you're trying to dress a family, you'll be surprised at the nice clothing available. More and more people are starting to realize they're not so bad.

If you stick to these places and be on the lookout for sales, you should be able to easily dress like a million bucks -- but spend pennies. Remember to never pay full price for expensive clothes. My wife and I dress well, but always use patience to find things we like at a huge discount.

The truth about sweepstakes and how to improve your chances of winning:

Most of us haven't won the big one yet. But it doesn't hurt to keep trying. There really is big money at stake. Government regulations enforce sweepstakes. So if there is a prize advertised, it must be given out. So how do you get your share? It will take a little extra work, but you really can increase your odds of winning.

1) One way is to subscribe to a contest news letter. This will provide you with information about all the current sweepstakes and how to enter. If you use this to track and enter them you will have multiple chances all the time.

2) Unless you have unlimited postage funds, you'll want to pick and choose what you enter. If the prize is other than cash and you don't really want it, use your postage for ones you do want.

3) Send multiple entries. This will increase your chances a lot. But don't send them all at the same time. Send a few everyday. Some sweepstakes pick a few entries each day and choose the grand prize winner from those. So if you have one arriving everyday you'll have a better chance of wining.

4) Follow the contest rules. That may sound basic, but if you don't, they will just throw it away.

How to get college aid in the 90's:

In the last few years, things have changed when it comes to getting college aid from the government.

Simplified application process: Now a family needs to only fill out one form. If you earn under $50,000 a year, you will only need to supply basic information.

More borrowing power: Loan limits for almost all aid programs have been increased. Now parents, regardless of income can borrow a full year's tuition plus expenses. These loans will need to be paid while the student is still in school.

Penalties dropped for home and farm equity: From now on, real estate assets will not be calculated for eligibility. This will give about 1.1 million more students money for college.

Direct-loan Experiment: This new law allows the government to loan up to $500 million in loans directly to students by passing banks and other loan agencies. This will save on paperwork and administrative costs.

NOTES

_____
_____
_____
_____
_____
_____
_____
_____
_____

Chapter
_____

Pay less Taxes

4

How to save $200,000 in estate taxes:

If you have or plan to have a sizable estate when you die, you could lose 35% of it to taxes. You could even lose up to 60% if it's a very large estate. In order to protect your estate for your beneficiaries, use these smart secrets.

1) Give gifts. The best way to not be heavily taxed is to reduce your taxable estate. You can give up to $600,000 in $10,000 gifts to your family per year.

2) Set up a living trust. This in effect hands over the money to a beneficiary and it continues to be a trust. This way it will not be considered taxable.

3) Use a MDW. A Marital Deduction Will will save you from taxes if your estate is bigger than your spouses. It works like this. When you die your spouse inherits your estate tax free. But, when your spouse dies the estate will be taxed.

How to avoid paying twice
on mutual fund taxes:

If you're in the middle to upper tax bracket then you need to look into investing in Tax-Free Municipal Bonds. This type of fund allows you to draw dividend payments annually, semiannually or quarterly with tax free status. It is best used as a way to keep your money in an interest bearing account without paying taxes on interest. It should not be used to build your estate. Some good recent choices are:

1) USSA Tax Exempt Short Term - 1-800-531-8181.
2) General Muni Bond Fund - 1-800-645-6561.
3) Value Line New York Tax Exempt - 1-800-223-1818.
4) Flagship All-American Tax Exempt Fund - 1-800-227-4648.

How to save hundreds with a new tax loophole:

If you have kids in college on a scholarship, you may be able to avoid paying some taxes. Typically scholarships are taxable income. However, whoever grants the money does not have to report withholdings for room and board. So find out if your kid's college reports these funds.

How to legally deduct 100%
of your hobby costs and save thousands:

Do you have a hobby that you do during most of your spare time and dream about doing the rest of the time? Then this will be good news for you. With a little effort you can enjoy your hobby and deduct all your costs. This is especially helpful if your hobby is an expensive one. Here are the rules you must follow:

1) You must turn your hobby into a business. If you can show a profit for 3 out of 5 years, you can deduct all expenses with no questions asked. If you don't make a profit, you will still be O.K., but if the IRS questions you, you must prove that you intended to make a profit but failed.

2) To provide proof, run your hobby like a business. Register your business by filing a "DBA" (doing business as) statement with the County Clerk's Office. Keep accurate books, set up a business account, get a business phone line, a listing in the yellow pages and get cards and stationary printed.

3) Find a way to show a profit even if you didn't. Do it by selling some equipment, or serve as a speaker or consultant for a nominal fee.

4) Associate with other enthusiasts. Maintain a client list for your business. Show that you have consulted experts for advice.

5) Every few years revise your business procedures to show that your are trying to correct the business problems that led to your past losses.

NOTES

_____
_____
_____
_____
_____
_____
_____
_____
_____

Chapter

Investment Secrets

5

How to invest now for the future:

A lot of people wish they only had money to invest. It can be overwhelming -- retirement and college education for your kids slowly creeps up on you and you have nothing to set aside. Well just about everybody can start investing now. If your response is "no I can't because I can barely pay my bills," well there is a way. Because the time will come when you'll need it. And if you don't start now, you'll still have nothing when the time comes. But you might need to make some adjustments.

1) Pay yourself first. When you get your paycheck, take $5 or $10 dollars out if that's all you can afford. Put it in a bank account. Not a savings account or emergency fund. But another account and promise yourself you will not touch it. Chances are if you take it out immediately after you get paid, you'll never miss it. Rearrange your other bills by paying less or try to take it from your grocery allowance. It is somewhere. Your task is to find it and save it.

2) When you have $50 or $100 dollars saved, find a financial planner. Just look in the phone book and find one that will consult with you for free. Most of them will and they will often give you a very good education in planning and investing. They can give you several options where you can put your money so it will grow substantially over time.

3) Talk to your employer about a 401(k). This is a great way to invest. You will not miss it much from your pay check because it is taken out before taxes. So if you put in $20 a month you may only miss $10 from your paycheck. Then if your employer will match some portion of it that too, will earn interest.

4) As your investment grows, look for other options. Take half and put it into something else. A bond fund or another mutual find, or a CD or something to spread the risk around and find higher yield investments.

Doing this will take minimal effort now, and provide a financial cushion for the future. Just set to work on how much you can start paying yourself and then watch it grow over the years.

Mistakes even smart investors make:

Any time you invest money there is always going to be a risk factor. And anything you can do to keep from losing your money will help. Because humans make mistakes, even the "professional" investors make costly mistakes. Here's what you can learn from mistakes they've made.

1) Don't always follow the crowd. If you buy or sell just because everyone else is doing it, you will come out with an average loss or profit at best. If you're the last to join the rush you'll take a worse loss. Often stocks go down, but they'll also go back up. And if you wait and sell when everyone gets excited again you can make a bigger profit.

2) Understand risk and reward. If you fail to take risk seriously, you can end up flat broke having lost everything. If you take it too seriously, your returns will be low. Choose investments that are balanced with high returns and moderate risk. Remember an occasional, temporary loss is OK.

3) Diversify. A good investment portfolio includes many different investments. CDs, money markets, stocks, mutual funds, bonds etc. Putting all your money in one place increases risk. Having your money spread out helps soften a hard hit if one investment goes for a loss. And at the same time, some may skyrocket to make up for the loss in another investment.

4) Look to foreign investments. Most people just think of investing in the U.S. It's wise to invest up to 25% in foreign investments. This will curb your losses should we have financial crisis.

5) Set up a regular investment plan. Instead of just investing here or there or trying this and trying that, set up a regular schedule. Your goal should be to grow your portfolio and get as much money working for you as you can. Plan to invest quarterly or more if you can, regardless of the price.

6) Get rid of greed. Don't invest like a person desperate to make a killing. This is when you will take a beating. It's like shooting craps. Instead, invest to make long term money. Make wise, thought-out decisions on current trends.

7) Don't rely on any one money manager. Money managers, newsletters and advisors all claim they have the winning answers for you. But they don't. No one source will have all the correct answers for you. Instead of having ultimate faith in one advisor, listen to their advice, but develop your own plan that works for your situation. Often their plans call for much more money than you'll have anyway and aren't much help.

8) Don't invest to avoid taxes. Many people, as their income rises, want to start aggressively investing to lower their taxes. This can be disastrous if tax laws change or economic conditions change. Invest to build capital.

9) Keep good records. If you don't know what you own, you can't keep track of how it's doing. Take the time to get organized so you can keep track of your investments.

How to make money with dollar cost averaging:

It's a very simple thing to do. It's just a matter of investing on a regular basis. Every month you invest a certain amount of money. So whether it be a mutual fund, bond, etc., you will add to the capital every month. And every month the interest will grow on a larger amount. Over a long period of time your investment will grow and grow and interest will also increase. If you start young enough, by the time time you retire having invested $2,000 a year, you could end up with over a million dollars by retirement.

Money tricks
financial managers use to make money:

Most will tell you they handle their own money the same way they handle yours. For some it may be true, for some it may not. Here are some of the strategies they use on their own money that they might never share with you.

1) Have patience. Good mangers understand that it takes years for some investments to pay off. Most people want to see a quick turn around. And then want to sell if it doesn't happen.

2) Do not look to invest in things like art, cars, antiques etc. They are not easily liquidated and you need time to find a buyer. Even real estate is only good sometimes. You can get more for your money with other financial investments.

3) Don't buy stock only because it's down and it's cheap. You are putting money in something you hope is just down for a short time. The problem is, you never know. It may never go up again.

4) Look for companies that will grow in the future. If it seems that a company has reached its growth potential, don't invest. They will never mature and your money will be wasted and idle.

5) Pick a trend and stick with it. What do the insiders say are major trends and growth capabilities? For example, 20 years ago if you invested in IBM because you saw the trend in computers, you'd be a millionaire right now. Look for these big growth opportunities.

All about annuities:

Annuities are a great retirement investment because they are are low risk, and high yield.

The way an annuity works is that you invest a lump sum of money or make payments into an annuity over years. This money earns tax deferred interest until it matures. When it matures you have two options, you can cash it in or draw payments from it. Annuities are good if you are in a high tax bracket because of the tax savings or a person with a lot of money to put aside.

There is a penalty for cashing in a annuity early. It is usually 7% for the first year and 1% for the next 6 years. After 7 years it has matured.

If you have a large amount of money, say $100,000, to put away, after 7 years at 10% you would have $170,000. Then you could take out your initial investment and leave the rest to earn interest. If you want to invest in an annuity, talk to your financial planner about your options.

How to avoid mutual fund tricks
to make 40-50% more when you retire:

An investment your broker will never mention. Many of the leading mutual funds have had incredible performance, but very few people know about them. You must go looking for them. There are no-load funds, meaning your broker will never tell your about them because he receives no commission from them. One such fund had a 69% return. You could be missing out on thousands of dollars. 20th century has a number of good funds that are worth looking at. To get a prospectus, call 1-800-345-2021. Or write: P.O. Box 419200, Kansas City, MO 64141.

Beware of "churning"! Churning used to be a way of turning big profits for brokers in the stock market. Although lately it's found its way in to the mutual fund market. If you don't watch what your broker is doing it could cost you big money. Churning is the constant buying and selling of stock to turn a profit. And every time a broker does that he gets a commission. To avoid this, never give your broker permission to make an unauthorized trade. Make sure you are notified in advance. This will cut down on him trying to steal your money. Also, make sure you are dealing with a reputable broker. To find out if he is, call the National Association of Securities Dealers at 1-800-289-9999.

Buying vs. renting: Which is for you?:

You'll find people in both arenas claim buying is better than renting and vice versa. So who do you listen to? You will need to make that decision yourself. And here are some pros and cons of each.

Renting:
Renting may or may not be cheaper than a house payment. Look around your area and get some prices on homes you like. In some cases your house payment may be equal to or less than rent.

Renting makes you more flexible. You are free to move around as you wish or need to. If a sudden job change comes about, you are not stuck with a mortgage.

As a renter you may or not be responsible for utilities. And if you are, they will be less expensive than if you were in a home. Also you are not responsible for a yard or grounds to maintain. Repairs are not your problem. If the refrigerator breaks, they give you a new one instead of having to come up with the money yourself.

Buying:

Whey you buy a house you have made a wise investment. It will most likely appreciate and you can borrow the equity or sell the house for a profit and buy a bigger and better house. Plus the tax breaks are super. You can now write off all the interest you pay when you file your taxes.

Once you own a home your utility bills will be greater, your cost for upkeep and maintenance will be more. You will have to go buy a lawn mower, lawn tools, and many things you didn't need before.

Also, when you buy, you must have a down payment plus closing costs. This will mean you'll need several thousand dollars on hand.

And now that you have a mortgage, you should plan on staying a while. You no longer have the flexibility to move like you did.

So are you ready to make a decision?

You should work the numbers before you make a decision. Figure out what you can afford. (2 1/2 times your annual earnings is a good estimate). Are you are ready for the responsibility? Do you want to make a sound investment instead of throwing away money to rent every month?

Take the time to think about it . Talk to a realtor and a bank loan officer. They will help you make a good decision.

How stock brokers rip you off
and how to avoid it:

Stock brokers sometimes have a bad reputation. These are people that live and die by the stock market. It is a stressful job and they can be rich one day and broke the next. What this means for you is that they may try to steal your money because they need it themselves. Here are the 3 most common ways they will try to rip you off and how to avoid it.

1) If your broker recommends a stock you've never heard of or if he can't find a prospectus on it, stay away. No stock is so hot that there is no paperwork or information. Never take his word only on it. This is done especially with over-the-counter stocks and new issues. If your broker keeps pushing these on you, get a new broker.

2) Be careful of churning. This is only a ploy to constantly buy and sell your stock so he can make a commission.

3) Don't let him talk you into investing in low paying investments like Ginnie-Maes. All you are doing is loaning him or his firm your money so they can use it as working capital. All you get is a low return.

How to avoid investment mistakes
that will cost you money:

Keep in mind it's your money you're playing with and if you lose it, no one will return it to you. Use the information below to avoid making costly errors.

1) Before you begin investing, build up a cash reserve. Experts suggest that you have 6 months living expenses set aside before you begin. If you have considerably less to invest then this won't be necessary. Remember, you should never risk more than you can afford to lose.

2) Set goals before you invest. What is it for? Retirement? College? A vacation? Is it for the short term or a long term? Decide what your goals are and discuss this with a financial planner to make sure your money is working to help you achieve your goals.

3) Make sure you understand everything that you are getting into. Ask questions about things you don't understand. Understand how you are going to be paid from your investment's profits, penalties and other things that could cost you money just because you didn't understand.

4) The best way to reduce your risk is to diversify. Spread your money around in mutual funds, stocks, cash, bonds, real estate etc. This way if you lose one you have several to fall back on.

5) Begin with low risk investments. Remember the higher potential return, the higher the risk. Decide how much risk you can afford to take. And if you are going to invest in high risk things, also invest in low risk things like U.S. Treasury Bonds and money markets.

Insider tip: Be careful when you buy a no-load mutual fund. Today more than half of them actually carry a fee called a 12b-1. This fee can be as much as .25% of average daily net assets per year. This will lower your expected returns. Make sure you ask about this before you invest.

How to buy the best REITs:

A REIT (Real Estate Investment Trusts) is basically a money market for real estate. REITs are becoming very popular again, and with the rising real estate market they may be a good investment for the future. If you are going to get involved be careful of some things.

1) Some require high start up fees. Look for ones without them.

2) Look for REIT discounts that specialize in one type of property like, industrial, business or homes. It's easier to manage and become familiar this way.

3) If it looks like it may be a limited partnership, be careful. You may think you're investing in one thing and later find out you have gotten yourself into a partnership and you are not solely in control.

Costly money errors even smart people make:

1) Living paycheck to paycheck. Rich people, poor people, smart people, and not so smart people do it. It's easy to do, and it stems from poor money management and living beyond your means. Put a stop to it by altering your lifestyle. Even if you make a decent living, if you aren't making ends meet, it will hurt you eventually. Try cutting back on things that are not necessities. Put that money into savings so it can earn interest for you. This is how you build true wealth.

2) Failure to plan ahead. What will your needs be in the future? What do you need to start saving for? Put a budget in place. This will help you see where your money is being spent. If you know you will need to have money for things in the future, you need to start putting it aside now. As the Boy Scouts say, "Be prepared."

3) Failure to set reasonable goals. Many people get frustrated with the slow growth of their investments in the beginning and stop investing. It may seem like all you're doing is putting money into a savings account. It takes time to see the big rewards. Set small goals until you reach the big one. Plan to have $10,000 after 5 or 10 years, and so forth. Whatever you do, don't give up.

4) Failure to adjust investments. Don't just invest your money and leave it unchecked. Be a little aggressive with it. If something isn't doing well, move it. Review your investments at least yearly. There are so many investment choices. Don't forget you have the right to put your money where it will work best.

5) Paying too much in taxes. There are plenty of ways to shelter your investment profits from taxes. Your money will grow at a much faster rate if it is tax-deferred. Find tax-deferred investments to protect your money. To illustrate the difference, $10,000 in a taxable account at 9% will grow to $15,814.30 in 10 years and $25,009.40 in 20 years. The same money in a tax-deferred account will grow to $19,671.50 in 10 years and $38,696.80 in 20 years!

How to borrow money at 8% and make 12%:

It's easy to do, the options are endless, and people do it all the time. If you are in good enough financial shape to get a personal loan from the bank, or borrow the equity in your home, you can use that money to invest. Chances are that right now you can borrow money at a lower rate than 8%. Any number of common stocks, mutual funds or others could yield you a 12% or greater return. So you will be making a profit from your borrowed money that you can reinvest or draw on for income.

How to buy stock at the right time to make an extra $10,000:

You can profit from a little-known phenomenon called the "January effect." No one is quite sure why it is, but small stocks go up starting in November through January. So a good time to buy is in October. Then you'll want to sell at the end of February before they go down again.

Also large stocks are highest from September to April. Plan to buy at other times to get the best price.

How to choose a great financial planner:

When you're trusting your hard-earned money to someone to invest and make you a profit, you can't be too careful in the selection process. At the same time a good financial planner can help you tremendously and really help you to make the most with your money.

His job is to tailor-make a financial plan for you and your needs now and in the future. A good one can be hard to find. With 200,000 people calling themselves financial planners today, only about 40,000 are really qualified and certified to give you good advice.

How to find a good one:

The first thing you need to check is for a "CFP" on his business card or on his firm's letter head or brochure. This means he has had the 30 hours required training every year. Plus a good CFP is registered with the SEC and state regulatory agencies.

Before you seek one out, decide what you need him to help you with. Are you just starting out? Do you need help in finding tax-deferred investments? Next, compile a list of planners in your area. You can call all of them or just a handful.

When you call them ask them these 4 questions:

1) What is your fee structure? They should be more than happy to disclose their fees. Get a written estimate from him. Many will do their consultation work for free. They make money on commissions if they sell you a product.

2) Do you have a working network with other planners? It is unlikely for him to know everything about all investments. He should have an information network available to find all the necessary answers.

3) What is your investment strategy? Ask how they would invest a sum of money in today's market. Make sure you let him know that you expect a return.

4) Who are your references? Ask him to supply several references. It's important to see how he did with clients during high and low times in the market.

Make sure you meet face-to-face with your planner. If you have trouble with a planner and want to report him or her you can contact: International Board of Standards and Practices for Certified Financial Planners, 1660 Lincoln Street, Suite 3050, Denver, CO 80264. (303) 830-75453.

How to get out of debt in 90 minutes without bankruptcy:

If you are feeling squeezed by your debts and need a way out, bankruptcy should be your very last resort. It will cost you money for attorney's fees and ruin your credit for 10 years. Instead, here's a better non-damaging way out. There are a number of credit counseling agencies out there that will do the following:

- Help you for free.
- Help stop creditors from hounding (or threatening) you.
- Consolidate your debts.
- Devise a payment schedule you can afford so you can pay off your debts.
- Help you work out a budget and help you manage and save money.

They can be light in a dark tunnel if you are at the end of your financial rope.

Below is a number that you can call to find a reputable credit counselor near you.

The National Foundation for Consumer Credit Counseling: 1-800-388-22267.

Chapter

Travel Secrets

6

How to choose the safest airline:

E ven thought experts claim flying is safer than driving, it doesn't make crashing in an airplane any more appealing. There are very real threats when flying. And all airlines are not equal. Cheaper airlines can afford to do so because they skimp on maintenance. Basically the two big flying threats come from discount airlines and third world country airlines.

When making reservations, if you really want to be safe, stick with the major carriers. They have the money and the history to provide the best planes and the best service on them.

One of the problems with the small discount airlines (and they are popping up all over) is that they often buy old, outdated planes. They are in need of repairs and reconditioning, and often don't get it. If you choose one of these airlines stick with older ones. Southwest is a small discount airline that has an impeccable safety record.

If flying overseas, especially in poor countries, you are really taking a risk. For example, if you want to fly within China, you must fly CAAC which is one of the worst airlines on the planet. Other bad ones are: Aeroflot in Russia, Air India, Egypt Air, Nigerian Airways and China Airlines in Taiwan.

How to get a free vacation home anywhere in the world:

Do you live in an attractive, popular area? Do people come to your town or city as tourists? If so, you are in a prime position to travel to another desirable spot FREE. Put a classified ad in newspaper like The New York times, Wall Street Journal etc., offering to "swap" houses with someone in a different place. You will need to work out an agreement and so forth. But this way you and the person you are swapping with get to go on vacation to a great place, and lodging is free!

Cruise wholesalers that will save you up to 60%:

It's a little known secret that some travel agencies specialize in cruises only. And they specialize in getting deep discounts on cruises. A general travel agency will never tell you about these, so you'll have to make some calls yourself. They are the same cruise packages the big agencies use and the same quality. They get discounts by buying in bulk and selling the rooms themselves. And the closer to the cruise date, the larger the discount for you. If you have an open schedule it may pay to wait until the last minute. So if you have been dreaming of a cruise for a long time and are looking to be pampered, get in touch with one of the companies below and Bon Voyage!

The Cruise Line
Miami, FL
(800) 327-3021

Spur of the Moment Cruises
(800) 343-1991

Landry & King
Coral Gables, FL
(800) 448-9002
(Great for special interest cruises)

World Wide Cruises
Ft. Lauderdale, FL
(800) 882-9000

How to save up to $100 dollars a week on your rental car:

The cheapest car you can rent is a subcompact. And it will also give you the best gas mileage, which you usually pay for. What some agencies do is ask you if you want to upgrade to a bigger, more expensive car which will always be $100 more. If you want to, that's fine. But they won't always mention the inflated price and it may come as a surprise when you pay your bill. Plus, many times if you order a subcompact, they will be out and you will get the upgrade for free. Also, beware of advertised discount rates, they are usually on the luxury cars and you don't really get a discount at all.

Be sure to call your credit card company to see what rental car coverage your card provides. You can probably decline the agency's overpriced insurance and save the money.

How to save 20% off the lowest price on airlines, hotels, rental cars and cruises:

The best and easiest way to make sure you're always traveling for dirt cheap is to join a travel club. Because they have so many members, they can get huge discounts on everything you need. It is worth the annual fee. Especially if you love to travel and do so often. Annual fees range from $19 to $99 a year. Here are 4 regional clubs you can contact for more information:

Ambassadair, (800) 225-9919
Nomads, (313) 941-8000
Ports of Call, (800) 843-6774
Sky Cruisers, (813) 536-2267
Infinet, (800) 966-2582 Infinet is one of the very best, and you're always guaranteed to save at least 50% off cruises, hotels and airfare. When you call, mention their $19 dollar a year offer from their direct mail package.

How to save vacation money
when exchanging for foreign currency:

When you travel to a foreign country you will get more for your money if you use the local currency. Although many foreigners gladly accept U.S. currency, you still usually get a better deal with local currency. What's bad for you is that most currency exchange operations give you a bad rate. They, in effect, charge you a fee for exchanging your money for you.

Instead, leave your cash home and use local ATM machines. That way you get the same good wholesale rates the bank got. You can save as much as $10 dollars on a $200 dollar exchange.

This is true for traveler's checks, too. To find ATM machines, call American Express and ask for their office locations in the country you're going to. They will always have an ATM machine.

The one catch is that your PIN number may not work in a foreign country. You'll need to check with your bank first.

How to save thousands on hotel bills worldwide:

You should never have to pay full price for a hotel room again. You have several options to get the lowest rates in any hotel or motel worldwide. Here are the best ways to slash your hotel bills forever:

When you are trying to book in a major hotel, first call the chain's 800 number and see what the rate is. Then call the hotel itself and find out. Many times they will be drastically different. With the hotel itself having a cheaper rate.

When you call the hotel ask for discounts. They won't offer the information freely. You'll have to ask. If business is slow you may get a big discount. Also ask about group or organization discounts. Many hotels offer 10% to 20% discounts for certain corporate employees, military or government personnel or auto club members. And if you're a senior citizen or a member of AARP you'll almost always get discounts up to 30%.

Making reservations early can save you 50% or more. During busy times they can charge high rates. But during slow times they are hungry for business.

Use a hotel broker. A hotel broker buys blocks of rooms at a discount and sells them at discounts of 50% or more. You'll need to call a broker in the city you want to visit. You can find one by calling the Chamber of Commerce or the Visitor's Bureau in the city you will visit. Here, too, is a list of some hotel brokers for certain cities.

Capitol Reservation,
(800) 847-4832. For Washington, DC.

Central Reservation Service Corporation,
(800) 548-3311 or (800) 950-0232. Offers discounts in several large U.S. cities.

Hot Rooms,
(800) 468-3500. For Chicago.

Hotel Reservations Network,
(800) 964-6835.
Has listings for more than 20 U.S. cities.

Quickbook,
(800) 789-9887.
Has listings for more than 20 U.S. cities.

RMC Travel Center,
(800) 677-1550.

Half price programs. For a $30 to $100 annual fee you can join a half price program and get 50% off hotel rooms. You must make reservations in advance and ask the hotel if it participates. Here are several of the most popular ones.

America at 50% Discount,
(800) 248-2783. Fee is $49.95 a year.

Encore,
(800) 638-8976. Offers a list of 3,000 hotels. Fee is $49.

Entertainment National Hotel and Dining Directory,
(800) 445-4137. Directory costs $37.95.

Entertainment Publications,
(800) 477-3234. Fee is $30.

Great American Traveler,
(800) 548-2812. Offer discounts at over 2,000 hotels. Fee is $49.95

ITC-50,
(800) 342-0558. Fee is $36.

Insiders tip: What about the YMCA? Before you brush it aside you should know that many of them are very nice and one of the best deals around. It won't be a 5 star hotel, but you'll get a clean, safe, comfortable room for $20 dollars a night. You'll find lodging in 39 U.S. cities, and in 25 foreign countries. I happen to know that the one in Hong Kong is very nice and looks like a regular hotel. To find out more, send a SASE to The Y's Way, 224 East 47th Street, New York, NY 10017.

Try college dorms. Many colleges are looking to make some money on empty dorm rooms during the summer. You can a get a nice dorm room for $15 to $30 dollars a night. And many times colleges are conveniently located right in the heart of a nice city. You should know, most times children are not allowed. Contact the college you want to stay at for more details.

How to get cash paid back by travel services:

There are different ways to get money back from travel services.

1) Travel cancellation insurance. In case you get sick or a personal problem comes up so that you can't go, but have prepaid, this is a good buy. You can get coverage for about $5 per $100 spent. You will need to have a letter or certificate from your doctor vouching for your illness.

2) Reduced airline prices. This has happened to my wife and me several times. We have bought tickets months in advance at one price, then during a fare war the fare drops. The catch is, if you don't call your travel agency and ask for a refund of the difference, you will probably not hear from them. So you need to keep a watch on your fares.

3) Getting a refund for a non-refundable airline ticket. Most of your discount fares have a stipulation of no refunds. However, when you book and pay, the travel agency still holds your money for a few days. That is your window of opportunity to get your money back if needed. They don't have to refund it, but one who wants your continued business will.

4) Use a Discover card. If you use your Discover to charge your travel, it pays cash back at the end of each year.

Chapter

Being Organized

7

How to end procrastination:

E veryone does it. And we all do it for the same reason. We are putting off something we don't really want to do. We never procrastinate vacation, eating dessert or doing something we enjoy. We put off those things which are work or unpleasant. The bad news is for the rest of our lives those things will come up. And sometimes the longer it goes undone the worse off we are. So how do you make yourself become quick to get to those things done? Take a look.

1) Learn why you procrastinate: The first thing you need to do is ask yourself, why do I procrastinate? Or more specifically, why don't I want to clean out the closet? Are your reasons just excuses? "I don't feel like it right now." "I have more important things to do." "I don't feel well." You'd be surprised how many times we tell little lies to ourselves to avoid doing something. Or is self-doubt keeping you from doing something? Often that is the real key. People doubt their ability to do the put-off task adequately. Once you understand your most common reason for procrastinating you can start to do something about it.

2) Do projects or tasks in pieces: Many people don't start something because they don't think they will have time to finish. The task seems overwhelming so it's never begun. Instead of trying to tackle the whole thing at once, try breaking it into bite-size pieces. If you need to clean your basement, start with working on it for one hour a day until it's finished. Many times you'll find, once you get going you'll want to do more. And if you really get going but get tired of it, think of other things you'd like to do, and do it while your energy is up. Write a letter, clean your cabinets, rake the leaves or organize a drawer.

3) Obey the "now" principle: This is where your will-power comes in. When you think of a project that needs to be done and you have time, just go do it. At least tell yourself you'll start on it. The key is to do it now. If you really want to change this bad habit, this will get you used to doing things immediately. Even if it's just a start.

4) Make a list: Some people can't get through a day without a list of things to do. If this helps, great. If you have never tried it, do. It will give you a sense of needing to accomplish things so you can cross it off.

Procrastination really can be beat. It's a bad habit and can be hard to overcome. But it's definitely possible with a little focused thinking.

Planning secrets of the rich and famous:

Planning your time wisely will effectively give you more free time, help you get your priorities done. (And help you decide what your priorities are!) Undoubtedly, the most successful people in this world are amazing planners who use every second of their day wisely. Here are some of their secrets.

1) Keep a daily "to do" list. Decide what must be done today. Prioritize them. And the next day make a new list starting with any new things plus the old items. Realize only about 2 out of 10 things are really important. Concentrate on those most important things. Don't waste valuable time doing things that can wait.

2) What's your most productive time of the day? Determine what that time is, and set this time aside for the most important projects. Don't waste it on small tasks.

3) Schedule routine tasks for times when your energy is drained. Like reading the mail, making a shopping list, reading the newspaper, talking on the phone.

4) Make time to relax. Even if it's only 15 minute a day for you and only you. Do it to gather your thoughts and catch a breather.

5) Make wait time productive. How much time do you spend waiting for doctors, for kids from school, in traffic jams? Use this time to get things done like reading a book or a magazine.

6) Plan for a crisis. If you have kids, a crisis a day is pretty common. If you don't get one, great. But plan some leeway (an hour is adequate) to deal with things that come up unexpectedly.

7) Keep a calender. Write down everything you need to remember to do. Even keep it months in advance if you can. Make sure it's in a place the whole family can see. Make it a rule that if someone needs to go somewhere or do something it must be written on the calendar.

How to interpret dreams and unlock their power:

Dreams can help us unlock tremendous inner power. They show us things we are afraid of, anxious about and things we wish we could do. You can use dreams to know more about yourself, and also to gain more insight into problems, challenges or obstacles in life. Dreams also help us unlock great creativity -- even if you think you are not creative. Here is a technique you can use to make the most out of your dreams.

1) Keep a dream log. This is the first step in interpreting your dreams. You must have something to refer to. Put a pad and pencil by your bed. It's guaranteed, if you try to just remember them and write them down later, you'll forget. You must capture them immediately. Write down as much detail as possible. Including your feelings during the dream and other people or characters and objects. Also, include settings and conversations.

2) Control your dreams. Believe it or not, you are in a state of semi-consciousness as you dream. The more aware you are, the more you'll be able to find a dream's meaning. Try looking for things that will help you in your dreams. As you go to sleep think about what you wish to accomplish. Is it a new painting you want to work on, a business presentation, how you want to organize your basement or how you'd like your yard to look? Really concentrate as you fall asleep on your purpose and the most wonderful ideas will come to you. It's a great resource that goes unused by most people. This "creative dreaming" will give you unbelievable fulfillment.

3) How to interpret your dreams: No one is better able to interpret your dreams than you. Keep in mind, your dreams are a mixed bag of your thoughts, experiences, fears, hopes and beliefs. Start looking at your dream log look for reoccurring events, or people or objects that keep popping up. Do you see patterns or similarities? If you have weird or "different" characters in your dreams, these are thought to represent other sides of your personality. Perhaps a side you know exists, but you keep hidden. Seek to start a conversation with these people in your dreams. You may learn some enlightening things about yourself.

4) Use dreams to confront your fears. Some people have recurring nightmares. Either someone is chasing them or they are about to fall off a cliff or some other frightening event. If you want to rid yourself of these inner fears you must try to

confront hem. Next time the dream comes up remember that you were going to put a stop to it. Try walking up to the person who is chasing you and tell them to stop. If you put this kind of thinking into your head often you will remember to do it. It's worked for many people. And it can work for you.

How to reach all your goals:

There is a saying, "a goal unwritten is only a wish." It's easy to have goals, but reaching them is a whole other task. What are your goals? If you want to reach your goals your first job is to set some. Whether they be long term or short term goals. Reaching goals can be a frustrating road if you aren't sure how to reach them. Here are some tips to help you reach all you goals.

1) Be realistic. Trying to get through medical school in 5 years instead of 8 is not a realistic goal. Losing 10 pounds is a realistic goal. Most failure comes because people aim too high. Not that that's bad, but be reasonable with yourself. Or set short term goals that will lead to a bigger one. Setting a goal to be president is fine but do it in steps rather than having that as a goal without knowing how to achieve it. Many people get discouraged because they set very ambitious goals, failed, got depressed and never tried again. Instead do some planning.

2) Try to visualize the outcome. What will you look like minus 20 pounds? What will your dream home look like? How will you look in your new office after the promotion? How will the new recipe look after it's done? How will you feel after you finally get your degree? Continue to always have these thoughts. It will internally help you do things to bring you closer to it. You will start thinking of new ways with new determination to bring it off just like you want to.

3) Write out a plan. Use a numbered order of steps you will need to accomplish your goal. Once you're able to formulate a plan and get it written, you will have a clear vision of how you will accomplish your goal.

4) Don't ever give up. If the goal you set was something important enough to do once it must be pretty important. It takes a lot of determination. Give yourself a reward for reaching your goal. Decide that you'll take a vacation, or go out to dinner or buy yourself a new stereo. Let that motivate you to achieve it.

5) Tell others about your goal. This way you will have their support as well. They can help you move along and cheer you on. You'll know when they see you they'll ask how you're doing and this can be a great motivator to help you reach your goal.

How to gain 10 hours a week of free time and eliminate wasted time:

Do it right the first time. It pays to take they time to do things right. If you don't, you'll just end up doing it again. Now you've spent twice the time, plus the aggravation. If it's worth doing, do it carefully.

Combine activities. If you need to go return a video, and you need to go the the store and pick your kids up, do it all at once. You spend a a lot of time just driving around. Take a little time to plan and only do it once. Plus, you'll save money on gas.

Stick to priorities. Decide what must be done today. And do those things first. Then move on to other things that must be done. You'll find lots of little things to eat up your time throughout the day and still feel like you got nothing done. So get the important things out of the way first.

Plan your work, work your plan. Make a daily agenda including meals, activities and errands. Build in some extra time for things that come up suddenly. The important thing is to make a game plan for the day then let it guide you.

Get up a 1/2 hour earlier. Losing just a 1/2 hour of sleep won't make a difference that you"ll notice, but you'll gain a 1/2 hour more time. If that seems too easy, try getting up an hour earlier. That's 7 hours a week you'll have to do what you like. Make it personal time for a walk or a book or whatever you feel you don't usually have time for.

Turn off the TV. If you're like most people you spend an average of 4 hours a day watching TV . That's 28 hours a week. More than one full day a week you just sit and watch TV. Turn it off. Only watch those shows that you really enjoy. Use the left over time to do other things. Or if you must, do things while you watch TV, too. Make better use of your VCR. Record shows and watch them later at a more convenient time.

Plan working meals at work and home. Plan meetings during lunch and breakfast so you can accomplish more. The same goes for home. Use mealtimes to plan and make family decisions. It's probably one of the few time you're all together to talk.

Set aside a time for the phone. If you have one of those phones that rings all day, let it ring. Let the answering machine get it. You can spend hours a day talking on the telephone. Not to mention the interruptions it causes every time you have to stop what you're doing to answer it.

Try to do things at the same time each day. This will help you develop habits. Things like getting up, showering, eating meals, going to the store, holding meetings, shopping, doing bills and yard work. Those things will get fixed into your schedule and you won't have to worry about finding time to do them.

Stay organized. Do you spend a lot of your day searching for things? Shoes, papers, bills, toys, etc. Keep things in their place. Reward your kids for doing the same.

How to get organized and stay that way:

Do you feel like your life and your home are a scattered mess? If so, then it's time to do something about it. If you just take it one step at a time, soon you'll be the organized person you never knew existed.

1) Start with yourself. Get a planner so you can organize your time better. Write important dates and events down so you always know where you must be. Organize your days. Make a daily plan. (See preceding topics on planning)

2) Organize your office. Whether it be at home or at work, start sifting through all your personal things and throwing away things you don't need anymore. Put things in file folders and in drawers. Make everything have a place. And always return things to the proper place. Get more file drawers if you need them and clearly mark what is inside. Just making it look neat isn't necessarily organized. Remember, from now on everything has a place. You'll find it fast and get it out of your way faster.

3) Organize your home. It's easiest to do this one room at a time. Don't try to get it all done in few hours or even a day. Just pick a room at random. When you do children's rooms, make sure they are with you so they see how things will be organized from now on. You may need plastic bins, racks, shelves and so forth to give everything a place.

You may think this is all easier said than done. It's really not though. You are the one that must change your habits. You must decide "from now on I will be more organized." Everything must have a place and things should always be in their place. Set aside an hour each week to do bills and throw away papers you don't want or need. File everything else.

Give it a try. It will take a lot of initial work, but after that it will run like clockwork.

How to simplify your life:

Use these 5 steps to make your life simpler and enjoy more time for yourself.

1) Set your priorities. What do you really want to do with your time? Are you spending lots of time doing things that you don't want or get no enjoyment from? Get a pen and paper and write down your top three priorities. Then write down everything else that takes up your time and see what you can eliminate.

2) Set your finances in order. Are financial worries stressing you out? If so, then seek to set them straight so you can put it behind you. See a credit counselor, make a budget and do without things you don't need until you are in better shape. Learn to live within your means and don't over spend. It's not worth the grief and worry it causes.

3) Find a comfortable routine. Are you one of those people who is always coming and going at different times. Set some time frames and get into a regular schedule. If you have no time limits you have no control over your day-to-day life. You be the one to dictate your own time. You may think a routine is boring and monotonous, but it will help you spend your time better.

4) Don't sweat the details. How much time and energy do you waste on things that usually turn out O.K. in the end? Most of us do. Life is full of stuff that can be potentially harmful or distressing, but we usually make more of it than it is. Try to keep that in mind and wait to see how things develop before you go nuts over it.

5) Always make time for yourself. It's important for you to take some time to relax and do something for you. Take a bath, go for a walk, go for a drive, read a book or just sit in a quiet room and collect your thoughts and meditate. If you spend all your time running around for other people life will just be a big burden. Don't forget about you.

Chapter
_____

8

Mental Fitness

How to stay calm in tough situations:

Tough or tense situations can shut some people down. Whether it's a car wreck, a constantly crying baby or a disgruntled employee, it takes some cool to remain calm and collected.

You must realize, whatever the situation is it's only temporary. Keep telling yourself to stay clam and logical. A lot of people overreact to tough situations and make bad choices. Count to ten before you make any rash decisions. Take the time to assess the situation and discover the best way to endure it or fix it.

Leave the situation if you need to. If you think you may say or do something that you'll be sorry for later, leave until you've calmed down. Also, try to view the situation in its entirety. Why is it happening? What's the solution? Will patience be my best help? Think before you act.

How to defeat the fear of failure:

What have you got to lose by trying? There are a lot of people out there that are afraid to try anything because they don't want to fail. If you are one of these people, use the following steps to overcome your fear.

1) Find out what you are really afraid of. Is it financial loss, fear of what others may think, lack of confidence? It could be one of these or something else.

2) Take calculated risks. If you are afraid to fail and you take a risk too great you may be right. Everyone needs to take risks. Figure out how much you can afford to put at stake. And take that much risk.

3) Change your attitude. If you constantly tell yourself that you will fail, you probably will. You need to absolutely believe that you will succeed.

4) Failure is part of life. Everything is a learning experience. Thomas Edison had hundreds of versions of the light bulb before he got one that worked. Abraham Lincoln was not elected several times before he was. Failure should not be feared, it should be looked at as a step in a process.

5) Be realistic. Don't set standards so high you can't reach your goal. Set out to achieve what you know you can. Then start taking a bit more risk.

How to reduce stress when you travel:

Traveling has a tendency to cause ulcers in many people when, in most cases, traveling is supposed to be an enjoyable experience. Use these 5 tips to replace your stress with calm, relaxed assurance.

1) Plan in advance. The #1 thing you can do is to plan well in advance of your trip. Make airline reservations, car rentals, hotel room bookings well in advance. And check every place you want to visit and make sure they will be open. Always confirm every so often to make sure nothing has changed. Occasionally airlines change flight times and so forth. Make sure nothing is left undone.

2) Make a list. Days or weeks before you go, make a list of everything you need to take. Do it in advance so you will have time to add on things as you think of them. When you go to pack, simply use your list and check off things as you go.

3) Always plan more time than you need. You never know what may come up at the last minute. Always give yourself plenty of time to get where you're going.

4) Find all you can about the place you're visiting. If you're going to a new place and you're nervous, go to the library and get a book or a video about the place. Even try to find someone who's been there to ask questions. Learn all you can so you'll feel more comfortable.

5) Have someone look after your house. Make arrangements with a neighbor or friend to watch your home when you are gone. A lot of people can't enjoy a vacation because they think their house is burning down. Have them get the mail and newspaper, check doors and even leave a light on inside.

How to handle conflict and control anger:

1) Don't let your anger control you. When you are provoked by someone they want you to fight back. Don't let them have that satisfaction. Be the one to stay calm. It disarms them and gives the message that you won't handle the situation that way. Then the person may accept a calm approach.

2) Try talking about it. Look for areas of agreement. Try to reason with the person and ask them to calm down so you can talk it out. Explain that yelling and screaming will not solve the problem.

3) Try to understand the problem and then to fix it. Try to understand what the problem is. Until you know what's wrong you can't get anywhere. Once you understand, start working toward a solution.

4) Don't get defensive. If you get defensive and start blaming the other person this will just make matters much worse. Instead do what you can to calm the person down and talk. Blaming and being defensive only fuels the fire.

5) Don't back down or act scared or submissive. An angry person will thrive on his apparent control. This will just make him more aggressive. Stand your ground while maintaining calm. Don't show any fear.

How to make a great first impression:

You only get one chance to make a good first impression. It can mean getting a job, or not, having in-laws that like you, or not, getting into the school of your choice, or not. It's important that you know how to really "wow" someone for instant appeal. Here are 5 steps to follow to make a dazzling first impression.

1) Make and maintain eye contact. Always look the person right in the eye. Don't stare or fix your eyes in a trance-like state. Looking down, or looking away when you speak shows fear and lack of confidence. Looking around shows disrespect for the person while they are speaking.

2) Speak clearly and loudly. You don't need to scream, but if you mumble or talk soft they will have a hard time understanding you. Be a bold speaker. And speak a couple decibels higher than normal. Don't speak too fast either or you will sound more nervous than you might already be.

3) Walk and stand tall and upright. Don't slouch while standing or sitting. It will make you look lazy and too relaxed. Standing or sitting up straight shows you are paying attention.

4) Don't get too close. People need about a 12" bubble around them for a comfort zone. Don't invade it at a first meeting. Stay far enough away to still carry on a conversation.

5) Keep up your end of the conversation. Don't make the other person do all the talking. Be gracious and talk casually. Don't dominate the conversation, but be as interesting and articulate as you can.

How to control moods and emotions:

It's never good to attempt to stifle your emotions. But you should seek to control them and not let them get the best of you. You should know how to express them appropriately at the right time. Use these tips to help control your emotions and moods.

1) Get enough sleep. If you are constantly tired and fatigued, it is much harder to control your emotions. Getting enough rest will help you think and reason more clearly and stay in total control.

2) Colors. Believe it or not colors can affect your mood. When bright colored light enters your eye it triggers your pineal gland to produce hormones that make you happy. Dark colors have the opposite effect. Decorate your home in light colors and wear them also. You'll notice you are more cheery and positive.

3) Use positive self-talk. It really works. Even if you feel like you don't believe it, tell yourself that you are a good person. It has worked for millions of people who felt otherwise. Continuously hearing yourself talk positively helps it slowly (or quickly) come true.

4) Watch your diet. Foods like sugar, caffeine and alcohol have an enormous effect on your emotions. Caffeine and sugar make you jittery and nervous. Alcohol will depress you and even impair you. Avoid these foods in excess.

5) Be objective. You can't save the world or solve every problem. Some people get very angry or upset and feel helpless. We all need to do what we can, but it's important to remain objective and see things in a realistic way.

How to overcome stress and anxiety:

Stress and anxiety are common in just about every-body. But they cause many unhealthy symptoms and relat-ed health problems ranging from insomnia and fatigue to ulcers and headaches, and the list goes on and on. There are ways to control stress and anxiety. In extreme cases, therapy and prescription drugs are used. But for most peo-ple with a fair amount of stress and anxiety there are sim-ple ways to deal with it.

1) Identify the source of your stress. Take a moment and try to think about what is really eating you. You may think it's one thing, but after sorting through your thoughts you may find it's something else. After you know what it is, either try to eliminate it, solve it or put it in perspective and ask yourself if it really is worth the agony.

2) Use meditation. This doesn't mean dressing in a loin cloth and chanting. Meditation is becoming very popular as a stress reliever. Just find a quiet place and a good time of day that you can set aside regularly. Sit upright on the floor or on a chair and close your eyes and try to clear your head. Think about nothing. You may spend a half an hour or 10 minutes. It's your choice. Begin to relax your whole body. Slowly let all your muscles relax. Think pleasant thoughts of blues skies or warm oceans. Also, pay attention to your breathing. Take long deep breaths. Soon you'll find yourself refreshed and better able to face each day.

Secret to attain real inner happiness:

Real inner happiness is your choice. You'll meet people who have always had a rotten life and always will, who are still happy. And you'll meet people who have everything in the world going for them and still moan and complain that they are so unhappy. Why? Because that's the choice they make. It may not make sense to everyone why so many people would choose to be unhappy, but they do. The good news is that you can learn to take control of the situation.

Unhappy people start when they're young. Negative thought patterns develop and they can't shake them. Thoughts such as "I'll never get what I want," or "It will never work out, it never does" continue to haunt unhappy people into adulthood. And most people turn these thoughts into a self-fulfilling prophecy. The secret is to wash away these thoughts and replace them with gratitude and an "I'm happy for what I have" way of thinking.

The process of unlearning these negative thoughts may take a while. It took a lifetime to learn them. The first thing to do is realize that if you're unhappy, it's your choice. The unhappy person always views them self as a victim. They need to realize they are not victims of external forces, they only perceive it that way. It is usually the stress of a situation that causes these feelings.

Controlling stress using relaxation techniques is a good way to start deprogramming negative thoughts. It takes a concerted effort to remove negative thinking. If you want to really be happy inside, you must make a concerted effort. If you aren't willing, it will never happen. Stop speaking out loud your unhappiness. Make a list of everything you have that is good. And be vigilant in your control of negative thoughts. Progress will come if there is determination.

How to overcome mistakes:

If we all beat ourselves up for every mistake we made we'd all be in bad shape. "To err is human." Use these 6 ways to get over your mistakes.

1) Learn to laugh at yourself. Don't take yourself too seriously. Learn to laugh at your dumb mistakes. If you can't, you are too uptight.

2) Everyone makes mistakes. Is your goal to be perfect? Well sad but true, it won't happen. You, me and everyone on this planet makes mistakes on a daily basis. So why should you be any different? Making mistakes is a necessary part of life.

3) Learn from your mistakes. Do your best to learn from your mistakes the first time so you don't have to repeat them. That's where you do have some control. Use your mistakes as a learning experience so from that point further you can eliminate that one from your life.

4) Use your new found knowledge to help others avoid mistakes. Be it a big one or small one, you can really help someone if you can share with them what you did and why you wish you hadn't.

5) Make restitution. If your mistake involved hurting another person or doing damage, do everything you can to make up for it. It may be as simple as an apology, or it may involve making a cash payment to repair a damaged item. It will make you and others involved feel better.

6) Lighten up. Don't view life as a perfection game. Take time to enjoy life and put mistakes behind you. You can't reverse time so why let it weigh you down?

Staying mentally fit:

So many people are concerned about their physical health and neglect their mind. It's just as important to keep mentally fit as it is to stay physically fit. There are some simple habits you can adopt that have already helped people stay mentally fit and in some cases have turned their lives around.

1) Get rid of negative thoughts and replace them with love. A mind that is only full of hate and dislike can not remain healthy. It may take some forgiveness on your part or it may mean shaping a new attitude toward people and life in general. Replace this negativity with love for life, for other people and most important for yourself.

2) Confront your fears. Everybody has fears. Some are very real and some are exaggerated. You may need to seek counseling to eliminate them. But most often you just need to let them out by talking to someone about it. Fear breaks down your mind and body with stress. Sort out your feelings and see what your real fears are and work on overcoming them.

3) Use positive thinking. Always look for the good in all things and situations. Some people look at a situation and only see the bad. Some people have learned to see the good. And there is almost always one thing good to be seen. Try to focus on what's good.

4) Challenge your mind. Fill it with knowledge. Read good books and always learn new things. If you don't exercise it just like your body it will diminish. Remember to always do something everyday to keep it active.

How to get what you want peacefully:

Or call it the art of negotiation with a difficult person. When you need something from a person you dislike or is hard to deal with it can be a tough situation. To provoke them will just make matters worse. There could be a lot at stake. Maybe it's a large sum of money, or a favor, or something in a real estate deal. Whatever it is you can have the upper hand by knowing these few rules.

1) Keep your anger in control. If you loose your cool you will decrease your chance of getting whatever it is you want. Getting mad will only start a fight and make it impossible to communicate clearly. Be the one to stay in control.

2) Point out negative consequences. What can you hold over their head. "You'll lose your job," "your credit rating will be ruined," "I'll call the police," "you'll regret it for the rest of your life." Try to find a consequence that will make them likely to give in.

3) Let the person know your reason for asking for what you want. Most times you'll have a good reason. Let them have a little sympathy for you. It can turn an angry person soft when they see you're sincere and that you are not just being selfish or greedy.

How to deal with change:

The majority of us don't like change. And it can stop us from really enjoying life like we should. It can rob us of happiness. If this is a problem for you, try these 4 steps to make change easy.

1) Accept change as a part of life. As they say, "the only thing that's constant is change." That doesn't always make it easier. But you can remember that it's not just you, everyone changes. Jobs change. Seasons change. People move. Kids come and go. You can't stop it. But if you'll just let it happen instead if fighting it you will relieve a lot of pressure.

2) Try to see the good in the change. Is it a new job with more money? A bigger house in a nicer neighborhood? Or maybe now you can make some more new friends? Whatever it is, try to focus on the good and not who you miss, or why it's different.

3) Get busy and involved. Make the very best of your new situation. Do everything you did before. Seek new opportunities to get involved. If you keep busy, you won't have time to think about what it was like before.

4) Prepare for change.   Take opportunities to go outside your comfort zone. Do things you normally wouldn't do. Go home from work a different way, eat things you never tried before, etc. This will help you get used to not always having the same routine in the same place.

How to calm an angry person:

Angry people can easily become violent and do harm to you or someone else. And if you're trying to solve a problem, there's no way you'll make any headway until the person calms down. Use the 3 steps below for success.

1) Stay calm. Don't raise your voice, yell, scream or act hostile. Then it's hopeless. You've been drawn in and the best thing to do is leave. Talk calmly and slowly. And show some concern in your voice for wanting to resolve the situation peacefully. You'd be surprise how your calmness will rub off.

2) Reason with the person. Tell them that you'd like to discuss the problem just as soon as they calm down and can talk rationally. Explain that it's too hard to solve a problem if they are upset.

3) Stay there until they calm down. Never turn your back and walk off, or hang up a phone. That will just infuriate them. Hold your ground until they calm down and are ready to talk.

How to avoid feeling lonely or sorry for yourself:

Scientific studies have shown that being or feeling lonely has nothing to do with how many people are around you. You can live with or be surrounded by people and still feel lonely. And this can have negative side effects. They found that people who feel lonely are more susceptible to illness and die sooner. There are things you can do to eliminate lonely feelings and have a happy, fulfilling life.

Many times loneliness is actually just acute boredom. Never just sit around. Read a book, get a pet, take up a hobby or two, go for a walk, get a bike, write letters, learn a musical instrument, volunteer your time. There are plenty of opportunities to make your time alone more enjoyable.

You also must become secure with who you are. Learn to love and appreciate yourself for who you are. Gather some confidence and self- esteem. If you don't like things about yourself that are negative, change them. If you like being who you are you will not feel so lonely by yourself. Learn to look to yourself for company instead of others.

Take time alone to discover who you are. Find out what makes you tick. What are your likes and dislikes? What are your goals and aspirations? People will be drawn to you if you have a sense of success and accomplishment with you.

Give your time to help other people. Hospitals, nursing homes and so forth love to have people come in and talk to patients. Become a big brother or big sister. Volunteer at a soup kitchen. Giving to others is very rewarding.

How to use the ERA technique
to overcome major problems:

ERA, Effective Repositioning Approach will help you overcome major obstacles and problems your life. It's easy to do and very effective. Pro and con lists aren't really very helpfully. All they do is make matters confusing by pointing out 2 equally arguable sides of a problem. The ERA technique uses imagery and creative problem solving. Take any problem you face at work, at home or in a relationship and apply the following steps for success.

1) First think of the very worst situation this problem could lead to. And also visualize the very best situation. How close to reality are they? How much work do you really need to solve the problem? Now that you've "seen" the best and the worst you can start to work towards solving it. Also, you must ask yourself how realistic are the best and worst scenarios? Maybe the problem is smaller than you think.

2) Now get out a piece of paper and a pen. Write down "I want" and then write down the problem you want to overcome. "I want to have a better relationship with my spouse." "I want to budget my money better.", etc. Then write down "However, I" and then write down your 1 or 2 biggest obstacles that are stopping you from solving this problem. Make sure this focuses on you and not someone else. Now cross out the "however" part and you're left with the situation you are trying to overcome.

3) Now it's time to start brainstorming and coming up with as many solutions as you can. No matter how silly they may seem, write them down. Then use this list to start solving the problem. It may go slow, but at least you have taken some positive action that will ultimately work.

Chapter
_____

Communication Secrets ⑨

How to use body language
to make others do what you want:

With just a little insider knowledge of what people are saying to you through their body language you can get them to do anything. You will know how to "read" them and shift gears depending on what they are showing you. It's fun and it will give you a hidden power.

People are most willing to do what you say when they are displaying, openness, insecurity and cooperation. Look for these signs, then ask for what you want.

Openness: Open hands, coat unbuttoned or off.

Insecurity: Chewing on pens or fingers, pinching themselves or doing "thumb over thumb."

Cooperation: Sitting on edge of chair, standing very upright and erect, gesturing with hands, open hands.

Whether people are displaying defensiveness, confidence, nervousness or frustration, these are signs. Nervousness and frustration are signs of indecisiveness, while defensiveness and confidence are signs of perceived power over you. These will tell you that you need to do some more talking to sway them your way. If they seem defensive, shift gears and put them at ease. If they are nervous or scared, give them confidence and stroke their ego. Watch for these signs.

Defensiveness: Rubbing nose or eyes, arms crossed, backing away, looking sideways.

Confidence: Hand holding lapels on coat, hands behind head, back straight, hands steepled in front of them, hands in pockets with thumbs out.

Nervousness: Smoking, pinching themselves, clearing throat too often, whistling, hand over mouth, jiggling money, keys or pens, tugging on earlobes.

Frustration: Rubbing back of neck, making gestures with a fist, clenched hands, rubbing hand through hair, wringing hands.

How to meet interesting people and get to know them:

Interesting people are all around us. We often sell ourselves short by thinking interesting people are only rich and famous. Your next door neighbor could have a riveting life story to tell. Someone at your church, at school or at the grocery store could be very interesting. You never know.

The key to meeting and developing a social relationship with them is by knowing how to talk to them and have them open up to you.

It helps if you are an outgoing, friendly person. If you are, people will have no problem talking to you. The very biggest tip is to focus on the other person. When you meet someone new and want to to get to know them, focus 100% of the conversation on them. People love to talk about themselves. Especially people with a interesting story to tell.

As you talk, smile, look them in the eye and nod. These are all cues for them to continue talking. Ask them questions for clarification. As they talk, be thinking of questions you want to ask so if a pause comes along you can fill it with that question and hear more. Once they are comfortable talking you can ask them just about anything and they will be more than happy to talk. Using this approach you can have a large set of very interesting friends to talk about.

How to negotiate like a pro:

There have been volumes written on powerful, effective negotiation. But by mastering just a few simple rules, you can negotiate and win every time.

Get the home court advantage. Always try to negotiate on your own turf. In your home or your office or on your front yard. If you do, the other person is out of their element and not as confident. If they refuse or can't, go somewhere neutral.

Use proper seating. Try to be at the head of the table, or in whatever direction faces the door so you can see who's entering. If there is a window, sit with your back to it so the glare is in his eyes.

Get all his demands first. Before you lay anything on the table, urge him to lay his out first. This gives you the upper hand because you can alter your demands after you see what his are. Don't let him talk you into a point by point forum. This is just slow and confusing. When it's your turn, offer them one by one and get an answer on each one before you go on to another one.

Getting a good final offer: If you've ever dealt with a car salesman you know a final offer is anything but final. You need to take this as only the final approach to a final offer. In most cases you can go for more. When given a final offer you have several choices. You can 1) get angry and act insulted 2) be nice about it, but politely tell the person it is not acceptable and offer to end the deal 3) start talking about something else to give you time to think about it. Depending on the situation these approaches will sweeten a final offer.

How to nicely decline. If a "no" decision sounds like it is your decision, that could make the person mad. Instead blame it on a 3rd party, my boss, my wife, the company, lack of funds, a policy or regulation. This gives you an out without a bad feeling and shifts the blame to someone else.

Deadlocked situations. If you are at an impasse and going nowhere, take a break. Maybe even an abrupt one. Just stand up and leave. Come back with a good idea. This gives you time to get out while they are still stuck in a room.

A pill that helps you overcome shyness:

For some people shyness can be a difficult day-to-day obstacle, even crippling for some. But it doesn't have to be with a new pill that actually helps you overcome shyness. Scientists have discovered that a pill, Dilantin, can help you overcome shyness. It helps calm anxiety, fear and depression. Ask your doctor about Dilantin for you.

How to make easy, stress-free conversation:

Having a strained, dull or stressful conversation can be a real downer. The best thing you can do its learn how to be a brilliant conversationalist so no one can ever label you a hard person to talk to.

1) Relax. Few conversations are life and death situations. Pretend you are talking to your best friend. Let the words hop out of your mouth. It may take some acting at first, but with practice you will form a solid habit.

2) Make eye contact. This will build your confidence. If you look around or hang your head you will look and feel uncomfortable. Look the person right in the eye and speak with confidence.

3) Focus on the other person. This will draw the attention away from yourself and relieve some pressure. And it will also put you in the lead so you can direct the flow of the conversation.

4) Learn how to "duck out." If the pressure is too intense there are several ways to gracefully leave a conversation. Say "I have to go to the rest room" or "Excuse me, I need to talk to her before she leaves." Or "I must go find my wife or husband." Or "I think I'll go out for some air." Or just say " It's been great talking to you, call me sometime," and leave.

How to write letters that get results:

Letters are a great way of communication. They are cheap and great if you want to communicate without being face to face. They are especially good if you have a sensitive message or if you want something. You can take your time to prepare a well-crafted letter that says exactly what you want it to so get what you want.

1) Be careful what you write. When someone reads your letter you will not be there to clear up a misunderstanding. Write clearly so you will not be misunderstood and upset someone.

2) Writing a letter as a unhappy consumer. This can bring valuable rewards if you say the right things. Explain your situation and why you are unhappy. Explain the hassle and inconvenience it has caused. Then write that you will never buy from them again and will tell everyone you know not to go there because of what happened to you. Ask for a full refund and tell them that if they value their customers they will right the wrong. This can be done and most companies will do all they can to help you even if it means a reimbursement or free merchandise.

3) Writing a letter for a job. After you write the letter, count the"I's." If you have more than 5 in a full page, turn them around and make them "you's." Employers want to know what you will do for them, not what you think is great about yourself. Sell yourself in terms of how you'll increase their market share or sell more popcorn than anyone ever.

How to meet new people:

Some people just don't feel comfortable meeting people in person. Luckily there are several ways for you to meet people and develop a relationship without meeting them face-to-face until you are ready.

Dating service. With a dating service you can go and watch a video of perspective people you might want to meet. Most times you can get a a phone number first so you can talk to them.

Internet. The Internet has become the hottest place to meet people. If you are able to go on-line you can get into a chat group and talk to all kinds of people. People love the fact that they can be a different person on-line where no one knows them. Most libraries will provide Internet access if you aren't set up at home.

How to effectively communicate with your children:

If you and your children are communicating well, your family will run much smoother. Effective communication sets the stage for an ideal relationship. Use these tips for better communication.

1) Encourage your kids. Let them know how proud you are of them. Pick one thing they each do really well that's different from the other children. Let them know how great a job they are doing.

2) Admit when you are wrong. As adults we sometimes have a hard time letting our kids know we actually were wrong. Telling them when you are wrong sets a good example for them and doesn't make you a domineering or controlling parent in their eyes.

3) Establish house rules. A house without rules is a house in chaos. There must be limits and rules they should abide by. And there should be a punishment for breaking them. Make sure you let them know these while they are young so they can learn them as they grow.

4) Take time to listen. So many parents are too busy these days to really listen to their children. Talk to them as a friend would. Set side uninterrupted time to listen to their problems and successes and offer your love and support.

5) Let them make decisions. Sometimes it's easier to decide for them because you know best. But they can't learn about consequences. Let them make their own decisions and carry them out.

6) Communicate clearly. A lot of mistakes and failures of children are because they misunderstood. Make sure you make clear your instructions so you set them up for success, not failure.

How to get your spouse to really listen:

With 50% of all marriages ending in divorce, effective, two-way communication is very important. It can make a night and day difference in your relationship. Use the secrets below to get your spouse's undivided attention.

1) Choose your time and place. Don't choose to have an important conversation in the middle of a favorite show or during the ball game. Do it when you have some free time together to talk. Go for a walk just to talk. Or if you have to, schedule a time to get together to talk. If the reason for getting together is clear, you will have a devoted listener.

2) Don't approach a conversation angry. If you need to have a discussion and you are mad, calm down first. Nothing turns off a person quicker than an angry person coming after them. They will get defensive and all attempts at a controlled conversation will be gone.

3) Start the conversation out right. Say "thanks for talking about this" or "this is really important to me" or "we really need to discuss this now." Or something else to grab their attention right off the bat and show your concern for the matter.

How to handle difficult people:

They come in all shapes and sizes. The annoying guy who talks all the way through the movie. The coworker who's music blares out of his office. The brother who is rude and obnoxious. They all have one thing a common, the need for attention. Most difficult people do it to stand out and be noticed. They don't realize how offensive they really are. Here are some tips for dealing with them.

1) Don't let them bother you. If they see you're being bothered then they chalk it up as another victory. They win. You fuel their fire. Be as unaffected by their behavior as you can. When the attention doesn't come, they're more likely to change. But be prepared to have a lot of tolerance. Before it gets better they will step up their bad behavior to make it worse before they will abandon it.

2) Talk to them confidentially about how you feel before it turns into a huge battle. Explain the advantages of changing their bad behavior and the consequences if they don't.

How to communicate better with your family, coworkers, and others:

Effective communication is vital to getting along and succeeding in society. Not saying what you mean can get you in a lot of trouble. Putting your thoughts into words that are easy to understand takes some practice.

1) First learn to be a good listener. A lot of people forget that communicating has 2 parts, speaking and listening. Get into a habit of being a really good, attentive listener. People want to be listened to and always appreciate some-one who is really paying attention to them.

2) Ask questions. Do this just to be sure you really under-stood what they are trying to tell you. Restate what they have said. This will ensure you don't make them mad or hurt their feelings by not understanding correctly.

3) Don't get angry. There are many situations where you feel yourself getting steamed. If your boss tells you your project is terrible, or your husband tells you dinner was "interesting." Keep your cool. And after you have calmed down, explain how you felt when you were told something that hurt you . Or in the case of your boss, ask how it can be better and that you must have misunderstood.

4) People love compliments. When you give someone a compliment it reassures them that they are OK. This helps communication flow better. Don't throw them around just to be appreciated. But a nicely given compliment makes you easier to talk to.

5) Don't be accusatory. This is especially helpful in an argument. Once you start blaming and saying a lot of "you's," you will quickly turn off the other person. Talk about what you might be responsible for and how you will try to fix it. Blaming just shuts down communication.

How to learn from, forget and overcome past failures:

Mistakes aren't all bad. They may be at first, but we can learn some of our most valuable life lessons from our mistakes. A lot of people make one bad one and it ruins, or nearly ruins, the rest of their life. It doesn't have to, and shouldn't, be that way. Learning to view them as learning experiences is a necessary part of living.

1) Learn to forgive yourself. That can be the hardest thing to do. The reality is you can't change the past. You can only go forward. This is easier said than done, but it's the only way to pick up the pieces. Do what you can to repay what you've done, forgive yourself and move on.

2) Try again. When you've failed at something, you may have great reservations about trying again. But most often that's exactly what you need to do. If not, you will live with that failure forever.

3) Do something else. If you failed at something that is final, you need to refocus your energy on something else. Set new goals and reach them.

Chapter

Your Family

10

Choosing the best day care or babysitter:

With so many 2 career couples today, more children are being watched during the day by someone else. You can never be too careful about choosing someone to watch your kids. There are lot of bad day care providers and lots of abuse and neglect. Follow these rules to make sure your children are in very good hands.

Choosing a day care: Don't ever choose a day care out of desperation. Many parents feel like they must reserve a space or they will not get one. And hasty decisions lead to trouble. First find out the fees and the times.(Most are open weekdays from 8am to 6pm, but do vary.) Fees vary from place to place. Also, make sure your child is old enough. Usually a baby needs to be at least 4 months old, but some will accept them at 2 months. When you go to visit the day care check out these things.

1) Environment. Is it clean? Does it look safe? Are there adequate fences and protection from roads, streams and ditches? Is it bright and cheery? Does there appear to be many things to do?

2) How will they treat the children? How do they discipline the kids? Are they willing to potty train? Or will they force the child to try even if you haven't at home? Do they have a variety of activities to help them learn? Such as reading, painting, playing, songs etc.?

3) Meal times. Are meals provided? If so, what will they be fed? Get a menu and check to see that they are sticking to it.

4) What is the ratio between kids and staff. You don't want your child to be one of 20 kids with only 1 or 2 adults watching them. You can bet that individual attention will be scarce. They should have 1 staff member for every 3 children.

5) How are the kids? Do they look happy and involved? Or bored and in need of attention?

6) Are the furnishings "kid style." Are there plenty of small chairs, tables and toys?

Ask your child how he/she feels about the place. Let them play there for a while and see how they are treated. They will be spending a lot of time there and you should make sure they will be happy and well taken care of.

Choosing a baby sitter: It's always best to choose someone you know and trust. If you can't, then use these rules of thumb to choose a good one.

Ask for references. Ask for names and numbers of other families they sit for. This will give you a good indication of how well they do. If they have none, it shows lack of experience.

Ask if:
> They are willing to cook a meal?
> Have ever watched a newborn?
> How would they punish an unruly child?
> How much she earns per hour?
> What they would do in an an emergency?

After answering these questions you should feel confident or not about their ability.

Keys to a long-lasting marriage:

Marriage is a lot of work. It's those that quit working at it that end in divorce. It's not enough to just be married. Your goal should be a happy, long-lasting marriage. Use these 3 keys to a splendid marriage.

1) Show affection. This is one of the first things to go after the honeymoon is over and kids come along. Holding hands, hugging, and kissing convey much more than a verbal assurance. Let your kids see this display so they know you do love each other.

2) Go on a date every week. When you were dating you were having fun and getting to know each other. Unfortunately, many couples stop dating after they get married. Why cut such a great part of a marriage out? You should continue to go out each week to have fun and spend time alone. You'll find yourself looking forward to that date each week and it will keep the romance alive.

3) Say "I love you." It's not enough to assume your spouse knows this and doesn't need to hear it. Set a goal as a couple to tell each other everyday. It's difficult to drift apart if you make it a habit to say "I love you" everyday.

How to make sure
your kids are getting a good education:

A shiny report card packed with A's and B's doesn't necessarily mean your child is learning. Report cards don't reflect growth in common sense and reasoning skills. It's easy to skew a report card when the teacher puts down a better grade than has really been earned. Don't just let your child's education go unnoticed. Waiting for a report card 4 times a year and relying on that is not enough. Monitor your child's progress yourself and make sure what you see on the report card is accurate with how they are progressing.

Secrets to being a good Mom or Dad:

Being a mom or dad is tough work. But it's also important work if you don't want your kids to be a burden to society. Even perfect parents have hair raising times with their kids. So don't feel bad if you do, too. Here are some basic guidelines that will help relieve some of the stress of child raising.

1) Unconditional love. What your kids need more than anything you can give them is love. Not just love when they deserve it, but love all the time. Often they need it most when they've done something wrong. Let your kids know you love them frequently.

2) Time. As busy as you and many parents are, kids need time. They need to see that you care enough to spend time with them. Go for walks, do a puzzle, read a book, go fishing and do it often. It doesn't really matter what you do as long and you do it together.

3) Talk with your kids. Starting when they are just old enough to talk. They will amaze you with their ability to carry on a logical conversation as young as 2 years old. It's important to keep in touch with them as they grow up to help them overcome their fears and share their triumphs.

How to prevent
your home from being burglarized:

Most people who get burglarized have left an open invitation for the burglar. Burglars don't like to work to get into a house. They go after the "easy" houses. If you take some simple precautions you can avoid being robbed.

1) Keep shrubs around windows cut low. Burglars can use them to hide in. If they are big they can sit and watch your house without being seen Also, plant pricker bushes under windows to act as a deterrent.

2) Use locks on doors that are pick-proof. This will stop a thief cold. Also, if you have a door with glass in it, use a lock that must be opened with a key from the inside. Otherwise they will smash the glass and reach in and open the door.

3) Keep stuff off your yard that will help them get in. This includes ladders, chairs, tables etc. Anything that will be an aid to breaking in should be stored inside.

4) Nail unused windows shut. If you have windows that you never use, pound a nail into the window frame from the inside.

5) Make sure your yard is well-lit. Nothing helps a burglar more than darkness. Leave a front light on. Also, you can buy inexpensive motion detectors for the back and sides of your house. If motion is detected lights go on.

6) Going on vacation. Make it appear as if someone is home. Leave a light on inside. Have a neighbor collect your paper and mail. They can even turn on a light every night. Stop all other deliveries and have your grass cut.

7) Make sure all doors from the outside are solid wood doors. Anything else will be easily kicked in.

8) Put iron gratings around basement windows.

9) Get a security system. There are many options available. Go with a reputable company that's been in business a long time. Or call the police department for a recommendation.

10) Use window locks that are jimmy-proof. A burglar will usually enter through a window. Keep them locked tight with good locks.

How to find time together for 2-career couples:

A lot of 2-career marriages end in divorce because there is so little time to devote to the relationship. Plus there tends be a competition that drives couples apart with both trying to succeed. Below are 4 ways you can make it work.

1) Share responsibilities. With both of you equally busy, there is no room to say that one person is in charge of cooking, or cleaning or the yard. Whoever has the time and inclination to do something, should do it. This will lift a lot of stress.

2) Strike a balance. If one spouse takes time off work to spend more time with the other, and work suffers and then in turn hurts the marriage. It can be a vicious cycle. Decide what is more important, the marriage or the careers. And if you take time away from one, do it without regrets.

3) Change together. If you've been doing the same routine for a long time, one of you changing it all of a sudden can send your marriage into a tailspin. Take to time to discuss changes like children, a new job, etc.

4) Schedule time together. And it probably will take scheduling. You need time to go on dates and put your jobs aside for each other. This is vital to keeping your marriage alive. Meet together for lunch if you can. Try to reserve weekends for each other also.

How to be a parent your kids will love:

Deep down inside every parent wants to be perfect or better yet a "cool" parent. If you really want to have a good relationship with your children from the time they're small all the way through adulthood, consider the 7 keys below.

1) Do lots of stuff together. Kids love to go places and do and see new things. Take them out and show them the world. It doesn't have to cost a lot. Take them to the cemetery to see their ancestors. Take them on a picnic. Go for a long bike ride on Saturday. Kids don't need to have lots of money spent on them to appreciate your time together. Just make it fun and interesting and they will remember it for the rest of their lives.

2) Eat meals together. This may sound strange or impossible to some parents. But this is the best time for a family to get together and talk. Starting when they're young, reserve a dinner time every night for all of you to get together and eat. It will build harmony and give you a chance to talk about the day's events.

3) Let them make their own decisions. Kids need to learn to think and act for themselves. If you constantly order them to do things and never let them do things for themselves they will either rebel, or never develop those skills on their own.

4) Befriend your kid's friends. Go out of your way to get to know your kid's friend and encourage your kids to have them over. This does two things: 1) You can see the kinds of kids they spend their time with, and 2) they are likely to stay out of trouble if they're in your house. It also lets your kids know you accept their friends and have made good choices.

5) Be their biggest fan. No matter what it is, a dance recital, a football game or a speech competition, be there.

And be the loudest supporter there. Support your kids as much as possible and let them feel like what they're doing is more important to you than anything else.

6) Keep your word. Children of any age get very hurt when a parent says they're going to do something and doesn't do it. It teaches them that a verbal promise is no good and they will start to do it also. If you make a promise, keep it. Unless it is life threatening, your kids are more important.

7) Always be there for your kids. Never tell a child you are too busy to pay attention to them. If you do it enough times they will quit coming to you for help. Make it clear that you are always available for your children to help them.

How to divorce-proof your marriage:

A good marriage is a blessed thing to have. A healthy one can be a glorious partnership. A bad one can be miserable and will end in divorce. Everyone goes through bad times, but they can be overcome. Here are 7 ways you can divorce-proof your marriage.

1) Agree never to get divorced. While you're on your honey-moon -- or after -- decide that divorce is not an option. No matter how bad times may get, agree to do what it takes to stay together. Just having this behind you will help solve problems without considering divorce as an option.

2) Be financially wise. A majority of fights, and eventually divorces, are a result of financial disagreements. Set up a system and make some rules you will both abide by. Such as, "I will never make a major purchase without your consent." Learn how to live within your means. Decide who will balance the budget and be happy with it. Smooth running finances regardless of income level will keep the peace.

3) Communicate. Be interested in each other. Don't shut each other out. It can happen easily. Take time together and be the kind of spouse who listens without judging or reacting harshly.

4) Be positive. No one likes to hear a negative spouse all the time. Make the very best of the bad times and be grateful for the good times. Remember, you are trying to fight your way through life together and you need to have a good attitude to make it successful.

5) Fight fair. Every couple will fight. But how you fight will determine how strong your marriage is. Seek to resolve the problem quickly. As as a rule, don't go to bed angry. It takes a strong person to admit they're wrong and apologize. Don't be rude or demeaning. Instead of one being wrong and the other right, try to compromise.

6) Don't let extended family interfere. The dreaded in-laws or siblings can put a lot of pressure on a couple. Discuss how you will deal with demands from in-laws. Make holiday arrangements fairly and in advance. Make it your job be get along with them as well as you can. This will ease lots of tension.

7) Be honest but not cruel. Many people confuse the two and really hurt their spouse. Be honest by doing it lovingly. Don't do it to make them mad or to get revenge. Tell your spouse how you feel with only the intention of helping them know the truth.

NOTES

Chapter
_____   **11**

Inner Strength

Why you shouldn't rely only on positive thinking:

Positive thinking is definitely a part of living a happy, productive life. However that alone is not enough. You'll meet plenty of people who are brimming with positiveness -- who are going nowhere. Why? Because it takes action to move forward. It takes courage and determination to achieve goals and make your life successful. Along with positive thinking, you should also:

1) Set goals.
2) Evaluate your progress.
3) Keep active and busy.

If you do this you will go a long way and be a happy person.

How to have instant willpower
and achieve your goals:

Losing 5 pounds, quitting smoking or studying for an exam is easy ... if you can muster up the willpower to focus and do it. Willpower is a great force inside of us that has a hard time coming out. But can move mountains if we can harness it.

Whatever it is you need willpower for, it must be very important. And willpower comes in bursts and is hard to sustain over a long period of time. Which means you need to continually recharge it.

Effectively using willpower is best done by doing what you would do before jumping into a cold pool. Hold your breath and just do it. It may hurt at first, but you'll get used to it.

Willpower is all mental. It's mind over matter. What you really want to do, you will. If it's going on a diet, it's strong mental control that will help you do it. One of the best things to do is keep a mental image in your mind of your goal's end. What will you look like? How will you feel? If you can just make it. The final reward is what gives willpower it's energy.

How to determine what you want -- and get it:

Do you know anyone who seems to have everything going for them? These are the people who have mastered the art of accomplishment. They are able to figure out what they want and then figure out how to get it. And you can, too. You can be one of those people who always gets what they want. It has nothing to do with money, riches or power.

All you need is a little brain power. It's called "success imagery" and it works. Scientists aren't quite sure how, but it does. All you have to do is daydream. That's right. Focus on something you want to have happen. Picture it. See it clearly in your mind and see the end result. What you are doing is mentally making a picture of it.

This imagery takes place in your right brain. And what your left brain sees in your right brain, it does. It works to make it happen. Of course you have to do the work, but your inner brain will help you figure out what is your best course of action. It will guide you backwards from the end result. It really can work. So give it a try and see for yourself.

Visiting a mortician for a better life:

Having a bad time? It happens to you and me and everybody else at some point. For some people it leads to drugs, alcohol or even suicide to ease the pain. Even if life isn't close to being that bad, wouldn't you like to be able to shake it off? Well here's a suggestion for you that might help.

Take a field trip to your local funeral home and have a talk with the resident mortician. You don't need to see any dead people, just talking to the mortician will be sufficient. Almost guaranteed, as you talk to him and spend time there the finality of death will creep in your thoughts. You will realize how short life really is. And how suddenly death can come. You'll start to appreciate everything you have. You might find out what kind of regrets those people left behind. What they did to bring death upon themselves, that you should avoid. You can continue to live while they miss out. You'll leave feeling better about yourself and hopefully with a new zest for life. Try it.

How to make better decisions:

If you want to be known as a down-to-earth, on-the-money decision maker, then follow the steps below that many top executives use.

1) Go with your gut feeling. A lot of people don't, and later wish they had. That "gut" feeling is your intuition that, more often than not, is right. Don't just ignore it. It is probably your best bet.

2) Set a deadline. Instead of putting it off, give yourself a deadline. Say a week. By then you must have a decision. That way you can have some time to think, and still have a deadline in your mind to help you get it done.

3) What are your other options. For example, if you need to decide what to do about a potentially bad roof problem, call 4 roofers to tell you how urgent it is and what it will cost. This may help you find a solution. Of if you can't decide where to go on vacation, get several prices for different packages and see which one is the right trip for the right price.

4) What are the consequences? If you imagine the very, very worst consequences of a decision you might find it's not as bad as you think. It will put your decision in proper perspective.

5) Let friends or family help. Sometimes you can't see the whole picture clearly. Get 2 people to sit with you and each argue a different side while you just listen. One side may make a whole lot more sense than you had previously thought.

How to develop a photographic memory:

Your memory is one thing you can improve. As you get older it may start to fade. Then you might try some of these things to regain it. But if you just want to have a steel-trap memory, follow the instructions below.

1) Don't spend time trying to remember everything you see or hear, keep your mind uncluttered with only those things that are important. Einstein never memorized his phone number because he said, "Why should I, it's in the phone book."

2) Use the first letter of a list of things to make an acronym. For example, West coast states, California, Oregon, Washington, make "COW."

3) Repeat important things over and over. When you memorize phone numbers, just keep repeating them over and over until you know it from memory.

4) Tell yourself that you have a good memory. If you tell yourself you have a bad one, you will. Let positive thinking go to work for you.

5) When you meet someone for the first time, look them in the eye and repeat their name back to them. This will help you make a name-face connection.

6) Make up a mental image of something or someone you want to remember. If you meet Ron Jones, remember "Ron Jones has lots of bones."

7) To remember numbers, say them out loud the long way. Instead of one, two, three, four -- say one thousand two hundred and thirty four. This will help you remember it better.

NOTES

_____

_____

_____

_____

_____

_____

_____

_____

_____

_____

Chapter

_____ **12**

Healthful Healing

How to reduce stress
and lower your cholesterol in 2 minutes:

Studies have shown that besides fatty foods, stress causes high cholesterol. If you're concerned about your cholesterol and have already made dietary changes, there's one more thing you can do that will have an affect.

By taking just 2 minutes of your day to do some relaxation techniques, you will lower your stress and also your cholesterol.

1) Pick a good time. For most it is in the morning before the stress begins. For some it is in the middle of the day as a break from the stress.

2) The rest is easy. Pick a quiet place where you are alone and undisturbed. The goal is to relax, breathe deep and concentrate on being relaxed. Focus on being calm and flushing all the stress and fears out of your body. 2 minutes is the minimum for effectiveness. The longer you can afford to do it, the better.

Signs that you have a prostate problem:

Prostate problems are very common and usually affect men over 60. But also, on occasion, affect younger men. The prostate is a donut shaped tube that sits under the bladder. Its main function is to transport sperm. Problems can go unnoticed for a long time before it is treated. The sooner you know you have a problem, the better. Here are 3 tipoffs you can use to tell if you have a prostate problem.

1) More frequent urination. If you find yourself suddenly going to the bathroom a lot more than normal and several times during the night, this could be why.

2) Difficulty starting urination. If getting the flow started is difficult this may also be a sign.

3) Dribbling. This is when urine continues to come out after you thought you had "run out."

If you have any of these signs, consult your doctor for a diagnosis.

How to sleep like a log every night:

Few things are more frustrating than spending the night -- or every night -- tossing and turning. And when you finally do fall asleep, it's time to get up. It can physically and mentally drain you and make you sick. If this happens to you, use the 10 tips below to cure your own insomnia.

1) Don't try to sleep more than you need to. For most adults, 7-8 hours of sleep is adequate. Don't take naps. This only makes you more awake at night. Look at how much you are trying to sleep and if it's too much, cut back.

2) Avoid stimulants. Anything with caffeine will keep you awake. Avoid them completely, all day.

3) Avoid exercising at night. During the day or in the morning is OK. But if you exercise at night you will get all wound up and your body will be ready for more action when you want to sleep.

4) Stick to a schedule. Go to bed every night at the same time and wake up at the same time. Your body likes the routine. And your body will "know" when to wake up in the morning, and gear down for bed time at night.

5) Don't use over-the-counter sleeping pills. For one reason, they have shown to be non-effective. And also because, if you are affected by them and they help you now, they will not help you in the long run. Plus, many people get hooked on them. If your problem is severe, go to a doctor and get a prescription.

6) Only use your bed for sleeping. Don't lay in bed and read or watch TV. Condition your body to relate your bed and bedroom with sleeping.

7) If you are not falling asleep. Get up and do something else. Often the longer you lay there the more frustrated you get, and this only makes it worse. Do something else out of the bedroom until you feel tired again.

8) Eliminate some of your stress. Many restless nights are due to stress. Do things to take care of that first and the insomnia may go away. Meditation or therapy may be what you need.

9) No alcohol. This may put you to sleep at first, but it will wear off and will not help your problem. You are best off to avoid it altogether.

10) Make your room sleep- friendly. Adjust the temperature (cooler is usually better), quiet all noises, turn off the phone so it can't wake you and make sure your clothes and bed are comfortable.

How to reduce blood pressure during pregnancy by 65%:

It's common for your blood pressure to rise while you are expecting. Still, it is not good for you or the baby. Research has found that a high calcium diet during pregnancy will reduce blood pressure. If you get 1,500 mg. of calcium a day, your blood pressure is likely to stay at normal levels.

How to sleep better with a natural sleep inducer:

Believe it or not there are foods that will make you sleep better. If you're at the end of your rope with insomnia, or just have trouble sleeping, try eating one of these foods before going to bed.

1) Any dairy product, milk, cheese, ice cream.
2) Eggs.
3) These meats: salmon, turkey, chicken and lamb.

The reason these foods will put you to sleep is because they all contain high amounts of Tryptophan and Tyrosine.

Mind exercises to increase your brain power and intellect:

Do you want to be smarter? Well you can. It's common knowledge that the average person only uses about 10% of their brain. That leaves 90% for you to fill with knowledge. It's not hard to do. You just need to shut off the TV and do some simple things to keep learning and expanding your brain's capacity.

1) Read. Reading can be fascinating and is proven to make you smarter. You fill your mind with images and knowledge as you read. Read novels, cereal boxes, magazines, how-to books. Anything you can get your hands on.

2) Do crossword puzzles. They help you think and use recall. They are great brain exercisers.

3) Read editorials. See what other people think. Editorials are opinions of other people. They are not fact . See if you agree or disagree with them. Learn to form your own opinions.

4) Use your dictionary. When you hear a word you don't know, instead of just letting it go by, write it down so you can look it up later. Expanding your vocabulary is a great thing to do. And while you're in the dictionary, browse through it to see what else you can learn.

Insider's tip: Speaking of minds and exercise, studies have found that people who exercise have greater mental capacity. Exercise increases blood flow to the brain and makes intellect keener, decision making easier, and thinking power greater.

A laxative better than the most popular brand on the market:

While it is not necessary to have a bowel movement everyday, you may have a problem if whatever is normal for you has changed. There are several natural laxatives that many swear to be better than anything you can get in a drugstore.

1) Sun flower seeds.
2) Escarole. It's a lettuce. Boil it and drink the juice.
3) Unprocessed bran. 2 spoonfuls a day.
4) Raw fruit.
5) Papaya. You can buy it in pill form.

And the king of them all:

In a blender, blend some apple and spinach into a juice. You may have to add some water. Drink this and watch out!

How to conquer all your fears:

There is only one way to conquer your fears. That is to confront them. If you don't confront them and deal with them, they will always be there waiting for you. Most of the fears we have are unwarranted. Of course many are legitimate, but most are really fear of the unknown. Fear of spiders because we think they will hurt us. Fear of a plane because we think it will crash. The majority of the time the fear we have is of something that will never happen. So, what to do about it?

1) What are you really afraid of? This is what you must figure out before you can do anything. Are you afraid of dogs? Is it because you got bit once? Is it because you think they will bite you? Is it a fear of rabies? Is it because they are dirty and you don't like dirt? Write down what you are really, truly afraid of.

2) What's the worst that will realistically happen? Pretend you are trying to tell a child not to be afraid of something. Even though children are not great followers of logic, use everything you can think of to dispel the fear. You may even want to jot it down.

3) Think how free you would be without the fear. Imagine if the sight of a bee no longer sent you running. Imagine being on a ladder that didn't make you dizzy. Imagine being free of your fear.

4) Confront it. This will be the hardest step. But once you do it and see that it's OK, you will be well on your way to getting over it. You will have to be strong, and may want to have a friend help you.

How to use self-hypnosis to stop smoking, snoring and more:

Many people discount any type of hypnosis, but this is a little different. And it may be the answer you're looking for if you are trying to kick a bad habit. Self-hypnosis is about talking to yourself. Giving your mind subtle messages. It's easy to do, and is best done as you go to sleep. You might want to go to sleep a little early before you are too tired to do it properly. Follow the directions below and see if self-hypnosis works for you.

1) Develop an affirmation and a trigger word. An affirmation is no more than 5 or 6 sentences that your subconscious mind can hear and then act upon. One thing you'll want to make sure and add to your affirmation is your reason for changing whatever you are changing about yourself. For example, you would say, "Because I will die young and cigarettes are slowly killing me, I want to quit smoking."

From this sentence you will choose a trigger word. This is to help you remember your affirmation. You should be able to at some point memorize your affirmation. The trigger word is one or two words to say out loud that will start your mind saying the whole affirmation.

Your affirmation should be positive and motivational. Like: My mind is relaxed, my body is relaxed and I feel better about myself. Or instead of a cigarette, all I crave is a long breath of fresh air.

2) Make sure you are comfortable. You can lie down on your bed or sit in a comfortable chair. Then for a few moments, just sit and relax.

3) As you sit or lay, count backwards from ten slowly. Try to relax. Imagine you are sitting in a very beautiful, peaceful garden. Feel your body relax. When you feel relaxed, start saying your affirmation. Concentrate only on the words you are saying. Imagine the new you. The one that is thinner, sleeps better, doesn't smoke, has more confidence.

Repeat this exercise everyday or several times a day until you feel yourself in control of making the desired change.

The good news about natural remedies:

The truth is natural remedies are becoming more popular than ever. Why? Because they work! They are working miracles. The scary part is that the medical profession and drug companies are doing everything they can to keep this from you. Why? Lost profits. Doctors will never tell you about natural cures because they can't prescribe one and they are not accepted by doctors.

Everywhere stores are popping up, and hundreds of very resourceful books are being published. And even better news is that these natural cures are 100% safe and have no side effects. Many people have stopped pumping harmful drugs into their bodies and are seeking natural cures instead. Check your local library or bookstore for the book of your choice. After you try some of them you will be amazed. The testimonials are incredible. This is news you will never hear from your doctor.

How to recover from illness faster:

You probably know people who are always sick. Or never seem to quite get over an illness. Or you or someone close to you has suffered from an illness and you wished there was a way to recover faster.

Well there are things doctors can do with medicine and drugs to help you heal faster. But beyond that there are only things you can do to heal yourself. Here are some suggestions you can try next time you want to recover faster.

1) Start exercising. People who exercise are just plain healthier. And are much less susceptible to illness. And when they do get ill, it doesn't last long. The hardest part is getting into an exercise routine. But if you're sick a lot and have a hard time snapping out of it, this may be for you.

2) Use positive thinking. A lot of people get depressed and down when they get sick. This only makes matters worse. Your mind tells your body that it doesn't care what happens. Be positive. Really know that you will get better and it will take a short time. Don't let your defenses down or be negative.

3) Repair your body yourself. This method is not often talked about, but many swear by its power. As you lay sick, close your eyes and envision your body healing itself. Imagine you can see inside where the illness is, and with your mind, fix it. Repair it and make the harmful things vanish. It may sound strange, but a lot of people claim your mind can control the illness in your body.

4) Be as active as you can. I personally have found that the best cure for a cold is to put on heavy sweats and go running. I feel the illness being flushed from my body. Depending on your illness, try to stay active.

5) Try alternative methods. There are hundreds of books on cures that are safe and natural. Many "miracle" cures are contained in them. No one can explain why they work, but they do.

How to calm an overactive child
without drugs or therapy:

Kids can be difficult enough as they are. Adding overactivity to their list of behaviors can be maddening. No one likes the thought of using drugs to calm them down or sending them to therapy. So here are some other things you can try.

1) Provide a careful diet. Cut way back or eliminate all sugar from their diet. This is proven to get kids all wound up. Also avoid soda. This has sugar plus caffeine. Try warm milk. It has a soothing sedative effect on adults as well as kids.

2) Establish a reward system. Hand out prizes for good behavior. Try to focus on the good, and not punishment for doing wrong. Make sure it's something the child desires. Maybe a movie, or special activity.

3) Keep a routine. Kids need routines. That is their only sense of time and order. Everyday, eating, reading, watching TV, getting dressed, errands, should all be done at the same time. Children have a very difficult time when they are not on a schedule or deviate from theirs.

A vitamin to improve your memory:

Yes it's possible. Studies have shown that your memory is very sensitive to your body's balance of certain vitamins and minerals. The ones which have shown the greatest effect on memory are:

B-1 - Controls ability to recall stored memories.

B-12 - Choline- Involved in memory loss and comprehension.

Magnesium - Involved in the ability to learn and comprehend.

Iodine - Assists in the thyroid to function properly. (A memory problem is one symptom of a poor thyroid.)

Foods that are good sources for these vitamins are, wheat germ, eggs, fish, soybeans, cheese, beans, nuts.

Try adding these foods to your diet if you want to improve your ability to remember things.

How to slash medical bills
and get the same quality of care as before:

Medical costs can add up to a fortune. Especially for a big family. Even with medical insurance you can end up paying hundreds or thousands of dollars a year in medical costs. Here are 8 ways you can slash yours.

1) Get itemized bills. This is the only way you know you're getting what you pay for. Find out before you go to the doctor what it will cost you.

2) Don't go to a specialist unless it's necessary. Many times people go to a specialist when they can get the same care from their physician for much less cost. Always check with your doctor before you go to a specialist.

3) Don't pay for insurance coverage you won't collect. If you have a disease, don't buy extra insurance until you've checked your regular policy. A lot of times it is already covered. And you can't collect more than 100% on a claim.

4) Get a second opinion. Whenever considering surgery or other treatment, get several opinions . Ask your doctor for referrals. You may find a cheaper or better alternative.

5) Get vaccinations. Immunization for you and your family will save you a bundle by preventing illnesses. Keep accurate records and get boosters as well.

6) Take preventive care. Do all you can to stay healthy. No smoking, no drinking, control your blood pressure, stay at your ideal weight, eat well and exercise. The healthier you are the less you'll pay for medical care.

7) Join an HMO. These organizations encourage preventive care and are usually less expensive.

8) When getting prescriptions, always ask if there is a generic brand available. They are a lot less expensive.

Insider tip: Don't be afraid of young doctors. Younger doctors are just as good and often much less expensive.

4 easy ways to relieve back pain:

Just about everybody suffers from back pain sometime in life. Pregnant women, hard laborers and weekend warriors all suffer the same. Here are 4 easy ways to stop the pain fast.

1) Exercise. Research has shown time and time again that perhaps the best cure for back pain is regular exercise. Even if it's 10 minutes of stretching and jump rope. Anything you can do to keep the muscles loose and flexible.

2) Lay on your back and raise your legs about 12 inches with a pillow under them for support. This will relieve the pressure on your spine.

3) Get down on your hands and knees. While you lower your rear end to your feet, stretch your hands directly out in front of you.

4) When sleeping, lay on your side with your knees bent and a pillow between them. It will relieve tension on your back muscles.

New ways to put an end to constant pain:

There are other ways besides drugs and pain killers to put an end to pain. Here are some things your doctor probably will not tell you about.

1) Acupuncture. For many people this is a last resort, and then they wish they had come much sooner. People get acupuncture for anything from allergies to back pain. See your phone book for an acupuncturist near you. It is painless and very effective.

2) Music. It has shown to reduce migraine pain, reduce high blood pressure and ease pain. It has been said that an hour of soft, relaxing music is as good as a dose of Valium.

3) Magnets. It may sound weird, but magnet therapy is held in high esteem by many people. They claim it removes pain entirely. It's done by placing magnets on the body part that hurts. A good source for information is an acupuncturist.

NOTES

_____
_____
_____
_____
_____
_____
_____
_____
_____
_____
_____
_____
_____
_____

Chapter

Diet, Beauty and Sex Tips   13

You can reverse the aging process:

Everybody's goal is to live a healthy life. It's obvious that some people age better than others. And it's not chance. The term "aging" refers to the process of your body's cells breaking down. The free radicals in your cells start to slip out. And science has found that besides exercise, low stress and a good diet, there is something that seems to be working to help people stay young.

Vitamins. In Vitamins A,C, and E are antioxidants that, if taken daily, will help repair damaged, broken-down cells. So if you want to live longer, increase your dosage of these vitamins. However, toxic levels can do serious damage. Don't overdo it.

How to look younger without plastic surgery:

Plastic surgery can cost thousands of dollars. If you want to look fabulous on a budget, follow the tips below and save a lot of money.

1) Exercise. If you want to look like a new person, exercise is the best thing you can do. It will build and tone muscle, make your skin glow, make you feel better and younger and help you lose weight. It can be a simple routine if you want it to be. If you exercise you may not need to consider plastic surgery.

2) Make-up. If you're a woman, by having someone show you how to professionally do your make-up, you can make yourself look dazzling everyday. Go ahead, spend the money to see how it's done.

3) Clothing. How's your wardrobe? Does it need an overhaul? Great fitting clothes make a lot of difference. Go shopping and get some help to find the right colors and styles for you.

4) Diet. Most everybody could stand to lose weight. You'll look better and feel better. Don't pay to have fat removed. Remove it yourself with a sensible diet that includes exercise.

5) Melatonin. You can buy melatonin in any health food store. Research has shown it to increase your life span and turn back the clock. Although they aren't sure why, melatonin reverses or delays debility, disease and decline of muscles.

6) Skin care. Using a good moisturizer and a good mask to tighten the skin will make it glow and reduce wrinkles. Make it a weekly or biweekly routine.

7) Natural breast enlargement. Many women have discovered that specific exercises preformed regularly will result in a higher, firmer chest.

8) Baldness. If you would like to see more hair on your head without costly implants, here are some little known foods that might do the trick. Foods that are rich in Biotin may help put more hair on your head. The best sources of Biotin are, whole grain foods, nuts, organ meats, vegetables and milk. You can also get it in supplement form.

How to have great looking skin:

If great looking skin is important to you, then use the tips below to make your skin look years younger.

1) Wash your face everyday. There is a lot of stuff on your face that you can't even see. Washing it off will keep pores from getting clogged. Use luke warm water and a mild soap for best results.

2) Moisturize your skin. One of the results of aging skin is dryness. A good moisturizer seals moisture in. Moisturize when your skin is already wet, right after you've showered.

3) Protect yourself from the sun. This is one of the 2 major causes of skin problems. Up to 80% of skin damage is from the sun. Never go out in the direct sun without sun screen no matter how light or dark your skin is. SPF 15 or higher is recommended to get adequate protection.

4) Stop smoking. This is the #2 cause of poor skin. Studies have shown that the carbon monoxide from smoking causes premature wrinkles.

5) Drink plenty of water. Water hydrates your skin and makes it softer. 6-8 glasses a day will keep your skin looking younger.

6) Exercise. Studies show that exercise keeps the skin healthy and taut. People who exercise have shown to have healthier skin than those who do nothing.

Insider tip: Here's a wrinkle cream that is claimed to be the best there is. And you can make it yourself. Take 2 egg yolks and beat them with 1/2 cup of olive oil. Brush the mixture on wrinkled areas and leave it there for 10 minutes. Now beat the egg whites until they're stiff and put them over the egg yolk and olive oil mixture. Leave the mask there or 1/2 hour, then wash off with warm water and soap. Reports say it tightens the skin and diminishes wrinkles effectively.

How to eat less by listening to music:

Anything to help make a diet more effective is greatly appreciated. It has been discovered that the kind of music you listen to while you eat affects how much you eat. Slow, calm and relaxing music slows you down. It calms you and you tend to eat slower. And if you eat slower you will eat less because you'll feel fuller. So try listening to some slow music and see if it makes a difference.

The truth about fat-free foods:

The disturbing truth is that fat-free foods don't make you less fat. If you look at the label, often you'll see that they've only replaced the fat with carbohydrates. Carbohydrates, when eaten, are stored as fat unless they are burned off right away. So anything with sugar, rice, pasta, bread, etc., becomes fat even if it's in a fat-free food. People often make the mistake of thinking that since it is a fat-free food they can eat as much as they want.

Wrong.

Look for foods that are low in calories as well as fat. Don't just assume a fat-free food is going to help.

How to lose 30 pounds in 30 days:

There are 2 new diets out now that are rather unconventional, but are working miracles for people.

1) One of the latest diets is the high protein, low carbohydrate diet. Basically you can eat all the fat and meat you want. But you must limit your sugar and carbohydrate intake. The developers claim that U.S. diet norms are backwards and can't work. This protein diet is working and many happy people swear by it. (I've seen its results myself with a co-worker.) Check your local bookstore for this book.

2) Many diet pills on the market today are working miracles for people. They contain 2 main ingredients. Garcinia Cambogia and Brindle Berries. You can find these in any health food stores. They help your body burn fat faster. They're also all-natural.

Both of these diets suggest an exercise program to get maximum effectiveness.

How to choose a good diet:

You could literally choose from thousands of diets that are available. So how do you choose one that will really work for you? Before you choose anything you need to realize that there is no "easy way" to lose weight. It will require willpower, determination and lifestyle changes. If you aren't ready to give it your best effort, you'll probably fail. But if you're good and ready, here are some suggestions for picking a good diet for you.

1) Avoid diets that promise huge results in a short time. This is merely a sales tactic to get you in. Their promised results are probably true for a very small percentage.

2) Avoid diet plans that require a large amount of money up front. They don't guarantee results. You don't need to spend money to lose weight.

3) Be careful of diets that involve an appetite suppressant and no eating limits. This never has worked. The pills can be addicting and result in bigger problems.

4) Choose a diet that includes exercise. Dieting without exercise is futile.

5) Choose a diet that has proven medical support. Juice diets, cabbage diets and so forth are diets that someone saw limited results with. But they do not work for the average dieter.

6) Choose a diet that you can do. Lofty goals are great, but don't start something you aren't sure you can do.

7) Ask your doctor what he recommends. If he is tuned in, he should be able to tell you what's best.

The truth about cooking oils: Which are best:

Oil in general is not good for you. But it's needed on occasion. Below are the 7 best oils (in order) for unsaturated oils. Avoid any animal oil, fat or lard. They are very bad for you.

The very best:

1) Canola(rape seed) oil
2) Safflower oil
3) Sunflower oil
4) Corn oil
5) Olive oil
6) Hydrogenated sunflower oil
7) Sesame oil

The very worst:

1) Coconut oil
2) Palm kernel oil
3) Palm oil
4) Cottonseed oil
5) Peanut oil
6) Soybean oil

How to lose weight with vitamins:

There is a vitamin, Chromium Picolinate that has shown to aid in several ways in weight control. It suppresses appetite, keeps your body from storing fat and burns it instead. Many say you can lose weight without diet or exercise. However, for best results, exercise and moderate eating will help. Any health food store carries this miracle weight loss vitamin.

Foods dangerous to male potency:

Impotence is one of the most treatable things that can go wrong. Over 85% of all impotence problems can be overcome. Many of them are psychological and many are due to things taken into your body. Here is a list of things that will cause short or long-term impotence

1) Alcohol. It dulls the brain and in turn numbs your sex drive and ability to perform.

2) Cigarettes. Also have been shown to inhibit performance by causing blood vessels to restrict.

3) Fatty foods. What's bad for the heart is bad for your sexual ability. Fatty foods clog veins, arteries and capillaries and restrict blood flow, causing impotence.

4) Drugs. Many cold medicines, depression drugs, epilepsy drugs and ulcer drugs also cause impotence.

How to have great sex:

If your sex life is anything less than fireworks in the bedroom, you may benefit from what therapists say are the key things you must do to have a phenomenal sex life.

1) Have fun. How "fun" is your sex life? For some it's not very fun. It's too serious. It should be playful and carefree. Therapists say you should be having a good time. And if you're not, lighten up. It doesn't have to be dramatic to be romantic. That's only in soap operas.

2) Relax. Stress is the biggest cause of lack of desire or lack of ability to perform. Your mind and your sex organs are very closely related. If you have too much on your mind it's not going to be very good. Try to "de-stress" your life. The difference in your sex life will be noticed.

3) Take your time. Rushed sex is not very pleasurable and if it is, it's only for the man. Take the time to please your partner. Enjoy the whole experience instead of just getting what you want and getting it over with.

4) Seek to improve your marriage. Most sexual tension and problems stem from a marriage breakdown. Sincere love for your partner will be a great spice to your love life. Once you overcome some barriers it will be like a 2nd honeymoon.

5) Aim to please. You'll have better sexual experiences if your focus is on the other person instead of yourself. Find out what makes them happy and content. It will heighten your pleasure even if you don't think it will.

A male fountain of youth:

Millions of orientals swear by it. It's called ginseng. It's an Asian root that is highly prized among orientals. You can buy it in pill form here for much less than they pay. Ginseng is claimed to be a male rejuvenator, as well as a "stay young herb." It rejuvenates the heart, sex glands, stomach, nerves and blood. It is definitely worth a try. Over a billion Chinese people couldn't be wrong!

The best time of day
for the greatest sexual pleasure:

There is no way to say for sure what is going to be the best for you. But here are some insights into different times of day that may make it more interesting for you.

Morning. For many people, especially men who are impotent, the morning can be a great time for sex. Why? You're rested and not as tired as you were the night before. Also, men have an easier time being aroused in the morning. It makes for a good start to the day.

Afternoon. This can be kind of care free. You might like a break during the day if it can be arranged.

Night. This is usually the hands-down winner. Mostly because of convenience. But also because it tends to be more romantic in the dark.

How to prevent eardrum pain on flights:

Eardrum pain on flights can be very painful. There are some things you can do to avoid that "my head is going to explode" feeling.

1) Chew gum. The chewing movement of your jaw will keep the pressure from building up.

2) Have a drink. Swallowing also will prevent pressure pain. Ask for a drink as soon as you get on the plane and continue to sip it as you take off.

How to cut your risk of stroke in half:

People who die from a stroke die almost immediately. Those who do not die are usually left impaired and crippled. There is a lot you can do to prevent having one yourself.

Basically what happens is, as plaque builds up on your artery wall it clogs the artery and causes high blood pressure. When a piece of that plaque comes loose and travels through your veins it can cut off blood to the brain, and if it goes on for several minutes you will have a stroke.

Here are things you can do to cut your risk in half -- or more.

1) Control your blood pressure. First you need to check it and see if it's high. If it is, your doctor will recommend a low fat diet and plenty of exercise. If it is too severe, there is medication to help control it.

2) Watch your red blood cell count. The more red blood cells you have, the thicker your blood will be. This will increase your chance of having a stoke. Many times you will be given a blood thinner such as aspirin.

3) Stop smoking. Smoking increases your risk by 70%. Research shows smoking may thicken your blood. It also causes high blood pressure. They've also found that 4 or 5 years after you quit, you may be as normal as a non-smoker.

4) Stop drinking. Drinking alcohol increases your blood pressure, weakens your heart, thickens your blood and causes your arteries to go into spasms that cut blood flow.

5) Lose weight. The heavier you are, the more your heart has to work to pump blood in your body. If you are overweight it is most likely because of your diet. All the fatty foods you eat build up on your artery walls, putting you at great risk.

6) Exercise. A good brisk walk or other moderate exercise will greatly reduce your risk of stroke. Exercise will help lower blood pressure, take off excess weight and control cholesterol.

How to naturally lower your cholesterol:

You could easily be part of the 20% of Americans that have high cholesterol. Many people think they don't have a problem. But they also can't see what their arteries look like from eating a typical fatty American diet. There are lots of ways you can naturally lower your cholesterol before it kills you.

1) Eat less fat. Animal fat is the main contributor to high cholesterol. In baked goods, meats, cheeses, dairy products, oil etc. You don't need to cut it out completely, but a significant reduction will be a big benefit.

2) Remove fat. Trim all the fat and skin from your meat and don't fry it. Bake, boil, roast or barbecue instead. Use fat free flavorings such as wine, tomato juice, lemon juice or orange juice.

3) Lose weight. Overweight people have high cholesterol. Most people can drop their cholesterol by dropping a few pounds.

4) Eat good snacks. Snack all you want, but snack on good things, like popcorn, carrots, yogurt, bagels.

5) Eat garlic. Many people have found garlic to be an effective way of reducing cholesterol. It works by dilating blood vessels and makes your blood less sticky. You can buy garlic in odorless pill form.

6) Fiber. Studies have shown oat bran to drastically reduce cholesterol levels.

How to beat a history of poor family health:

If heart disease, cancer, or other illness is prevalent in your family, you may be a sitting duck. There's no saying that you can't beat the odds if you are informed. Almost every illness has preventive measures you can take. The smartest thing you can do is see a doctor as a young adult. Tell him what your family illness is and explain to him that you want to know what to do to prevent it. Many people sit around and wait too long or do nothing. Take the information you have and get to work on a solution.,

NOTES

_____

_____

_____

_____

_____

_____

_____

_____

_____

_____

_____

_____

_____

Chapter
_____

Nutrition and Exercise

14

Nutritional weapon
in war on breast cancer:

Cholesterol-conscious dieters avoid eggs at all cost, But they may be making a mistake--especially women. Adding eggs to the diet may help prevent breastcancer.

Sounds incredible? There's a sizable body of scientific evidence behind this amazing assertion. Egg yolks and garlic are primary food sources of the antioxidant selenium--one of the 10 essential trace minerals. And selenium, as more studies are discovering, prevents cancer. There is even emerging data that selenium may help cure cancer.

This is not to say that, by itself, this mineral can protect all people from all types of cancer. What it can do is reduce the incidence of all types of cancer. It works to diminish cancer risk by strengthening the immune system and protecting vital cell components against free-radical attack.

Breast cancer protection: A study at the University of California at San Diego in the early 1970s concluded that optimal selenium intake could reduce the natural occurrence of breast cancer in mice by nearly 90 percent--to only 12 percent of the normal cancer rate. Concluded Dr. Gerhard Schrauzer: "If every woman in America started taking selenium today or had a high selenium diet, within a few years the breast cancer rate would decline drastically."

In fact, some surgeons and oncologists now use selenium (and other antioxidant nutrients) to treat cancer.

How much to take: Recommended supplementation levels are from 50-100 micrograms of selenium per day (taken with A, C and E and other antioxidant nutrients). Some studies used levels as high as 2,000 micrograms a day with no resulting toxicity.

Other selenium food sources (besides eggs and garlic): cashews, tuna, salmon and halibut.

Caution: Selenium supplements make better health sense than increasing egg yolk consumption. The American Cancer Society recommends reducing consumption of the saturated and polyunsaturated fats contained in vegetable and animal oils.

Miracle minerals for arthritis sufferers:

Millions of Americans suffer from various forms of arthritis, often with crippling and excruciating effects. Yet they remain the most neglected segment of the American population. Pain remedies help victims endure the daily agony. But doctors seem unable to provide curative or preventative treatments.

Nutritionists, however, don't share this pessimism. They do offer hope. And, increasingly, they provide scientific research to prove it. For instance, nutritionists claim that calcium can help arthritic conditions--dramatically, and in several ways.

Ironically, medical opinion for many years has mistakenly steered people with arthritis away from calcium-rich foods. But studies have long confirmed that calcium is removed from the bones continuously, both when under stress (such as from arthritic conditions) and when the diet is inadequate in calcium (as well as magnesium and vitamin E). Calcium has also been shown to decrease pain sensitivity.

Conclusion: Arthritis sufferers should have a generous intake of calcium.

Example: One woman suffering osteoarthritis upped her calcium intake to 2 grams daily from fresh and powdered milk, plus another gram from a mixed-mineral supplement.

Total: 3 grams daily.

Result: Her bone spurs disappeared and, along with them, her crippling pain.

Other food factors that combat arthritis: According to many nutritionists, the following dietary supplements can work synergistically to prevent or even reverse damage to arthritic joints:

* Pantothenic acid
* Vitamin A
* Vitamin B (Complex)
* Vitamin C
* Vitamin D
* Vitamin E

Other minerals can help, too:

Nutritionist Carlton Fredericks, Ph.D., has a further mineral prescription for rheumatoid arthritis sufferers in his book Arthritis: Don't Learn to Live With It--manganese and zinc. He would like to see diets of these patients supplemented with manganese and zinc, along with cod-liver oil, vitamin C, bioflavonoids and vitamin E. A deficiency of manganese, he points out, can cause disc and cartilage problems. In his own practice Dr. Fredericks has seen remarkable improvements in arthritis sufferers who increased intake of these nutrients, including zinc and manganese.

Mineral to avoid: Iron supplements and high-iron diets can actually worsen rheumatoid arthritic conditions, according to Dr. Fredericks and others. Indeed, many sufferers are already victims of an excessive iron load.

What about wearing copper bracelets to treat arthritis? This is one of those folk remedies that persists, despite persistent efforts of physicians to debunk it.

But there may be something to it after all. In recent clinical studies, patients suffering osteoarthritis or degenerative joint disease became significantly worse after discontinuing habitual use of the copper bracelets. The worsening effects were not seen in subjects who had worn "placebo" bracelets.

How can wearing a bracelet of any metal affect the body internally? There's an amazing answer for this: It turns out that copper from the bracelets, when dissolved in sweat, can be absorbed through the skin.

Minerals can also prevent osteoporosis:

Recent estimates put the number of Americans affected by osteoporosis at around 24 million. This crippling condition can destroy the quality of life and put someone in a wheelchair or bed forever. Even worse: It can often be life-threatening.

Osteoporosis-related hip fractures cause approximately 50,000 deaths a year. These people are not dying from falls. Hip fractures, for instance, increase vulnerability to illnesses such as pneumonia. Other fatal complications result from blood clots, which can cause stroke or heart attack.

What can reduce or even prevent this crippling bone loss? The answer is calcium. Increasing this mineral to reduce and even help prevent osteoporosis is not a secret. Mainstream medicine acknowledges that the loss of bone density is a calcium loss. Yet the prescribing of calcium, along with vitamin D, is still not as extensive as it should be.

Osteoporosis specifically targets older women, causing those familiar crippling conditions: dowager's hump, bent-over posture and an increasing risk of fractures. Men, with greater bone mass, have a lesser risk of developing osteoporosis. Women also lose more bone tissue after menopause due to a decrease in estrogen, the female sex hormone.

Some medical authorities, many who oppose food supplementation in principle, remain skeptical on whether calcium and vitamin D supplements can deter bone loss in postmenopausal women.

And yet many scientific research studies show the two nutrients have done precisely that. Among women in one test given calcium and vitamin D, loss of bone mineral density was reduced by 43 percent! (No reduction of bone loss was experienced by the placebo takers.)

One researcher, Dr. Robert Heaney of Creighton University in Omaha, Nebraska, concluded: "Although we do not know everything there is to know about calcium intake and age-related bone loss, or the mechanisms by which vitamin D impacts on calcium absorption, we do know enough to act now."

How much should you take? According to Dr. Heaney, "it seems prudent to increase the intake of calcium and vitamin D in most postmenopausal women--calcium to at least 1,000 mg. per day and preferably to 1,500 mg. per day, and vitamin D to 400 to 800 IU per day--without waiting for more information."

Other osteoporosis treatments and therapies: Estrogen- replacement therapy is also effective. And exercise is a proven preventative.

Sedentary women are at greater risk, according to most research studies. In fact, exercise is critical early in life to help build bone mass. Children, especially girls, should begin to build as much bone mass as possible by engaging in regular weight bearing exercise (running, walking, aerobics, etc.) and by eating foods rich in calcium and vitamin D.

Fat-burning pills -- myth or breakthrough:

There's a lot of "buzz" these days about two over-the-counter nutrients that are supposed to help metabolize fat and curb appetites. These nutrients (often combined in one supplement) are:

* Chromium picolinate, and
* L-Carnitine

Bodybuilders have been downing these hard-to-pronounce pills in quantity--and getting results. Now medical science seems to be catching up and weighing in positively. Here's are the findings:

* Chromium picolinate: Medical reports are confirming that chromium picolinate helps reduce body fat without cutting calories. And these supplements are perfectly safe: People taking 500 micrograms (mcg.) per day reported no adverse effects.

How it works: Chromium reduces insulin resistance, which in turn decreases the storage of fatty tissue by increasing its metabolism. Sufficient chromium helps build lean muscle pounds and interacts with the thyroid hormone system to help burn fat more efficiently.

Bonus: Chromium also diminishes appetite by helping to stabilize blood-sugar levels.

Why supplements are needed: Chromium deficiency is widespread, affecting--according to some medical surveys--90% of the U.S. population.

* L-Carnitine: This nutrient, synthesized from the amino acids lysine and methionine, works to metabolize fatty acids--and also reduces feelings of hunger and weakness from those with low- calorie diets.

L-Carnitine is available both in tablet and liquid form.

What supplements the experts take:

Ever wonder which vitamins and minerals all those scientific researchers and experts actually take? Here are some answers.

* The late Linus Pauling, Ph.D., who was president of the Linus Pauling Institute for Medicine, Palo Alto, California. In the years before his death, Dr. Pauling was taking the regimen recommended in his 1986 book, "How to Live Longer and Feel Better": a daily insurance formula plus 15 milligrams of beta carotene, 18,000 milligrams of vitamin C and 800 international units of vitamin E.

* Trish Ratto, R.D.,coordinator of Health Matters, the University of California at Berkeley wellness program for faculty and staff. "I hate pills and can't get them down, so no, I don't take vitamins. I did when I was pregnant, but it was a struggle. Of course, I understand the value of antioxidants, so I'm very good about eating fresh fruits and vegetables. I eat more than five servings a day, including lots of cantaloupe just about every day. It's packed with vitamin A."

* David Sobel, M.D., regional director of patient education and health promotion for the Kaiser Permanente health maintenance organization in Oakland, California: "I take a multivitamin and mineral supplement, plus 20,000 international units of beta carotene, 1,500 milligrams of vitamin C and 400 international units of vitamin E."

* Bonnie Liebman, director of nutrition at the Center for Science in the Public Interest in Washington, D.C. "I'm nursing a baby these days, so I'm taking a multivitamin and mineral supplement in consultation with my physician. After I wean my baby, I plan to take an adult insurance formula and probably additional antioxidants."

* Shari Lieberman, Ph.D., a clinical nutritionist in New York City and co-author (with Nancy Bruning) of "The Real Vitamin and Mineral Handbook." "I take a daily multivitamin/mineral supplement containing 5,000 international units of vitamin A, 50,000 international units of beta-carotene, 50 milligrams of the B vitamins (except for 1,000 milligrams of niacin), 3,000 milligrams of vitamin C, 400 international units of vitamin D and E, 1,000 milligrams of calcium, 150 micrograms of iodine, 25 milligrams of iron, 500 milligrams of magnesium, 25 milligrams of manganese, 200 micrograms of selenium and 50 milligrams of zinc."

* Sheldon Saul Hendler, M.D., Ph.D., assistant clinical professor of medicine at the University of California, San Diego, and author of "The Doctor's Vitamin and Mineral Encyclopedia." "Every day I take an inexpensive multivitamin/mineral insurance formula containing all of the 11 vitamins and 7 minerals for which there are RDAs. My supplement contains 100 percent of the RDA or a little more. In addition, I take 400 international units of vitamin E for prevention of heart attack."

* Gladys Block, Ph.D., professor of epidemiology and public health nutrition at the University of California at Berkeley School of Public Health. "I take a daily multivitamin and mineral supplement plus 2,000 to 3,000 milligrams of vitamin C, 400 international units of vitamin E and 1,000 milligrams of calcium."

Vitamin shopper's survival guide:

In addition to the bewildering choices of nutritional supplements at any health-food store or pharmacy, there is also the high-cost factor. A month's supply of a couple of nutrients can cost you $20 or more, and nutritional advocates give you a long list of things you should take.

Here are some tips to cutting through all the advertising claims and brands and prices:

1. Food comes first. Supplements are just that, something in addition to a sound diet. Get your five servings of fresh fruits and vegetables daily, then take supplements.

2. Forget brand names. All vitamins are essentially the same. A few drug companies supply all the hundreds of companies that sell them. Always buy the cheapest vitamins you can find.

3. Ignore the word "natural." Some packagers mix a tiny amount of a natural vitamin with a large amount of synthetic, then market the combination as "natural."

There are three exceptions to this, however: vitamin E, folic acid and calcium. Natural vitamin E (d-alpha tocopherol) is absorbed better than the synthetic vitamin (dl-alpha-tocopherol). Select a supplement that contains only d-alpha.

But for folic acid and calcium, avoid natural forms in favor of synthetic. Synthetic folic acid is more easily absorbed, and natural calcium can be hazardous--possibly contaminated with lead. Calcium carbonate, a laboratory creation, is the preferable form.

4. Don't buy the hype. Avoid fad supplements that claim to give you superhuman energy or sexual ecstasy. And don't fall for claims of "newly discovered" vitamins. There aren't any.

Don't pay extra for supplements that claim to be sugar-free or starch-free. Unless you're on a severely restricted diet, the little bit of sugar and starch in some supplements won't matter.

Don't pay extra for "chelated" minerals. Chelation combines minerals with other substances, often amino acids. Proponents claim that chelation increases the amount of the minerals that actually gets absorbed into the bloodstream. They call this increased absorption rate bioavailability. Technically, the claim must be true, but ordinary minerals are absorbed just fine. And also pass on timed-release supplements. They may not provide the steady flow of nutrients advertised. They may even cause problems. And it's usually cheaper to take a few pills a day than one timed-release supplement.

5. Make sure the pills dissolve. Look for a dissolution statement on the label. To do any good, pills must dissolve completely in the digestive tract. Some don't.

6. Check the expiration date. Steer clear of supplements within six to nine months of their expiration dates. They've probably been in the bottle for several years and may be past their prime.

7. Begin with an "insurance formula." Multivitamin mineral supplements--sometimes called insurance formulas--contain some of every vitamin and mineral. They're both convenient and economical. They take up less shelf space than a dozen bottles of single nutrient supplements. And it's easier to swallow one pill than a dozen.

8. Then supplement your insurance formula. These have breadth, but possibly not enough depth for your needs. For instance, the optimal daily requirement for calcium is 1,000 to 1,500 milligrams, but it's impossible to get that much from an insurance formula.

9. Pick beta-carotene instead of vitamin A. The body converts beta-carotene into vitamin A, so for all practical purposes they're the same. However, long-term use of vitamin A at doses above 50,000 international units a day may cause problems. Beta- carotene is non-toxic even at high doses.

10. Look for at least 25 micrograms of biotin. Biotin is the most expensive vitamin, and many packagers skimp on it. Biotin content is a quick, easy way to compare insurance formula pricing. Buy the cheapest one that contains adequate biotin.

11. Go easy on iron. Unless your doctor advises otherwise, don't take more than 100 percent of the RDA for iron. People with iron-deficiency anemia and women with unusually heavy menstrual flow may need more than 100 percent, but most people don't. Yet some supplements contain several times the RDA.

12. Check for selenium. For years researchers have touted this trace mineral as a cancer preventive. That view gained considerable credence when the NCI's study in China showed that it helped prevent deaths from esophageal and stomach cancer. (See first item in this chapter.)

13. Vegan vegetarians may need extra B-12. If you consume no animal products, you may become deficient in vitamin B-12. This can damage the nervous system, so make sure your supplement contains at least the daily requirement of B-12.

14. Keep supplements away from kids. This is especially true for iron. Although iron--and supplements in general--are safe for most adults at the optimal daily requirement, it takes only a few tablets of a high-potency iron supplement to kill a child.

15. Watch your wallet. Ten dollars a month should do it. If you pay more than that, you're paying too much.

Don't swallow fad diets:

Year after year, the slick magazines and best-sellers list tout the latest gimmick diets. If it's new, you can bet it'll be gobbled up.

Don't bite. Fad diets don't work. In fact, they're less than 5 percent successful. You may lose weight on them, but you'll gain it all back again. This is called the ping-pong effect.

Who falls for these diets? Professional dieters for the most part, people who lose thousands of pounds in the course of their lifetimes and gain them all back again. This is not only futile; it's extremely stressful to the body.

You can also lose weight fast with diuretics, but it's all water loss. Diet pills are another quick weight-loss gimmick that can be harmful and offer few benefits.

Best weight-loss secret -- undereat:

Exercise won't work if you sabotage it by indulgent eating. It takes 30 minutes of aerobic workout to burn off just a dozen corn chips. To metabolize a hot fudge sundae, you'll need to run a 10-minute-mile pace for 40 minutes. Play racquetball like a maniac for a half-hour, and you can eat a single slice of apple pie--and barely stay on your calorie count.

Put it this way, if you're only a pound overweight and run one mile, you've carried the equivalent of a ton of extra weight.

Ideally, 15 percent of your body weight should be fat. But the average male, by the time he reaches age of 40, will have 40 percent body fat--even if he maintains his ideal weight.

Solution: Maintain a sensible diet plus a regular exercise program. And, as you grow older, you need to increase your exercise--not decrease, as most of us do. Older people also need to cut back further on calories.

Stroke-fighting diet:

A recent Harvard Medical School study documented a one-fifth decrease of stroke risk by dramatically increasing daily intake of fruits and vegetables. Reason: fruits and veggies contain antioxidants, potassium and folic acid, all of which work to prevent oxidation of LDL (or bad cholesterol--good cholesterol is HDL). This, in turn, works to control blood pressure and blocked arteries.

Tip: Nutrients in vegetables can be lost through overcooking. Best advice is to steam, not boil, the veggies.

Low-fat restaurant dining:

You may eat a low-fat diet at home, but despair of following it when you eat out. This is especially a problem these days when eating out is more and more common. In fact, too many of us, with our hectic schedules, couldn't survive without take-out and drive-through.

Or if you simply go out for lunch every day at work and eat out a few other times each week, restaurants end up as the source of at least a third of your meals.

What can you do to maintain your low-fat program? It does require a few adjustments. But with a little forethought, it's doable. Here are some sensible menu picks from nutrition experts:

Plan ahead. A little forethought is better than hours of self-recrimination for what you should have done. It's no big deal to plan for low-fat dining out. If you're happy at home with a simple breakfast of toast and coffee or a bowl of cereal with skim milk, don't even look at the menu. Just order your usual meal and don't get tempted by the Belgian waffles or bacon-and-sour-cream omelet. If you're happy with a salad for lunch or a baked potato and a steamed vegetable for dinner, don't look at the menu. Just order them.

Think small. Patronize restaurants that offer a large selection of appetizers. Try one or two instead of an entree.

Order small portions. Before you and your companion are seated, suggest splitting part or all of your meals. And stay away from buffets, smorgasbords and all-you-can-eat specials. Besides being setups for overeating, these dishes are often high in fat.

Nibble before dinner. Never arrive at any restaurant feeling ravenous. You'll choose more wisely and feel better about yourself if you take the edge off your hunger beforehand with a healthy low-fat snack.

Beware of booze. Alcohol is surprisingly high in calories (more than 100 calories per ounce). If you drink beer, wine or cocktails with dinner, drink water or iced tea at the same time to quench your thirst and help you nurse your drink.

Become more assertive. Restaurants are in the business of service, so speak up. Let the staff know what you want. They won't resent it.

Ask for substitutions. Instead of a three-egg omelet, can you order a one-egg omelet with some egg substitute? Can you get skim or low-fat milk for coffee instead of cream or half-and-half?

Clear off temptation. As you're seated, ask that the bread and butter or chips be removed or served later with your meal. While you're waiting, sip water, club soda or herbal tea. If you do keep the bread basket, remember that breadsticks, rolls and French bread are lower in fat than croissants and most muffins.

Come prepared. If a restaurant doesn't serve healthful dressings and condiments, discreetly bring your own. Salsa makes an excellent bread spread, salad dressing and vegetable topping. Or prepare some herb-and-lemon-juice salad dressing and bring it in a small container.

Get skinned. When ordering chicken, insist on skinless parts and ask if the skin was removed before cooking.

Ask questions. Even such presumably healthful dishes as broiled or grilled fish or skinless chicken can be smothered in high-fat sauces. Ask how sauces are prepared; if they are high in fat, ask for no sauce or sauce on the side. Ask for salad dressing on the side as well. Then dip your fork into the dressing before you spear any salad. That way you get a little dressing--but not too much--with each bite.

Divide and conquer. If you can't resist a high-fat dessert, split it with your companion or take part of it home.

Stand firm. Don't let yourself be corrupted by your dining companion. Well-meaning friends sometimes sabotage low-fat dining plans by coaxing--"Come on, live a little."

Beware of salads. Not all are low in fat. A good one to avoid is the chef's salad with its cheeses, eggs and high-fat lunch meats.

Catch yourself in the act. Finally, whenever you catch yourself thinking, "Oh, what the heck..." stop a moment, close your eyes, take a few deep breaths and ask yourself if you really want that item.

Know where the fat is. Steer clear of anything fried or sauteed, anything creamed, breaded, Alfredo or Hollandaise, tempura, batter-dipped, au gratin. Avoid heavy sauces.

Know where the fat isn't. You can enjoy anything broiled, grilled, baked, boiled, roasted, poached or steamed. Also on the safe list: fish, seafood, skinless poultry, lean red meats, salads, pasta with pesto or tomato sauce, fresh fruits and vegetables, whole-grain items and frozen ices, sorbets, sherbets and nonfat frozen yogurts.

But never say never. You have to let your guard down once in awhile, and don't feel guilty when you do have a creme brulee. But cut back on the rest of your meals that day.

Some ethnics are safe, some aren't. Chinese, Indian, Vietnamese, Cambodian, Middle Eastern and Japanese tend to be low in fat. But stay away from tempura. But be careful around French, German, Mexican, Cajun and Italian restaurants. These all tend to serve food high in fat. Even there, if you're careful, you can find tasty low-fat foods. But if you're going to order pizza, ask for less cheese and more vegetable toppings. Better yet, skip the cheese altogether and ask for a pesto pizza. If you must have a meat topping, Canadian bacon is the leanest. Similarly, it's hard to find low-fat lasagna, cannelloni, manicotti or saltimbocca. Tomato-based marinara sauces are lower in fat than pesto, which is lower than meat sauces or cream-based white Alfredo or cheese sauces.

Be careful of meats. Always trim off visible fat. At delis, try a turkey sandwich instead of pastrami. Cole slaw, soup or salad are fine. At steak houses, order leaner cuts--sirloin, tenderloin and flank steak. Avoid prime cuts.

Stay out of burger shacks--or order a grilled chicken breast sandwich. So what if they laugh at you? If you must have a burger, though, order one topped with grilled onions and mushrooms, not bacon or cheese.

Pick your fish. At seafood restaurants, grilled or broiled dishes are quite low in fat--unless served with a sauce containing butter, cheese or sour cream. Stay away from breaded or fried dishes and those served with high-fat sauces.

Keep your oatmeal plain and simple. Don't add high-fat toppings such as nuts, butter, whole milk, half-and-half or cream. Stick with skim milk and fruit.

Don't order cream soups. At lunch, look for cup-of-soup-and-half-sandwich combos--as long as the soup is not "cream of something." Combinations satisfy the need for variety. Vegetable and bean soups are nutritious, filling and usually low in fat. Soups with a chicken stock base are higher in fat, but they're still a better choice than a croissant ham-and-cheese sandwich.

Beware high-fat sandwiches. Mayo and "special" sandwich sauces are high in fat. Stick to mustard, ketchup, salsa and barbecue sauce.

Forget french fries. Select rice, pasta or a baked potato instead.

5 fountain-of-youth secrets:

Baby boomers, now into their 50s, are intensely interested in the quality of retirement life. And more middle-agers and seniors are finding a veritable fountain-of-youth in the research of leading physicians, nutritionists and gerontologists. Extracted from these findings, here's a five-fold program for staying younger and fitter at any age.

1. Exercise daily
The benefits are apparently even more dramatic than previously thought. Increased exercise of the right kind can halt, even reverse, many effects of aging. This is true no matter when you start your fitness program--even at age 90.

Exercise is especially important for seniors tempted to cut back on physical activity. Lack of exercise can lead to many debilitating diseases associated with aging--heart disease, high blood pressure, diabetes, osteoporosis.

Check with your doctor before launching into any ambitious exercise program--like aerobic workouts, swimming, biking or weight training. But any of these, under medical supervision, can provide immense benefits to older Americans.

For many seniors, walking remains the best regimen, and one that is easy to maintain. A daily 15-minute walk can do wonders to increase life-expectancy and quality.

2. Watch your diet

People of all ages can benefit from shifting to foods richer in nutrients and leaner in calories. But this becomes more urgent as we grow older. Fortunately, in retirement years, without the pressures of the daily grind, people have more time to prepare inexpensive, but nutritionally balanced meals.

3. Take supplements

The case for nutritional supplements is getting more persuasive every day. While some doctors remain skeptical, many others prescribe vitamins, minerals and other basic nutrients to their patients. Ask your doctor to recommend a good multivitamin/mineral supplement. Other nutritionals to consider: Vitamin C, B complex, vitamin E and beta-carotene. C, E and beta-carotene are antioxidants.

Increasingly, physicians are also suggesting older patients take a daily aspirin tablet. Clinical studies show this can reduce incidence of heart attacks, strokes, even colon cancer.

4. Exercise your spirit

Seniors who take time for daily meditation, prayer, inspirational reading (or whatever they may call it), reap profits in terms of inner and outer health. Energy levels and well-being increase, while troubles and worries take a lesser toll.

Spiritual communion can also lead to fulfilling activities-- such as helping others or pursuing lifelong goals. These things-- in place of increased TV viewing--can really make years golden.

Another senior stress-reducer: a pet.

5. Sleep well
Those who live longest confess different longevity secrets, often contradictory. But most have one surprising secret in common: a good night's sleep. Lack of sleep prevents the body from mending the daily damage caused by stress and anxiety.

ABCs for more ZZZs: Stay away from coffee, tea or cola in the afternoon or evening. Take a walk instead. Or have a small glass of wine with dinner. And if there's a hot tub or sauna available, jump in.

Cheapest heart medicine:

Many doctors pooh-pooh the beneficial effects of vitamin E, but their numbers are getting fewer every year, and they are now in the scientific rear-guard. Studies verify that vitamin E lowers the incidence of heart disease in long-term users. How? Vitamin E reduces platelet adhesion--and fibrous plaque on arterial walls--by returning abnormal platelets to normal. This keeps the blood free-flowing, so coronaries are reduced.

Another long-term study, published in the American Journal of Clinical Pathology, concluded that vitamin E was helpful to those with heart disease. How? Because it is anti-clotting, improves oxygen utilization, controls the patch-scar that replaces damaged heart tissue and improves capillary permeability.

How much E is enough? A reasonable daily dose for those seeking coronary disease protection is 400 IU (International Units)--up to 800 IU daily.

Note: The antioxidant mineral selenium should be taken in conjunction with E for maximum effect. Reasonable amounts are 50 micrograms of selenium daily for protection and 100 mcg. daily for control.

The truth about coffee and cholesterol:

Medical studies as far back as the early '60s uncovered a cause-and-effect relationship between coffee-drinking and higher cholesterol. One study of 2,000 men over a seven-year period revealed that those who developed coronary disease drank 5 cups or more of coffee daily. Even a single cup of coffee causes a prompt rise in blood fats and cholesterol.

Solution: Decaffeinated coffee seems not to have these cholesterol-raising effects.

Herbs to hype your love life:

The ginseng root is a favorite Chinese remedy, used for just about everything. As a tea, chewing gum, soft drink and pick-me-up capsule, it has been a "cure-all" prescribed by Asian physicians for about 5,000 years.

Many of the claims are farfetched--for instance, you can see in the dark if you drink enough Ginseng tea. Its real claim to fame, of course, is as a supposed aphrodisiac. (In Chinese, ginseng means "man root," because the root resembles the human male figure.)

Unfortunately, there's no scientific evidence supporting any of this, despite centuries of anecdotal evidence. The FDA has outlawed sale of ginseng specifically as an aphrodisiac, but it can be sold for general health purposes. As one physiologist said, "When the buyer believes something will improve sexual performance, it may well do just that."

Another herb, Ginkgo biloba extract, from the ancient, ornamental Ginkgo or maidenhair tree, has shown an ability to lessen or eliminate impotence. How? Studies show that ginkgo increases blood flow into the penis. After six months of taking 60 mg. daily of the extract, half the men in one long-term study were able to sustain erections, while all but 5 percent of the remaining men noticed some improvement. Ginkgo biloba extract (GBE) can be found in most health-food stores.

How much? The safest recommended dosage for GBE seems to be 40 mg. three times daily.

Drug-free ways to drop cholesterol and blood pressure:

Health professionals agree on the dangers of high blood cholesterol--any level above 250 milligrams brings an increased risk of heart disease and strokes. People in that high-risk range need to bring their cholesterols down below 200.

There are drugs designed to do just that. Unfortunately, the most popular and potent one--lovastatin (Mevacor)--has serious side effects. These include liver and gallbladder problems, muscular disorders, rashes and psychiatric disturbances. And lovastatin is not cheap! The maximum recommended dose will set you back $200 a month--for life!

Drug-free solutions: Avoid saturated and hydrogenated fats. Increase intake of vitamin A, B complex, C, D, and E. Pioneering nutritionist Adelle Davis also recommended 250 milligrams a day of the specific B vitamins choline and inositol, plus lecithin and brewers yeast (a prime B-vitamin food source), along with the minerals magnesium and iodine.

High blood pressure (or hypertension) can result from a loss of kidney function caused by inadequate oxygen levels in the blood. Those with high blood pressure should consider taking vitamin E, which decreases the need for oxygen. And there are other nutrients, whose lack can elevate blood pressure. Foremost among these are the B vitamins--especially B-6 and choline--plus vitamin C and potassium. Including complete proteins in the diet is also important in order to decrease hypertension.

Test cholesterol at home:

Everyone with high blood cholesterol is a candidate for heart attack or stroke. Medical professionals recommend that everyone, regardless of age, have an annual blood cholesterol test.

Yet most Americans don't know their blood cholesterol level. Some are discouraged from doing so by the cost. Lab tests can run $50 and more. Others are too lazy or busy to schedule an office visit.

But such excuses should be a thing of the past. In most drugstores you can buy a home cholesterol tests-- Johnson & Johnson has one for around $20. And you don't have to wait two days for results. The test measures cholesterol level in a quarter-hour. According to most medical opinion, if used properly, these tests give an accurate reading 97 percent of the time.

Caution: Home tests are not designed to replace an annual checkup, including cholesterol reading, with your doctor. They are recommended for people with high or borderline cholesterol levels who want to monitor themselves between doctor visits. Others at increased risk of heart disease should ask their doctor about home testing.

And home tests should be avoided by hemophiliacs or those who take blood-thinning medicine, due to the danger of excessive bleeding.

Basic blood-pressure remedies:

Nutritional solutions aside, there are fundamental steps to bring down high blood pressure. Here are six:

1. Lose weight. Even 10 or 15 pounds off may bring an overweight person into normal range.

2. Quit smoking. Cigarettes may not hype your blood pressure, but they work in combination with elevated pressure to increase risk of cardiovascular disease.

3. Aerobicize. Even if you don't drop pounds, aerobic workouts will bring down your blood pressure. Some good aerobic activities: walking, running, cycling, swimming, stairclimbing. Make a point of exercising before any stressful event. This will help bring down your blood pressure during the event.

Caution: weight-lifting can increase blood pressure.

4. Shake the salt habit. The more salt you absorb, the higher your blood pressure will go. It's not enough to stop reaching for the shaker. Most dietary sodium comes from other sources- snacks, salad dressings, lunch meat, even cereal.

5. Have an occasional drink (no more than 2 a day). Teetotalers tend to have higher pressures than do moderate drinkers.

6. If these methods don't bring down your blood pressure after a few weeks, go to your doctor and take a hypertensive drug (if prescribed). No matter how it's accomplished, lowering blood pressure will reduce your risk of heart attack and stroke.

Advice: Have your pressure checked frequently.

Hands-on headache treatments:

All headaches are not equal. And they respond to different treatments. Aspirin is fine, but you may be able to deal directly with the cause instead of resorting to painkillers.

1. Sinus headaches. These are characterized by throbbing around eyes and nasal congestion. If you suspect an infection, you may need a prescribed antibiotic. Other treatments: Over-the-counter painkillers and decongestants.

2. Cluster headaches. These may be chronic, with sharp pain, often behind one eye, for a few minutes to hours. Ideal treatment would be to identify and eliminate the trigger cause--which can be foods, tobacco smoke or alcohol. Doctors may prescribe preventatives, including lithium or vasoconstrictors, such as beta-blockers.

3. Tension headaches. These are characterized by persistent pain and tightness in forehead, neck and shoulders. A massage may be the best treatment, simply rubbing under the temples to increase blood flow, or massaging the neck and shoulders. Warm compresses also help. If not, there's always aspirin.

4. Migraine headaches. The most intensely painful, sometimes involving nausea and light-sensitivity. Rest in a dark room can help. Most require treatment with prescription analgesics.

Other common headache causes:

There are many other common varieties of headaches. The trick is to match the treatment with the type.

Here's a brief rundown:
1. Hunger. Missed a meal? A quick drop-off in blood-sugar levels can set off a headache. Answer: If you're too busy to leave your desk for lunch, brown bag it.

2. Eyeglass problems? Squinting through an outdated prescription? A headache may be on the way. Answer: Don't skip your annual eye examination.

3. Caffeine. Too much, or too little, can cause headaches.

Too little, if you're used to your coffee or cola fix at work, and go into weekend withdrawal. **Answer:** Cut back the Monday- through-Friday intake caffeine intake closer to weekend levels.

Too much caffeine narrows dilated blood vessels, which can also trigger headache pain.

4. Bright lights. Are you parked all day in front of a glowing PC screen beneath a fluorescent tube? Fit a non-glare screen on your monitor. Switch to an incandescent light-bulb. If you're also staring at a bright window while on the computer, close the blinds.

Primer on painkillers:

The pain medication lineup on the pharmacy shelves is getting longer and longer. How do you know what to take? The fact is, the right medication for one person may not be right for another. The same goes for doses. The following is a quick rundown:

1. NSAIDS. This is an acronym for "non-steroidal anti-inflammatory drugs." They are designed for mild to moderate pain. Among them are:

* Over-the-counter ibuprofen, which includes Advil, Motrin, Nuprin and Aleve. Some NSAIDS are available in injection form.

* Aspirin is the original NSAID, commonly used for mild to moderate pain. While aspirin is non-narcotic, some sensitive patients can develop gastric distress or bleeding. Aspirin also has anticoagulant properties.

* Acetaminophens (such as Tylenol) are also used for mild to moderate pain. Tylenol has no anti-inflammatory effect and, unlike aspirin, does not irritate the stomach. But those suffering from chronic alcoholism and liver disease need to be monitored.

2. OPIOID ANALGESICS are designed to alleviate moderate to severe acute pain. They include:

* Codeine, a "weak" opioid for moderate to moderately severe pain.

* Morphine, a "strong" opioid, for moderate to very severe pain, comes in many forms and doses, including long-acting.

* Demerol, which is given by injection for moderate to severe pain, but can cause side effects.

3. ADJUNCTIVE DRUGS are used to provide additional pain relief, to reduce side effects or lessen anxiety. They include:

* Antihistamines, which have sedating and pain-relieving qualities, but can cause undesirable side effects in older people.

* Tricyclic antidepressants, which can provide analgesic effect and are sometimes helpful when used for chronic or cancer pain.

* Sedatives, tranquilizers, hypnotics, all used for anxiety and pain.

For more information on pain relief:

* Agency for Health Care Policy and Research Publications Clearinghouse. You can get a free copy of their acute-pain patient guide. Write P.O. Box 8547, Silver Spring, MD 20907, or phone 800- 358-9295. Guide is available in English and Spanish.

* City of Hope National Medical Center and Beckman Research Institute, 1500 E. Duarte Rd., Duarte, CA 91010. To get a free copy of "City of Hope Patient Handbook for Cancer Pain Management" call 800-679-4673.

* National Chronic Pain Outreach Association, Inc. To request a free information packet, send a SASE to 7979 Old Georgetown Rd., #100, Bethesda, MD 20814-2429.

Don't put up with acute or chronic pain:

It's now possible to control most pain. That means no one should accept acute or chronic pain, including cancer pain. If you're being subjected to that, something's wrong. It may be you simply don't know your rights. Here's a short list. If you're a pain patient, you have the right to:

* Have your pain prevented or controlled.
* Receive pain medication on a timely basis.
* Be believed when you say you have pain.
* Receive compassionate care.
* Have your pain questions answered freely.
* Know what medication, treatment or anesthesia will be given.
* Know the risks, benefits and side effects of any treatment.
* Know what alternative pain treatments are available.
* Ask for changes in treatments if your pain persists.
* Seek a second opinion or a pain-care specialist.
* Be given your records on request.

Heimlich made easy for choking victims:

Choking is a common breathing emergency. A person who is choking has the airway blocked by a piece of food or another object. The airway may be partly or completely blocked. If a choking person is coughing forcefully, encourage him or her to cough up the object.

Before doing anything: Ask the person if he or she can talk. If you get an answer, there's no crisis--the person has already got the object out of the airway and will be okay.

But if the person can't cough, speak or breathe, it's time for the famous maneuver invented by Dr. Heimlich:

Step 1. Place thumb side of fist against middle of abdomen just above the navel. Grasp fist with other hand.

Step 2. Give quick upward abdominal thrusts.
Repeat until object is coughed up or person becomes unconscious. (If another person is present, have him or her call 911.)

If victim is too big to reach around or is obviously pregnant, give chest thrusts instead of abdominal thrusts.

Caution: Special (and very careful) emergency procedures must be applied for infants and very small children, who could be seriously injured by adult-style abdominal thrusts.

What to do for infants who are choking:

Choking is a leading cause of death and injury in infants, who love to put small objects such as pebbles, coins, beads and parts of toys in their mouth.

Babies also choke often while eating because they haven't yet fully mastered chewing and swallowing. Foods like grape and nuts are particularly risky. Never let an infant eat or drink alone.

If an infant is unable to cry, cough or breathe:

Step 1. With infant face-down on forearm so that the head is lower than the chest, give five back blows with heel of hand between the infant's shoulder blades.

Step 2. Holding the infant firmly between both forearms, turn the infant to a face-up position on forearm.

Step 3. Using two fingers, give five chest thrusts on about the center of the breastbone.

Repeat the sequence of five back blows and five two-fingered chest thrusts alternately until the object is coughed up, the infant begins to breathe on its own or becomes unconscious.

Stop as soon as the object is coughed up or the infant starts to breathe or cough. Watch the infant and make sure that he or she is breathing freely again.

Call the local emergency number now if you haven't already done so. The infant should be taken to the local emergency department to be checked, even if the infant seems to be breathing well.

Don't get hooked on contaminated fish:

You can't rely on visual inspection of the fresh fish at your market or favorite restaurant. Chemical contamination may be invisible. You need to know in advance which seafood varieties to avoid, no matter how appetizing they look.

Here's a caution list:

* **Swordfish and fresh tuna.** Savor them as occasional delicacies, but mercury contamination can occur if eaten too frequently.

* **Lakefish.** There has been an alarming increase in varieties contaminated with PCBs (polychlorinated biphenyls). Avoid trout, bluefish and other freshwater fish caught in inland lakes.

* **Local catches.** In some tropical areas, there's a risk of parasites from eating fresh tuna, bluefish or mahi mahi. Other problem catches: barracuda, snapper and amberjack.

What's left? The good news is that the many seafood items are usually chemical-free. For instance: perch, sole, cod, flounder, halibut and salmon.

Shellfish are okay if cooked. Raw is risky. Raw oysters, clams and mussels may contain microbes, which can cause hepatitis or gastroenteritis.

7 ways to build a strong physique:

Want to look like Arnold Schwarzenegger, or just make your T-shirts tighter? Weight training is the way to go. What's more, it's recommended even for older adults-- under medical supervision.

To make the most of free-weight workouts, you don't need a thick book of exercises. Just follow these 7 iron-pumping principles:

1. Work large muscle groups first. That means the big thigh muscles (quads), chest (pecs) and back. Smaller muscles will be called into play during these sessions. If you've already fatigued them, they won't be able to do their supporting job.

2. Work out late. Many people pump iron in the early morning, before work or school. But they're fighting their own body rhythms. Body temperature, blood pressure and testosterone are at their highest levels in the afternoon, permitting a harder workout and a greater gain.

3. Use a workout partner. Solitary workouts are okay, but a gym buddy can push you harder and help maintain your intensity. Even more important, a buddy can make you show up for a workout when you're tempted to slack off.

4. Change your workout frequently. Don't stick to the same routine more than six weeks' running. Muscles adapt quickly to any exercise.

5. Zero in on your workout goal. Do you want bulk? Use moderate weights, increase number of sets to around 5, use 8 to 12 reps. If your goal is brute strength, increase weight and cut down on sets and reps.

6. Be consistent. Forty minutes three times a week is enough to get going. Don't attempt marathon sessions. You're too apt to skip the next workout.

7. Don't skimp on rest and sleep. After a hard workout, muscles need 48 hours to recover. And never work the same muscle group on consecutive days.

Bonus Advice: Many fitness experts recommend lifting and lowering weights at a slower pace than usual. The slower approach reduces the likelihood of injury and keeps the muscle loaded, thereby giving quicker results.

Shopping for the best health club:

Everyone agrees exercise is good for you, but picking the right gym or health club can be hazardous to your health--and your pocketbook. You'll work up a sweat just sorting through the lures and come-ons that promise rock-hard results for rock-bottom prices--available, of course, "for only a limited time." Some clubs also tout "$5 a month" introductory memberships.

Sounds too good to be true? Right. It's easier to bench press 300 pounds than to get a straight answer out of most health clubs. You can verify this by phoning clubs in your area and asking the price of a year membership. Be prepared for double talk. Basically you'll be told the information isn't available over the phone. You have to come in.

Guess what? Runarounds get worse when you walk in the door. You'll be shown a bewildering array of options, which boil down to this:

* Prices drop the longer the contract you sign;
* Renewing membership is cheaper than joining;
* Cash will get you a better price than credit.

The reason for all the flim-flam--particularly in the big chain fitness centers--is that salespeople work on commission, just like car hucksters. If they think they're losing you, they'll run into the back room to check with their manager, then come out with a better price.

How can consumers cut through all the high-pressure hustle?

* Demand to know the best cash price for a year membership (or by the month, if you prefer).

* Before signing any contract, examine it carefully. Some "no money down" come-ons may attach a whopping annual interest fee that runs for years, even if you decide to quit after two months. And some make you pay for things you don't need, like sessions with a trainer. Determine if fitness evaluation and training session are included in price? Ask if child care is available? If so, is it free? How about free parking?

Make sure the pricing matches your financial situation. And sign the minimum contract, until you're positive you want to stick with it. Are there membership discounts for families and students? Assistance granted for those with special needs? (YMCAs often provide these.)

Things to look for in choosing a facility:

* **Location.** If a club isn't convenient to your home or office, you'll think of reasons not to go.

* **Diversity of equipment and facilities.** Make sure the club offers things you want now and might want later on. Is there a full range of Lifecycles, StairMasters, weight machines? Free weights? Aerobic or yoga classes?

Swimming pool? Jacuzzi? Sauna and steam? Snack bar? Boxing? Racquetball and basketball? A dance center? A kindergym?

* **Congeniality.** Make sure you like the environment, and that you feel comfortable for your level of fitness. You don't want to wind up sandwiched between hard-core body-builders if you're into a light aerobics. What kind of "scene" prevails? Is it a hardbody pickup place or more family-oriented? Is there loud music? How crowded is the floor during peak hours--or during the hours you'll need it?

* **If it's a chain,** how many clubs are in your area? What's the reciprocity between clubs?

Tip: For straight answers, good value and a fair price with no sales pressure, check out your local YMCA.

Choosing an exercise-rider:

Sales are booming for exercise-riders, the newest home-fitness option that looks like a hybrid of an exercise bike and weight-training equipment. More than a million "riders" have been sold, according to industry estimates.

You've seen them on infomercials--the HealthRider, the CardioGlide, the E Force, the AeroMotion and about a dozen other models. You've heard the claims: How, in just an hour a week, these gizmos will tones up more body parts than a traditional exercise bike while improving your cardiovascular system. All this with no high-impact pounding and at a fraction of what you'd pay for most other home-fitness equipment.

Some exercise experts say these machines are here to stay, others claim they'll set you up for back problems.

What you should know before you shop:

On all designs, the concept's the same: to shape you up aerobically while building muscle. Your own body weight serves as the resistance. Most riders include monitors to display speed, calories burned, time elapsed, distance and other factors.

* Benefits:

Estimates vary, but an average person who weighs 155 pounds will burn approximately six calories per minute or 120 calories per 20-minute workout on these machines. That's a bit less than the calories expended during medium-intensity aerobics.

* Risks and Drawbacks:

Exercise riders require a fair amount of knee-bending, so people with knee problems might want to consider that. They also take a lot of hip flexion. Overworking the hip flexor muscles, which are attached to the lower lumbar vertebrae, can contribute to lower-back problems.

"People with knee and back problems should avoid riders," one exercise physiologist advises. "People with large bellies might be wise to bypass them, too."

Consulting your doctor before purchasing a rider or any other piece of fitness equipment is advised.

And these machines are not effortless, no matter how easy things look on the infomercials. They take work. You have to burn calories.

Best advice: Try a rider in the store and take advantage of any special trial offers. And consumers are advised to check with the retailer before buying because money-back offers vary from store to store.

Don't let exercise machines collect dust:

Growing numbers of exercisers, opting for the privacy and convenience of home, are buying home-exercise gear. Unfortunately, after a few weeks of intense workouts, this equipment is usually neglected by the once well-intentioned owners.

Stationary bikes end up gathering dust in a corner. Basements and garages are littered with Thighmasters, barbells and jump ropes. Eventually all this abandoned metal winds up in thrift shops.

Probably two-thirds of purchasers stop using home equipment. And the drop-out rate at health clubs is about the same.

Among possible reasons our exercise attention span is so short:
  * Not everyone is cut out to be a successful home-exerciser. Some return to gyms.
  * Some are suited to home workouts but choose the wrong equipment.
  * Some can't stay motivated.
  * Some have unrealistic expectations--they do too much too fast and end up sore and discouraged. (Always consult a doctor before beginning or resuming an exercise program.)

Others expect to see a quick and dramatic change in their appearance. But biology doesn't change that quickly. Infomercials show the fit--not the fat--working out, models who probably work out two hours a day, six days a week-- a schedule few people can maintain.

Another obstacle to home exercise: the lack of social reinforcement found in health clubs and at running tracks and walking paths. One way to recreate that environment is to ask family members to prod and encourage you--or even join you.

Sensible approach: Design a seasonal program planned around the home equipment and other activities. For instance, use the stair-stepper in the winter but abandon it in summer for walking and other outdoor exercise.

Cheap alternatives to home equipment:
* A $7 Rubbermaid stool (in lieu of the more expensive exercise step, which can cost $50 and up)
* Or home calisthenics (like the one described below) that require no equipment.

Burn flab at home:

Here's a do-it-yourself way to revitalize your body and reverse the unsightly bulges of the aging process. This simply daily exercise requires neither gym membership nor bulky health-club machines. If practiced consistently, it will give you a natural tummy tuck without having to go under a cosmetic surgeon's knife.

Six-step tummy tuck:
1. Lie on your back on a rug with feet next to sofa, couch or chair.

2. Raise your ankles and lower legs and place them on the couch or chair so your hips and knees are each bent 90 degrees.

3. Fold arms across your chest.

4. Pull chin to your chest. Tighten abdominal muscles, raise head, neck and shoulders off the floor and lift as high as possible. Keep lower back pressed to the floor. Raise up slowly. Exhale throughout this movement.

5. Hold a full second, then gradually lower head, neck and shoulders back down. Don't lower your shoulders all the way to the floor. Inhale throughout.

6. Without lowering your shoulders all the way down, repeat the crunch as many times as you can. Then relax back to the floor. This is 1 set. Most people can do 8 reps in the first set.

Bonus benefit: Unlike the situp, this "crunch" is unlikely to cause back-strain.

You'll need to incorporate other light calisthenics and aerobic exercises to elevate metabolism and burn off surplus body fat.

Keeping your mind in shape:

While exercise and diet are keys to retarding the aging process, you can also increase your vitality through brain power.

There's no reason, according to the latest research, why the brain can't be kept sharp, youthful and active throughout life. In fact, we can do better than that. We may even be able to reverse deterioration of the brain's cognitive function.

Studies have shown that an aging brain retains a powerful capacity to revitalize itself. Even if neurons are lost through disuse, other brain cells can take over their tasks. Stroke victims demonstrate this miracle all the time as they retrain their brains to regain lost skills.

Here are 5 proven techniques to maintain maximum mental fitness:
1. Try new experiences. Don't let each day be a carbon copy of the one before. Plan new and different things. For instance: Walk or drive along a new route to work. Spend an evening doing something you've never done before. Attend a meeting of a group or organization you've been curious about. Go bowling (if that's new), horseback riding. Start a garden.

2. Try mind puzzles. These may include word games, chess, checkers or crossword puzzles. Learn a new musical instrument, a new dance, a foreign language. You don't have to master these disciplines, just stimulate your brain by making a start.

Both short and long-term memory weaken as we grow older. Try some of the many excellent memory-enhancement techniques.

3. Challenge your brain. Take the plunge into cyberspace. Buy a PC, learn some programs, surf the Internet and the World Wide Web. Go to the library, check out books on subjects you've never studied, sign up for adult education, visit local art galleries, attend some lectures.

4. Exercise daily. This will stimulate blood flow to the brain.

5. Finally, to make the other steps possible, **turn off the TV.** You need active involvement in life, not passive stimulation.

5 steps to quit smoking:

Despite scary statistics from the FDA about how nicotine is even more addictive than cocaine, millions of people succeed in kicking the cigarette habit. Antismoking professionals have boiled their successes down to five secrets. Study them and you, too, can be an ex-smoker.

1. Quitting is tough--don't underestimate it. Remember, it takes a person years to build the habit. Don't expect to quit overnight.

2. However, if you smoke less than a pack a day, quit cold turkey. Once you're below the level of 15 a day, cutting down doesn't seem to work. Those few smokes become too precious.

3. If you're a pack-a-day smoker or above, taper off. Yes, we've all heard about heavy lifelong smokers who threw their last pack in the wastebasket and never smoked again. But with high levels of nicotine addiction, you'll face pretty severe withdrawal pains.

Quit on the installment plan: Don't reach for that first cigarette on awakening. Make yourself wait a half-hour. If you can do that, cut down to less than a pack a day, say 15 or less. At that level, your odds of quitting more than double.

If you can keep that level for a while, then attempt to quit. If you only last a week, don't give up. You're making progress. It's like running a marathon--you start with shorter distances.

4. Get help. That's the method of the world's most effective rehab program, Alcoholics Anonymous. One person pushes the other, and is always there in a crisis. This is especially critical during the first few days after you quit--when you're most tempted to backslide. Call your support person to talk you through the craving.

5. A nicotine patch is fine, but you'll need more. The patch combats physiological dependency, but doesn't address psychological addiction. You'll still have to deal with the daily stresses that made you reach for that nicotine fix in the first place.

Easy way to block bad breath:

You hear all kinds of so-called halitosis cures being touted these days, from costly breath- freshening tablets to chewing parsley--even gargling with industrial-strength hydrogen peroxide! Save your money, spare your gums and lick your problem by following the tried-and-true recommendations of the American Dental Association:

1. Brush your teeth twice daily, floss daily, and don't forget to brush and scrape your tongue at the same time.
2. Use a fluoride or antimicrobial mouth rinse.
3. Schedule regular dental checkups and professional cleanings.
4. Keep your mouth moist; a dry mouth can lead to bad breath.

5. Use a moisturizing nasal spray to control post-nasal drip, which can contribute to bad breath.

6. Smoking is a prime factor for halitosis. If you smoke, read the preceding item for help in kicking the habit, or ask your doctor for advice.

These six breath-freshening procedures also help maintain good oral hygiene.

ABC's of quick dental care:

Here are five simple, but unpublicized ways to improve dental hygiene.

1. Best toothbrush: Soft nylon is better than hard, which can damage gum tissue. Hard brushing can also wear grooves in tooth enamel. What's beneficial is to spend more time in the brushing. And two brushes are better than one. When used in rotation, each brush can dry out properly.

2. Best dental floss: Don't buy waxed. It may slide easier, but unwaxed grabs particles better.

3. Water Piks and other flushing devices: Never use them full-force. High pressure can imbed particles in dental recesses and cause infection.

4. When to visit the dentist: Morning appointments are better than afternoon. Reason: Pain sensitivity increases during the day.

5. Save on costly crowns: Fillings with reinforcement pins may perform the same function--for a lot less.

Chapter
_____

Trim Health-Care Costs   **15**

Exercise your patient rights:

Unless it's an emergency operation, it's the patient who decides whether to go ahead. The surgeon explains the procedure--duration of operation and recovery, possible dangers--then asks you to sign an informed-consent document.

Most people sign at the first request. They shouldn't-- not until other important questions are answered to their satisfaction:

1. Are there non-surgical alternatives that don't involve hospitalization? What are they?

2. Does the doctor know of people with symptoms similar to yours who have chosen not to have surgery--and recovered?

3. What are the risks of having the operation? Of not having it? Of postponing it to get a second opinion?

If a surgeon doesn't deal with these questions in his or her initial presentation, it may indicate a procedure is less than imperative.

Caution: Some doctors get around the second-opinion option by recommending friends or colleagues to confirm their opinions. Get your referral from a hospital your doctor is not affiliated with. Local, state or national medical societies can also help find qualified physicians or hospitals.

Other sources: The American Cancer Society, the American Heart Association and your local or state medical society can also help you find qualified physicians or hospitals. The American College of Surgeons, 55 East Erie Street, Chicago, IL 60611, can provide names of board-certified surgeons in your area and names and addresses of surgical-specialty organizations.

Don't forget to check your health insurer's policy on second opinions. Most HMOs and insurance companies require a second opinion before approving payment for the following procedures: Angioplasty, back surgery, cataract removal, coronary artery bypass, gallbladder removal, hernia repair, hysterectomy, knee surgery, prostate reduction or removal, tonsillectomy.

Note: Health-care organizations and some states have set guidelines for patient's rights. When you enter a hospital, look for the American Hospital Associations "A Patient's Bill of Rights," which is posted in all member hospitals.

Warning: future medicare squeezes:

To slash Medicare costs, Congress will be encouraging seniors to leave fee-for-service coverage and switch to lower-cost alternatives--such as HMOs.

Some plans would require recipients to pay higher premiums for Medicare coverage, with wealthier seniors bearing the brunt, and would reduce payments to doctors and hospitals.

Some proposals would also increase the deductible for doctor bills, and gradually raise the age of Medicare eligibility to 67 in the next century. For seniors on fixed incomes, increasing those costs could be hazardous to their health.

Although a switch to less expensive HMO's would not be compulsory under most congressional proposals, many senior citizens fear that ultimately it will become mandatory.

On the plus side, these plans give you a system with a lot more benefits. But for those who are really sick, the specialists they want may not always be in the same plan, nor the best hospitals. And many seniors want somebody who knows them when they walk in the door, not a place where you take a number from a receptionist.

Proponents of HMO's point out that many seniors already opt for the less expensive alternatives and are content with them. (About 10% of the nation's elderly belong to HMOs.)

Some plans even provide services geared to the needs of the elderly, offering such extras as vans to take them to doctors' appointments and bring them home, and special nutrition and exercise programs.

A study released by the Group Health Assn. of America showed that only about 4% of the elderly who choose HMO's return to fee-for-service. The same study, based on data collected by the Health Care Financing Administration, showed that 84% remained with their HMO's, 6% switched to another HMO in their area and 6% left for other reasons, such as moving out of the area.

Other experts warn that shifting millions of seniors into such programs might result in an excess of managed-care plans with no accountability, no oversight and no quality control, except the marketplace, which leaves them more vulnerable than with a federally supervised and sponsored program.

It's a hard call, and one that will vary from person to person. But Medicare, for better or worse, is going to be changed.

How to be a savvy health-care consumer:

Until recently, the medical industry has refused to give accurate information about doctors, prescription drugs, hospitals and health plans. But consumers are finally starting to ask hard questions of doctors and health plans. They want information so they can comparison-shop for health care, just as they do for cars or long-distance telephone service.

If the medical industry doesn't fork over this data fast enough, employers and entrepreneurs will do it for them. One California firm is collecting and analyzing hospital data for a group of Cincinnati employers. Another small New York company publishes slick consumer guides to medical care in several U.S. cities.

Here are the kind of questions savvy consumers (and employees with company HMOs) want answers for:

* Which hospitals in a city have the best outcomes-- and the best prices--for heart surgery?
* How do members of Brand-X Health Plan rate its doctors and hospitals?
* Which hospitals have the lowest and highest rates of Cesarean-section births?
* How much does a particular health-care plan cost?
* Is my doctor in the network?
* How do colleagues rank health plans?
* How long do they have to wait in doctors' offices?
* How long does it take to get an appointment?
* Are there translation services or Spanish-speaking providers?
* What is the procedure for emergencies? Does it vary based on type of emergency? For example, if your c h i l d has a bad fall and you're worried about a concussion, can you seek out-of-system care close to home, or must you go to an in-system doctor or hospital to get reimbursed? What about heart ailments, strokes, premature labor, asthma

attacks and broken bones? What if an emergency turns out to be a false alarm? Can your claim be denied after you've already received care?

* How are administrative problems handled? Is there an appeals process for denied claims? How does it work?

* Can you get a nurse practitioner on the phone if you can't get the doctor?

* Can a woman choose an obstetrician-gynecologist as her primary-care physician?

* Is there an evening telephone line to call for a sick child?

More and more consumers are starting to question charges along with the necessity of certain tests and treatments. Some savvy individuals are also actively shopping around, recognizing that the cost of different procedures can vary widely even when the quality of care is the same.

One patient called his hospital and demanded an explanation of charges and whether the procedures were necessary. In the end, the hospital slashed the bill 20%. Others, when facing expensive surgery, find a doctor willing to negotiate away some fees. It may not seem like your money, because the insurance company pays the bills, but since you're paying the premium, it is your own money.

For up-to-date hospital information:
Get the 221-page "Consumer's Guide to Hospitals," published by the Center for the Study of Services, a nonprofit organization founded in 1974 with funding from Consumers Union and the U. S. Office of Consumer Affairs.

The guide reports actual death rates, risk-adjusted death rates and trends in Medicare cases in each of the almost 6,000 short-term, acute-care hospitals in the United States. Send $12 (includes shipping and handling) to Center for the Study of Services, 806 15th St. N.W., Suite 925, Washington, D.C. 20005. Call: 800-475-7283.

Choosing cost-effective health-care:

How do you determine the most cost-effective health plan for your family? Plot your out-of-pocket costs in each plan by adding up health-care usage in a typical year. A look at last year's check register--or your family health insurance file--may help you complete such a worksheet.

Non-hospital options that save $$$:

The instant you walk through the hospital doors, the meter starts running--and at a faster rate than if you checked into the world's ritziest hotel. What can you do about it? Instead of checking in, check out the increasing number of procedures available on an outpatient basis or same-day surgery.

Examples: tonsillectomy, hernia repair, cataract removal, removal of a tissue lesion or cyst, dilation and curettage (D&C).

Cheaper solution: Some minor surgery and routine diagnostic tests can be handled at the doctor's office. Savings can be 50% or more. Doctors don't care, since Medicare actually reimburses more for doing certain procedures in office rather than at a hospital or surgicenter.

In some cases, a nurse practitioner or physician's assistant can provide routine care--and for far less than a physician. Some nurse practitioners maintain private practices. Check with your local medical society, or contact the American Academy of Nurse Practitioners, Capitol Station, LBJ Building, Box 12848, Austin, TX 78711.

Emergency Care for Less: Use a 24-hour urgent-care center for off-hour emergencies rather than a hospital emergency room. You'll probably see a physician faster and come out with a smaller bill.

Caution: Hospitals are imperative for procedures involving general anesthesia, but overnight stays may be unnecessary.

Perform radical surgery on your hospital bills:

Too many of us assume that hospitals bills are etched in stone. But cost- conscious consumers take an opposite approach: They negotiate up front for the best hospital deal, then, after checkout, go over all bills with a fine-tooth comb, questioning or disputing suspicious charges.

The rewards of this approach are ample, especially for those with fee-for-services plan, who must pay around 20 percent of hospital charges up to a maximum of $1,500.

How to do a "dollar-ectomy" on your hospital charges:
* Before undergoing diagnostic procedures or treatments, ask your physician if he or she will accept the insurance payment as total compensation and waive the usual fee. Some doctors won't, others will.

* To trim hospital costs, avoid unnecessary tests and explore outpatient options. Many services that patients assume are included in the daily rate are actually extras. This includes a bedside telephone. Ask what it costs. If you don't need a phone, ask that it not be hooked up. Other hospital non-freebies: tissues, slippers, toothpaste, other toiletries. Pack your own and say "No, thanks."

* Check bills for overcharges, which are often disguised with mysterious abbreviations and diagnostic codes. Bet your bottom dollar that most such errors will be in the hospital's favor. Ask your doctor or a member of the office staff to explain your hospital bill to in detail.

Consumer advocates also suggest you log all tests, medications and charges in a notebook, and use your log later to check the itemized bills (you should always demand an itemized bill). Question all items that don't match your log. If you don't feel up to making this record yourself, ask a friend or family member to keep track for you.

Common overcharges: billing for items or services never provided, such as lab work, medication, thermometers, wheelchairs. Items are often placed in the operating room and never used--but billed. Check with your surgeon later to find out if he or she used all equipment you were charged for. Ask the same question about medications.

Look for duplicate charges, especially for lab tests and medications. If several physicians ordered the same test, or one ordered a test repeated, ask why. If a technician performed the test incorrectly the first time or there were other mistakes, such as X-rays that weren't clear, you can contest the charge by claiming duplicate or shoddy testing.

Ask the hospital billing supervisor to check all suspect charges and correct the bill (within 30 days). If not satisfied, call the hospital administrator's office.

A commercial option: For a percentage of your charges, MedReview (800-397-5359) will audit your medical bills for obvious errors. But since you're out to save money, you might as well do it yourself.

Deciphering hospital jargon:

Hospital patients who glance at the charts at the foot of their beds will find themselves staring at a lot of strange symbols and abbreviations. Is that because the information is none of your business?

No! You have every right to that information. Here's a brief key to some commonly used gobbledygook, which may also prove useful in decoding the subsequent bill:
IV = intravenous (drip solution)
Force Fluids = increase intake of liquids
NPO = If this sign is posted by your bed, you won't get anything to eat or drink.
Void = urinate
Ambulate = you get taken for a walk.
HR = heart rate

BP = blood pressure
IPPB = intermittent positive pressure breathing
hs = medication taken before sleep
qid = take 4 times a day
tid = 3 times a day
bid = twice a day
od or qd = once a day
qod = every other day

Filing a medical grievance:

If you're in the hospital and have a grievance, ask to see the patient advocate. If not satisfied, work your way up the hierarchy toward the hospital administrator.

If you're still not getting the response you deserve, you can write the Joint Commission of Accreditation of Healthcare Organizations, 875 North Michigan Avenue, Chicago, IL 60611.

If your complaint concerns a doctor or staff member at a private medical office, first talk to that person. If the problem isn't resolved, contact the local medical society or your state's Board of Medical Examiners. Be prepared to document your case. Keep copies of correspondence and of all relevant incidents, conversations and meetings.

If still unsatisfied, consider contacting the media. Negative publicity in the local paper or on the local news can get quick results. But be prepared to produce documentation to whomever you contact. They'll want facts, not vague complaints or accusations.

Last option: Hire a lawyer. All that may be required to get your grievance addressed is a letter on a lawyer's stationery.

Get your baby born for less:

Newborns are a precious bundle of joy, but getting them delivered safely requires a bundle of money. Here are typical charges:

* Hospital charges--usually in the neighborhood of $3,000 to $5,000.
* Prenatal and delivery fees range from about $1,500 to $2,500 for an uncomplicated pregnancy.
* Anesthesia, lab and pharmacy fees used in the delivery can run thousands more.

The cost of prenatal care and a normal delivery averages $6,200 nationwide. Cesarean deliveries run about $3,000 more.

But expectant parents have several ways to trim such out-of-pocket costs, if they're willing to plan ahead and do some homework.

The biggest factor is your health plan.

If you belong to an HMO, your medical expenses are likely to be modest, because most plans cover both prenatal and delivery expenses with minimal co-payments. But those covered by indemnity plans, which give patients more choice over which doctor and hospital to use, are likely to pay hundreds--even thousands--more.

That's because you must first satisfy your plan's deductible. Then, typically, your co-payment will be 20% of covered costs. And certain procedures simply aren't covered. For instance, so-called "well baby" care at the hospital, which can run $300 to $600, isn't covered because traditional health insurance plans don't pay for check-ups.

If you're in an indemnity plan, you can save thousands by transferring into an HMO prior to the pregnancy.

What if you're sold on a particular doctor, who happens to be more expensive or who uses a high-priced hospital for deliveries? Haggle. Your doctor's billing department cuts discount deals with insurers every day. They'll negotiate with you too.

Another way to cut cost is by working out a prompt-pay discount. You may get a 5% to 10% discount by paying as you go.

If you're not insured, offer to pay cash up-front and you can shave the bill by 30% or more. Doctors "retail" rates are often 50% higher than their insurance reimbursement rates, so they often offer discounts to cash customers, too.

Cash rates aren't advertised. You have to ask. Also make sure you know whether up-front payments will be considered payment in full, even if actual expenditures exceed estimated costs.

Kids and air bags -- safety update:

The National Highway Traffic Safety Administration warns that the number of young children killed by air bags has increased rapidly and more tragedies will occur if adults don't adhere to guidelines about how to properly seat children in cars.

The agency said adults should adopt firm rules:
* Children should ride in the back seat, wearing seat belts or secured in a child safety seat.
* If children must ride in the front seat, belt them in (lap and shoulder) and move the seat back as far as it can go.
* Never put a rear-facing child safety seat in the front.

The potential for air bag injuries has been known for several years. Officials previously warned that infants strapped in rear-facing seats--the position recommended by safety experts--could be killed or severely injured if a front-seat air bag deploys.

In most such fatalities, the child was sitting in the front seat without a seat belt, although injuries have occurred in which the child was thought to be wearing only a lap belt. Because of pre-crash braking, the children were probably leaning close to the dashboard when the bag was deployed. An air bag unfurls at more than 100 mph.

Many of these deaths have occurred in low-speed crashes (less than 20 mph)--the kind of fender-benders that occur hundreds of times each day.

Even small adults can be injured by air bags if too close to the steering wheel. The NHTSA recommends drivers adjust their seats so they are at least 6 to 8 inches from the wheel.

Shopping for nursing homes:

Deciding to move an aged and infirm parent to a nursing home is almost always agonizing. Picking the right facility can be almost as difficult. For these reasons, most adults postpone these decisions until the last moment--then choose under pressure and in haste.

It's better to investigate all nursing homes, board-and-care arrangements and other options in advance, while beginning to prepare your parents for the inevitable relocation.

How do you shop for the best place? Start with friends and colleagues for recommendations. You'll be surprised how many people have gone through this painful process. If they've found a wonderful place, they'll be glad to tell you about it.

Listings of accredited homes can also be obtained from your church, business group, fraternal order, state agency on aging, the American Association of Homes for the Aging (Suite 770, 1050 17th St. NW, Washington, DC 20036), or the American Health Care Association (1200 15th St. NW, Washington, DC 20005).

Financial preparations:

If your aged parent's resources are minimal, Medicaid can step in and provide financial support for nursing-home care. Most homes in urban areas charge at least $1,000 a month--some charge twice or three times that--per parent. They may also require a substantial down payment. Though state rules vary, patients who begin paying their own way may be able to switch to Medicaid assistance after their savings run out.

Financial strategy:

There are steps you can take to protect assets if these would be gradually depleted before Medicaid takes over. The method is to move the parent's assets into a trust fund, which must be established so that Medicaid is unlikely to attach it. Which means it has to be set up in advance of need, since most states forbid asset transfer for a certain period (often two years) prior to admission to the nursing home.

In order to do this, you should consult an attorney who specializes in elder law. You can find one by writing or calling the National Academy of Elder Law Attorneys, 1604 N. Country Club Road, Tucson AZ 85716 (602-881-4005).

Checking out a nursing home:

1. Arrive without an appointment. Inspect public areas and patient rooms for cleanliness, overcrowding and safety features. Look in on the dining room during meals, also the kitchen. Ask residents their opinions.

2. Observe the staff. Are they friendly and respectful to residents? Are there enough employees to give attention to all residents?

3. What kind of medical supervision is available?

4. In the office, check accreditation, license and current certification for Medicare and Medicaid.

5. Don't sign a contract until your lawyer has checked it. Some give nursing homes the right to discharge a patient whose condition has worsened without returning any advance lump-sum payment. Insist on your refund right in the event plans change.

6. Make sure you know which services are included and which are "extras"--and how much extra they cost. Make a list of "extras" your parent will require and see which you can supply yourself.

7. Meet the administrator and all department heads. In case of problems or emergencies, you need to know faces and names.

Finding a care-giver for aging parents:

A tragic problem confronts the country's aging population: How to obtain safe and adequate help in their own homes as they become unable to care for themselves.

Long-term help with everyday tasks such as housework, cooking, bathing and shopping can be the difference between remaining at home or being forced into a nursing facility.

While many look to their own families, others must hire strangers. Largely unregulated by government agencies, in-home care can be crushingly expensive or even dangerous for the elderly, who sometimes are abused, neglected or financially exploited.

Getting Good Help:
Here are suggestions from experts in gerontology, social work and law enforcement:

* **Plan ahead:** Locate a trusted relative or friend--preferably more than one so there are checks and balances--to handle your affairs if you become mentally impaired.

* **Seek help:** Talk to someone you trust in selecting a care-giver.

* **Referrals:** If you go to a referral agency, ask how long it has been in business and insist on references from other clients or senior citizen organizations. Ask how the agency screens employees and monitors workers and

whether it provides substitute aides when necessary. Ask about the qualifications and training of workers. Ask whether the agency insures aides against accidents or misconduct. Find out exactly how much you will be charged and how much the worker will be paid.

* **Advertisements:** Be careful when seeking help through a newspaper want ad; exploiters look for such ads. Don't list your phone number or address in an ad; have applicants send resumes, including references and experience, to a post office box.

* **Interviews:** Conduct in-depth interviews with prospective care-givers. Insist on references and don't be afraid to ask detailed or personal questions. Have a person you trust sit in. Check references carefully. Get the phone number, address, driver's license and Social Security numbers of the prospective aide. Discuss details of salary.

* **Wages:** Don't pay wages in advance and don't lend money to or borrow it from the care-giver.

* **Duties:** Be sure the prospective care-giver understands exactly what tasks are to be performed. Managers at senior citizen centers or home-care agencies can help determine your needs.

* **Checking:** Have a trusted friend or relative make frequent, unscheduled visits to check on your care.

* **Dependence:** Beware of becoming overly dependent on the care-giver and don't be afraid to fire an aide who is not doing a satisfactory job.

* **Plan:** Have a backup plan to cover emergencies, days the aide is off and holidays.

* **Cautions:** Beware of prospective aides who ask questions about your finances. Also, get to know personnel at your bank so they will be able to spot a stranger handling your finances and will be more likely to notice unusual activity in connection with your account. Check out money management programs at your local senior center.

* **Help:** If you are victimized, call the Elder Abuse Hotline: (800) 992-1660.

Chapter

More Investment Secrets **16**

Start wealth-building now -- you've got a lifetime left:

Y ou may believe that if you want to accumulate any real money, you'll need to save substantial sums each month. But this is simply not true. You don't have to start with a $100,000, say, like super-investor Warren Buffett. (See below, "4 Commandments of the World's Greatest Investor.") The trick is to start with what you've got-- and start now.

Saving even small amounts pays off over time. For instance, if a 20-year-old starts saving just $1 a day ($30 a month) and continues to save until retirement at age 65, he or she will accumulate more than $314,000, assuming a 10% average rate of return.

If you start saving $200 a month from the time you're 25 until you retire at age 65 and earn 10% annually on your money, you'll have a cool $1.26 million to spend in retirement. A 401(k) with a company match would mean even more money.

What happens if you start at 40, but save twice as much--$400 a month? You'll end up with $303,747.

In both instances, you would have contributed a total of $96,000 to savings. But the person who saved early got the benefit of 20 extra years of compound interest--a powerful force.

It's too late to start early? Then start now. Every extra year helps.

The basic jumping off-place for any savings and investment program is this: Pay yourself first. Every financial planner says it; few people do it. Write yourself a monthly check--and stash it in savings. How much? At least 10% of your after-tax income, if you possibly can. Remember, regular savings is the key to wealth- building. Don't think it over, make it automatic, as if it was rent or mortgage. If you don't, your savings will never amount to much.

When things are tight, give up the night out, the new suit or the expensive pair of shoes--don't fail to contribute to your savings plan.

Saving regularly actually has two purposes: You accumulate wealth and you get in the habit of delaying gratification and living below your means. Why would you want to do that? If you ever hit a tough stretch--where you are out of work or face big, unexpected expenses--you'll have money in the bank and know how to make it last.

The easiest way to save regularly is to make it automatic by contributing to a 401(k) plan at work--where contributions are taken out of your check before taxes and before you get your fingers on the money. If you don't have access to a 401(k), consider setting up an automatic investment program with a mutual fund company.

Again, saving early is more important than how much you set aside. If you've put it off too long already, don't compound the error. Start today.

Which comes first, love or money:

The best-laid financial plan will go awry if it's not agreed up by both partners in a marriage. And the ideal time to reach the accord is before marriage.

Why? Because the vast majority of couples who split cite money as a main or a primary factor.

It's not easy, of course, to bring up this touchy subject. For some partners, money is a taboo topic. But that only makes talking about it more essential.

You don't have to lay all your financial cards out on the table, at least not at first. Don't demand to know the other's checking account balances or salary info or 401(k) plans? Not at first. Discuss financial goals and the way you handle money. What do you hope for the future? Your own house? A luxury car? Do you aim to take time off--or quit--if you have children? Do you save for major expenses or do you charge them?

One financial detail couples must share is whether they are coming to the altar with outstanding debts. Do you have thousands of dollars in student loans that must be paid off? Owe money to the IRS or credit card companies? What's your plan to pay those off? You don't want to inherit somebody's credit problems without knowing about it first, If you talk about it, both parties know what they're getting into.

Eventually you'll have to determine how you'll handle household expenses. If both are working, do you plan to have a joint checking account, keep accounts separate or have a joint account for joint expenses and separate accounts for individual discretionary spending?

If one spouse will stay home, will he or she get an allowance or a credit card that can be used up to some limit, no questions asked? Or will one spouse be in control of the purse strings?

People need to have some of their own money--even if only to buy gifts for the other. If one partner is too controlling, it will make the other feel helpless and, often, resentful.

What if the love of your life says he or she is not comfortable talking about money? It's a bad sign, that's what.

You wouldn't want to find out after you were married that your partner doesn't want to have children and you do, for instance. Money is the same. It's going to come up in your relationship, whether it's because of work or how to save or what to buy. If one person thinks the conversation invades their privacy, you are going to be in a pickle sooner rather than later.

4 keys to wealth-building:

You're not likely to get rich by scrimping and saving. But you will be taking a first step toward wealth-building if you use those savings in an ongoing investment program.

In fact, that--not inheritance--is how most millionaires are made. The average millionaire is a compulsive saver and investor, a person who follows all four of these keys to wealth-building and wealth-keeping.

1. Focus on net worth, not income. Study the lives of the real moneymakers (with the exception of the celebrity rich), and you'll find them reinvesting their take-home pay back into their businesses, or into stocks or other assets. They're not only building net worth, but keeping earnings out of the IRS' reach.

2. Don't spend, invest. The late Sam Walton of Wal-Mart drove a pickup truck. Super- investor Warren Buffett operates out of a small office in Omaha, with no computers in sight. These tycoons could afford a lavish lifestyle, but became accustomed to living simply as they clawed their way to the top.

And they knew that a rich-and-famous lifestyle can be a drastic financial drain. The same is true of fancy restaurants, accommodations, travel, housing, vacations. Wealth-builders don't burn their money to light cigars, but to fuel their enterprises.

And never borrow for consumption: When you buy a house, you're investing in a place to live. When you buy a car, you're investing in transportation that will take you to and from work. There's no sin in borrowing to make these major purchases--as long as it's not more debt than you can afford.

However, a big-screen TV is not likely to improve your earnings potential. If there are certain luxuries you simply have to have, wait until you can pay for them with cash.

Remember, wealth isn't what you spend, but what you accumulate. If you want to get rich, in fact, a good principle is to live way below your means. If your family earns upward of $50,000 a year, you should be setting aside 10% of that gross amount--or more--in savings. Even better, increase that contribution level up to 20%.

3. Define your goals. Successful people know exactly where they want to go, how much wealth they want to build, and usually have a clear idea of the intermediate goals en route to their ultimate destination.

For instance: Do you want to buy a bigger house, have an early retirement, leave an substantial estate to your kids? You won't get there with vague yearnings and haphazard effort. Draw up a timeline from where you are to where you want to go. Then work backward to calculate how much you need to make and save each year.

4. Seek the best advice--and pay for it, if necessary. Wealth-builders may be stingy about luxuries, but they'll pay top dollar for expert legal or financial opinions. There's no virtue in going it alone, when others can help you get there.

The 4 commandments of
the world's greatest investor:

According to Forbes magazine, Warren Buffett, chairman of Berkshire Hathaway, Inc., is the second richest person in the nation (after Microsoft's Bill Gates). Buffett who turned his startup investment of $100,000 into an empire worth nearly $20 billion, is legendary for picking winners.

How does he do it? His basic philosophy is so simple that you don't need to be a math whiz or investment analyst to put it into play. In fact, almost anyone can do it. Here it is, boiled down to four principles.

1. Invest in a business, not a stock. If you can't understand where the heck a particular company is headed in the market, stay away from it. Easily understood businesses have better long-term prospects. Ditto with company management. If you can't understand what executives are saying, chances are they're not making much better sense to the market either.

When Buffett finds businesses he likes and management that talks sense, he goes a step further, studying company financials to find those whose stock price is at a significant discount to their value.

2. Restrict your investment to 5 to 10 businesses you like. You don't need widely diversified portfolio. In fact, Buffett considers that a mistake, since few people can make hundreds of smart decisions. He'd prefer to concentrate his attention on a few sensibly priced companies, so he only has to make a few smart decisions.

3. Forget about economic trends. This kind of roller-coaster watching can drive you crazy--and it's a waste of your time and energy. Leave it to the paid pundits. Instead, concentrate on finding good businesses.

4. In fact, don't even track the stock market on a daily basis. Ignore it. Your eye should be fixed on long-term success.

Picking growth stocks
in a fast-changing economy:

All long-term investors would like to own a "worry-free" portfolio filled only with high-quality growth stocks. But these days few industries or individual companies enjoy longevity in the growth-stock category.

Many investment analysts believe that the pickings for classic growth investors are definitely slimmer today than in years past. Many of the buy-'em-and-put-'em-away growth stocks of the past are too expensive today relative to earnings, after huge 1995 price gains. A great stock-picker has to know not only what to buy--but when.

Major drug stocks, for example, suffered deep declines in 1992 and 1993 as the federal health-care reform threat shook the industry. And when Philip Morris slashed cigarette prices in mid-'93 in a bid to steal market share, some analysts declared that brand names in general had lost their cachet, and that with it went the brand companies' dependable growth rates.

Yet many of the brand-name growth stocks are again the market leaders, hitting record highs as they deliver above-average earnings growth. In retrospect, the sell-off in the stocks in 1992-93 was a great time to buy. And it's still not too late to get in on that trend.

So possibles to add to your "buy" list of growth stocks: Philip Morris, Reebok, RJR Nabisco and Bristol-Myers.

3 sleeper stocks to watch:

Historically, the stock market has performed well in the months prior to a presidential election. The explanation is not hard to find. The Administration naturally pulls out all the stops to hype the economy, hoping that voters will reward them at the ballot box. For instance, in 1996, both Congress and the White House began jockeying to pass a middle- class tax cut, with each hoping to get the credit.

Of course whether the market as a whole continues its bullish ways or experiences large-scale corrections, there are large profits to be made in overlooked areas. While no one can predict the Wall Street horse race, here are three entries that bear watching:

1. Natural Gas Stocks

The national outlook is for slack to falling oil prices, due to a glut of supply worldwide. But there are indications that natural gas stocks, after a lackluster year, are headed higher in the near future. One such indication is the fact that large blocks of natural gas stocks are being bought by top executives of those energy companies. This kind of "insider confidence" bodes well for natural gas prices and profits. Possible buys in this category: Pennsylvania Enterprises (NYSE:PNT); NorAm Energy (NYSE:NAE), Cross Timbers Oil (NYSE:XTO)

2. High-Speed Modems

Speed is "in," with the 55 mph limit raised, and the Information Superhighway taking off. In a couple years 'Net surfers may be propelled into cyberspace at much super speeds by cable connections. But in the practical future, high-speed modems are still the way to go--and the way to bet. One good company to bet with is U.S. Robotics (NAS-DAQ:USRX), a solid name in modems and a forward-looking firm in data communications. For instance: U.S. Robotics recently formed an Internet routing partnership with MCI, a deal that will lift U.S. Robotics over the billion-dollar revenue mark in 1996.

3. Wireless Communications

The Third World is racing to catch up with modern technology. And vast regions of these countries--China and India, for instance--have never really been "hard-wired" with copper. Oddly, this may work to their benefit, spurring them to go straight to wireless technology. This is particularly true in Asia--China, India, Malaysia. One company well positioned to take advantage of this explosive market is California-based STM Wireless (NASDAQ:STMI), with solid technology and international business expertise.

Surfing the millennium wave in stocks and funds:

No one expected the 1995 market rush. Last January, experts were almost uniformly bearish, but only the disciples of market timing--those who sell stocks and hold cash when they foresee a market decline--cashed in nearly everything to head for cover.

As the market took off, the timers still saw signs of impending doom. While stocks returned about 30%, the timers' cash earned about 5%.

Lesson to be learned: Stay fully invested and give up on timing the market. You'll be far better off determining the best approach for you and pursuing it than trying to duck in and out of the market.

Another approach: Buy funds that are fully invested. If you want that safe hedge as well as a stock fund, pick a good money-market issue and allocate your money between the two.

Another lesson to be learned from 1995: Develop and stick to a long-term investment plan. Most plans are not about chasing performance or making the most out of the market, they're about having enough to live and not risking everything. The market more often pays off for the people who stick to their plans.

Many historians still predict a growing anxiety as 2000 looms, a deepening sense that while the world isn't ending, great changes lie ahead that will dramatically alter the world as we know it, or knew it. And because a large portion of the markets' advance has come in 1995--the Dow's best year since 1975--there is widespread resignation that 1996 can't possibly top its predecessor, and even that some of this year's progress must be reversed in the near future.

But for many investment pros, the fear that markets may be buffeted between now and 2000 stems less from a belief in the power of that number itself to trigger change as from its potential to intensify societal and economic trends already underway.

Key trends:
    * The Aging Population:
The first American baby boomers turn 50 in 1996. The boomer generation in total numbers 76 million, nearly 30% of the entire U.S. population. In Europe and Japan the graying is even more pronounced, and birth rates even lower than in the United States. What that translates into are high savings rates, relatively low consumption rates and the potential for continued subdued inflation, experts say.

And yet if Americans' consumption continues to suffer in the name of saving, there may be plenty of companies-- and stocks--on the losing end of the demographic shift. Profits, remember, are what ultimately drive share prices: Without the former it's tough to support the latter for long.

Already in the 1990s, U.S. clothing makers and retailers, auto makers and furniture producers have typically been lousy stocks to own.

Industry winners, meanwhile, have included many health-care companies, financial services providers, semiconductor makers, entertainment providers and other companies whose products or services fill what people believe are the real needs in their lives.

If U.S. consumers' spending continues to decline, the secret in the stock market will be to own companies that provide what Americans truly want, or multinational companies that derive most of their growth from overseas, especially in the burgeoning Third World.

* The Spread of Technology:

The 1995 mania for U.S. technology stocks has unquestionably crested, and with the pullback in many of those shares some Wall Streeters are prophesying a widespread bust in the computer business in general.

Yet, looking ahead to 2000, most investment pros say it's inconceivable that technology will play a lesser role in the world economy's growth than it does today.

But while there is certainly money to be made in technology stocks in the near and longer-term future, picking the right companies in a business where product life cycles are measured in months rather than years won't get any easier.

Despite the technology boom of the last six years, the list of major computer companies whose shares today are below their year-end 1989 levels is sobering: Amdahl, Apple, Cray Research, Digital Equipment, IBM, Sequent and Tandem, to name a few. To invest in this exciting arena, you're better off in a diversified portfolio of tech issues.

Easy way to shift assets offshore:

From a diversification standpoint, investors would be wise to maintain a modest foreign stake. Foreign companies weigh in with two-thirds of the world's stock-market worth, and there's usually a couple of foreign nations performing better than the U.S. market.

The Value Line Mutual Fund Survey, a New York publication, suggests investors consider putting 20% to 30% of their stock allocations into foreign-stock funds, as a way of shifting assets away from the high-flying U.S. market.

Options include investing in domestic funds with big overseas stock holdings, or in one of two types of international mutual funds: conventional open-end mutual funds, and closed-end, single- country or single-region funds. (You can also buy shares directly in a foreign company.)

The 10 best-performing international stock mutual funds over recent years:

1. GAM International--annualized return 12.27%
2. Merrill Lynch Dev CapMkts A--12.19%
3. Smith Barney Int'l Equity A--11.19%
4. Harbor International--10.89%
5. Warburg Pincus Int'l.--10.75%
6. EuroPacific Growth--10.69%
7. Morgan Stanley Instl. Intl. Equity--10.42%
8. Templeton Foreign--9.53%
9. Managers Int'l Equity--9.42%
10. Ivy International A--9.41%

Taking a deceptive stockbroker to court:

If you have a dispute with a broker and can't settle it amicably, there is an easy and fairly low-cost way to settle it: binding arbitration.

Securities arbitration, which allows an impartial third party to resolve broker-client disputes, is the mandatory form of settlement procedure when brokers and their clients get into a rift. That's because most brokerage firms require customers to sign arbitration agreements when they open accounts.

Cases are heard fairly quickly--usually within a year, compared to up to five years in civil courts--and the cost is reasonable. The bad news is that there is little, if any, chance to appeal an adverse decision. Unless the arbitrator is biased or had a clear conflict of interest, the decision is legal and binding.

Arbitration filing fees range from about $30 for a small case in which the amount in dispute is less than $1,000, to $1,800 for cases where the amount is more than $5 million.

Plaintiffs can represent themselves or be represented by anyone they choose. They do not need to hire a lawyer or an arbitration specialist. But experts recommend hiring a professional when the dispute involves a lot of money. That's because the brokerage is almost always represented by an attorney. And a General Accounting Office study found that customers were much more likely to win when they were professionally represented.

Make sure to discuss fees and charges before you hire a professional. There is a wide variation in what experts charge to take your case to arbitration. Many attorneys work on an hourly basis, with rates ranging from $125 to $450. Some are also willing to charge a flat rate to prepare arbitration documents, if you want to represent yourself.

Tips From the Experts

To increase your chances of winning a brokerage dispute, here are some suggestions from the experts:

* **Document your case.** If it's your word against the broker's, your chances of winning a dispute are 50-50. But if you confirmed your conversation in writing shortly after you opened the account--and saved a copy of the letter-- your chance of winning is much improved.

* **Complain:** If you find or suspect problems--improper trading, misrepresentation, unsuitable recommendations--ask a trusted financial adviser to review your account. If the suspicions are warranted, complain to the broker, the brokerage firm's branch manager and the firm's compliance department immediately. Make sure you clearly state what the problem is, how you discovered it and what you want the firm to do about it. Make these statements in writing. And be sure to keep copies for your records.

* Arbitrate promptly: One of the biggest mistakes investors make is not filing arbitration claims until years after a problem occurred. Federal and state statutes of limitations could nullify your claim before it's ever heard. And arbitrators may question the credibility of investors who allow illegal or improper activity to continue for years before objecting.

Mutual funds made easy:

Mutuals have been piling up huge gains lately. If you still haven't profited from this growth, this could be your year to start. Here's a quickie intro:

Mutual funds are investment companies that pool the money from many people and invest it according to published guidelines. If you put $10,000 in a fund with total assets of $1,000,000, you have a 1 percent share. If the fund's value rises to $1,200,000, your 1 percent stake will be worth $12,000.

You can buy mutual funds from banks, brokers, financial planners or directly from the investment companies themselves. You may also be able to invest in mutual funds through an employee 401(k) plan.

On shares bought from brokers, financial planners and banks, you generally pay a "load"--an upfront sales fees between 3 percent and 8.5 percent of the invested amount. Shares purchased directly from a mutual fund company are generally "no-load," meaning your entire purchase amount is invested.

Why pay a load? The rationale is that if you buy through a broker, banker or financial planner, you're getting professional advice in selecting them. If you're willing to forgo the advice, you can forgo the fee.

Other costs: Fund companies also charge annual management fees, usually around 1 percent of your investment each year. Some also charge yearly marketing fees.

Caution: Some people think their investment is federally insured if they buy a mutual fund from a bank. It isn't. You're money is at risk. How much risk depends on what investments the fund buys. Government regulations, however, do protect investors from mutual fund fraud. Historically, bond or money market funds have lower risk than stock funds, but don't perform as well over long periods of time.

3 low-risk, high-potential mutual funds:

Here is a trio of mutuals with great track records and upside potential. Perhaps more importantly, all three have fund managers skilled at dodging downside risk.

All three have racked up solid-to-spectacular numbers in recent years. As always in investing, of course, the past is no guarantee of future earnings.

1. Zweig Strategy Fund (800-444-2706). This $41.1 billion mutual has averaged returns of 11.2 percent yearly since it's launch in 1989. More importantly for cautious investors, Zweig has done well during very bad market periods. In 1995, when the fund returned 25.1%, 30 percent of its equities were in technology stocks. It has since diversified into core industrial companies. Zweig Strategy Fund is available in 5.5% load shares.

2. Warburg Pincus Growth & Income Fund (800-257-5614). This fund, which returned 20.4% in 1995 and 75.9% over the last three years, has 40% of its money in tech stocks, but has shown an ability to do well both in up and down markets--experiencing fewer slippages than most equity funds. No-load.

3. Fidelity Puritan Fund (800-544-6666). This $15.6 billion balanced no-load is extremely diversified in its holdings. Puritan weathered the bear markets in 1987 and 1994 better than most of its competitors, and has returned 50.1% in the last three years, and seems well positioned for the future.

Top 10 investment newsletters:

The investment newsletter business is certainly a booming sector. The best ones beat the market, but the worst ones can lose you a lot more than the subscription price. With so many of them out there, and the price being high-- how can you know which ones are worth reading and riding with?

Here is a ranking based on performance over the last five years, based on a survey by the Hulbert Financial Digest:

TOP 5 INVESTMENT NEWSLETTERS/5 YR. TOTAL NET
1. OTC Insight .... **+185.0%**
(James Collins, editor, $195, P.O. Box 127, Moraga, CA 94556; 800-955-9566)
2. Oberweis Report .... **+176.2%**
(James D. Oberweis, editor, $249, 841 N. Lake, Aurora, IL 60506; 708-801-4766)
3. Turnaround Letter .... **+161.0%**
(George Putnam III, editor, $195, 225 Friend St., Ste. 801, Boston, MA 02114; 617-573-9550.)
4. New Issues .... **+138.5%**
(Norman Fosback and Glen King Parker, editors, $95, 3471 N. Federal Hwy., Ft. Lauderdale, FL 33306; 800-327-6720.)
5. MPT Review .... **+133.6%**
(Louis Navellier, editor, $245, P.O. Box 5695, Incline Village, NV 89450; 702-831-1396.)

TOP 5 MUTUAL FUND NEWSLETTERS/5 YR. TOTAL NET
1. Stockmarket Cycles... **+186.0%**
(Peter Eliades, editor, $198, P.O. Box 6873, Santa Rosa, CA 95406; 707-579-84444.)
2. Timer Digest .... **+124.5%**
(Jim Schmidt, editor, $225, P.O. Box 1688, Greenwich, CT 06836; 800-356-2527.)
3. Fidelity Monitor .... **+113.0%**
(Jack Bowers, editor, $96, P.O. Box 1294, Rocklin, CA 95677; 800-397-3094.)

4. Fundline .... **+ 93.9%**
(David Menashe, editor, $127, P.O. Box 663, Woodland
Hills, CA 91365; 818-346-5637.)
5. Professional Timing Service .... **+ 85.7%**
(Curtis J. Hesler, editor, $185, P.O. Box 7483, Missoula, MT
59807; 406-543-4131.)

Research and track investments
on the internet:

To keep current on mutual funds these days, you don't
have to subscribe to an investment newsletter or send
away for prospectuses. If you have a PC and Internet
access, you can scroll through performance data about
thousands of funds. You can even download prospectuses
and fund applications.

To get your financial feet wet, check out these sites
operated by the larger families of mutual fund offerings:

Calvert Group: http://www.calvertgroup.com

Fidelity Investments: http://www.fid-inv.com

Gabelli Funds Inc.: http://www.gabelli.com

Invest-or-rama: http://www.investorama.com

Kanon Bloch: http://investools.com/cgi-bin/Libarry/kbca.pl

Mutual Funds Magazine: http://www.mfmag.com

NETworth: http://www.networth.galt.com

Charles Schwab: http://www.schwab.com

The Vanguard Group: http://www.vanguard.com

Jack White & Co.: http://pawws.com/jwc

There are other ways to collect savvy investment tips
without tapping your much-needed funds. Probably the
most obvious and effective way is to visit your local public
library and browse any of several excellent daily and weekly publications:

The Wall Street Journal, Investors Business Daily, Money Magazine, Business Week, U.S. News, and Consumers Digest publications like "Your Money." Some of the most knowledgeable Wall Street experts are regular contributors.

Note: You may also be able to locate these publications on the Internet.

Picking a discount broker:

The war among discount brokers has been a real boon to investors, saving fees and giving a bonanza of services. These brokers now account for about a third of individual stock trades--and it's going up every year, as more and more investors abandon full-service houses.

It makes dollars and sense. Why pay hefty brokerage commissions, which average more than $200 per trade for the big firms, like Merrill Lynch and Smith Barney Shearson. With fewer services, discounters charge average per-trade commissions of $50.

Despite this, discounters do provide customers many basic services, such as research reports like ValueLine and Standard & Poor's. They can also set up margin accounts and automatically reinvest dividends. Some can even buy mutual fund shares.

What they can't do is provide individual investment advice.

The big three regular discounters are Charles Schwab (which pioneered the concept), Fidelity and Quick & Reilly.

Here are the top 10 deep discounters, as ranked by Mercer, Inc. To order their annual directory, call 800-582-9854, or try the American Association of Independent Investors, 312-280-0170, which also publishes a yearly survey. (After you've narrowed your choice to several candidate firms, ask for a commission schedule and description of services, fees and bonus discounts.)

TOP 10 DEEP DISCOUNTERS
1. Wall Street Equities (800-447-8625), $24 minimum commission.
2. Brown & Co. (800-822-2021), $29.
3. K. Aufhauser & Co. (800-368-3666), $31.49.
4. Lombard Institutional (800-688-3462), $27.50.
5. National Discount Broker (800-888-3999), $33.
6. R. J. Forbes Group (800-488-0090), $35.
7. Pacific Brokerage Services (800-421-8395), $29.
8. Kennedy, Cabot & Co. (800-252-0090), $33.
9. Recom Securities (800-328-8600), $35.
10. Barry Murphy & Co. (800-221-2111), $32.50.

For no-fee mutual funds, the choice narrows to Schwab's OneSource and Fidelity's FundsNetwork. Each offers 24-hour, toll- free phone service, and allows investors to manage a portfolio of funds from different families and switch among funds and cash- management accounts. For more information: Charles Schwab's OneSource (800-266-5623); Fidelity's FundsNetwork (800-544-9697).

Buy stocks with no broker and no commission:

If you make an initial purchase directly from the company offering the stock, you can bypass brokerage houses and commissions entirely. There are nearly a thousand companies that sponsor dividend-reinvestment plans, or DRPs. Here are a dozen that sell stock directly to investors at commissions of only a few cents a share:

Arrow Financial Corp
Atlantic Energy Inc.
Barnett Banks Inc.
COMSAT Corp.
Dial Corp.
Exxon Corp.

First Alabama Bancshares Inc.
Johnson Controls Inc.
Kellwood Co.
Kerr-McGee Corp.
Mobile Corp.
SCANA Corp.
Summit Bancorp. (NJ)
Texaco Inc.
U.S. West Inc.

(For further information: Evergreen Enterprises, 301-953- 1861, publishes a $30 quarterly guide and annual directory of companies that offer DRPs.)

College -- the most expensive bargain:

How much is a college degree worth? About $795,000 over a lifetime, if you're a man. Somewhat less for women.

The Census Bureau, which compiles statistics on annual income by education level, has found a definite correlation between how many years you attend school and how much you earn later.

The average male high school graduate, age 25 or over, earns $21,782 per year. But graduate from college and your average annual earnings expectations soar. The average male college graduate earns $41,649. Over a working lifetime--the 40 years between age 25 and age 65--the difference that four extra years of school makes adds up to a fortune.

And more than 70% of the families reporting annual incomes of $70,000 or more boast a college graduate in the household, according to the Bureau of Labor Statistics.

Of course, just because you didn't go to college, doesn't mean you can't be a success. It just means you're bucking longer odds.

3 strategies for building college savings:

If you've seen recent estimates of what college will cost when your youngsters are ready to go, you're probably in financial despair. But there's hope on the horizon. With sound planning, you can still afford those ivy walls. Here are three schemes that will help your kids get their sheep-skins--and leave you in a better economic position as well.

1. Pay Down the Mortgage Faster
Parents of toddlers could refinance a 30-year mortgage into a 15-year loan. By the time the oldest child is college age, the parents will be done with house payments.

They could then elect to continue making payments in order to finance education costs out-of-pocket, or they might refinance and get cash that way.

This method also eliminates the risk that the kids will use college money to finance a grand tour of Europe rather than their education.

How much extra would you need to pay to get rid of the mortgage by the time your kids reach college? That depends, of course, on the size of the mortgage, your interest rate and the your kids' age.

Here's an example:
Suppose a family has a $100,000 30-year mortgage at 8% interest and a 5-year-old child. Their monthly mortgage payment amounts to $734. If they want to pay off the mortgage in 13 years for their child's expected college enrollment, they'd need to pay $1,033 a month--about $300 more than they're currently paying.

A hefty bite, yes, but consider what they get in return. Not only are they free of mortgage payments 17 years sooner, they save a stunning $102,994 in interest expenses.

If you can't afford such a big a payment, pay what you can. It still builds equity, thus boosting your borrowing power. And that borrowing power can be tapped when college bills arrive. Even tiny additional payments will save you mightily in interest expenses.

2. Use Your 401(k)

Perhaps the smartest strategy is just ignore the kids and save as much as you can for your own retirement. A wonderful vehicle is a 401(k) plan, where your employer matches a portion of your contributions--if you can borrow from the account.

Roughly 90% of the nation's larger employers now offer these plans; 84% match a portion of worker contributions, and 81% offer workers the ability to borrow from their accounts.

How does that help your would-be scholars? Here's how: By the time your oldest kid is starting college, your retirement fund will be so substantial that you'll feel comfortable putting 401(k) contributions on hiatus while you get the kids through school. This lets you use current income for college bills.

And retirement plan contributions are not considered assets as far as federal financial aid calculations are concerned. That means your child also qualifies for comparatively more aid.

Another benefit: Many of these 401(k) plans let you borrow about half of the account value for major events, such as buying a house, dealing with a medical emergency or paying for college.

Caution: If you change jobs, you may lose your ability to borrow from the account. But having accumulated substantial retirement funds, you are in a better position to slow your savings while the kids are in college.

3. Get Serious About College Early

When babies come on the scene, relatives often sent checks. If you're the parent, don't spend that money on toys. Buy stock in companies with good growth prospects so that someday Baby will be able to attend an Ivy League university without drowning in debt.

In fact, you can do the saving in Baby's name to save on income taxes. Currently, the first $650 the child earns on his account is free of federal taxes. The next $650 is taxed at a 15% rate. If the money was invested in the parent's account, the federal government would tax it at a 28% rate.

Baby's investment plan can and should be aggressive. And since the money won't be needed for 17 years, you can afford to ride out temporary market swings. Over the long run, stocks have outperformed nearly every other type of investment, raking in 10% average annual returns over the past 50 years.

As Baby becomes a teen-ager, however, and his account gets bigger, you may want to shift new investments--and, if possible, the existing account balance--back into your name. This is because tax benefits begin to evaporate as the account grows in size. And if your teen has too much money, he or she won't qualify for as much financial aid. Finally, there's the question of non-college spending.

What if your young scholar is irresponsible with money--or doesn't want to go to college? Parents uncertain about their offspring's responsibility probably should save in their own names--regardless of federal income taxes.

Another college-saving investment:

U.S. College Saver bonds are technically the same as any Series EE U.S. Savings Bonds, with a few key differences:

* At purchase, these bonds must be registered in the names of the parents of the children for whose education they are intended.

* Bond buyers must be at least 24 years old.

* Tax breaks apply only to bond proceeds used for tuition and required school fees, not for books and room and board.

* The bonds must be purchased by the parents of the children attending college in order to be eligible for the tax break.

* At redemption, the family's adjusted gross income cannot exceed federal maximum limits. Income limits are set each year.

For more information, write for the free brochure, "U.S. Savings Bond Investor Information," from the Federal Reserve Bank of Kansas City, P.O. Box 419440, Kansas City, MO 64141.

You don't need a million to retire in style:

Investment companies and financial planners have been spreading the word that people need to sock away a million bucks if they want to maintain their current lifestyle.

Truth is, nobody knows exactly how much you'll need to retire comfortably. The amount will depend on inflation, your lifespan, your company pension and whether Social Security still exists when you retire. Your non-retirement assets--such as a home, stocks, bonds and mutual fund investments--are also involved.

So you may need $500,000 or $2.5 million, more or less. One thing you do know for certain: You'll need money, so start saving.

New investment strategies after retirement:

Investment firms and mutual-fund companies have made a convincing case for the need to save big for retirement. But what about people who already have retired? How should they invest?

It's a good question, because obviously financial priorities change after people stop working. Investing tips and approaches that make sense for younger people don't necessarily fit retirees. For instance:

* **Retirement plans.** It makes sense for younger people to put as much as they can into tax-sheltered retirement plans. But seniors need to concentrate on pulling the money out wisely.

That's because a stiff tax penalty awaits those seniors who don't withdraw enough cash each year from individual retirement accounts once they reach their early 70s. A penalty also applies to large IRA withdrawals--generally those in excess of $150,000 a year. And seniors over 70 1/2 generally can't even make IRA contributions, assuming they have earned income in the first place.

* **Dollar-cost averaging.** Socking away modest amounts of cash on a regular basis is great for people of any age to build up wealth and deal with market volatility. Mutual funds are fine vehicles for this, because they allow small monthly purchases of $50 or $100 or so.

But it's also important for senior citizens to consider systematic-withdrawal programs, which offer dollar-cost averaging in reverse. Mutual-fund companies routinely offer systematic-withdrawal programs, even if they don't publicize them as much as automatic-investment plans.

* **Estate planning.** Bequeathing their wealth is the last thing younger investors think about in building a nest egg. But not older investors. Those who want to compile a

handsome sum for heirs might have to take more risks to build it up. That usually means incorporating stock funds into their plans--and giving these riskier investments sufficient time to grow.

   * **Growth investments.** Generally, senior citizens should invest more conservatively than younger folks, and that means favoring bond- and money-market funds over stock portfolios.

   But a healthy 65-year-old who can anticipate living another 20 years, may be able to afford a little investment risk in exchange for greater growth. And that means including some stock-market investments. Younger retirees should consider earmarking anywhere from 40% to 60% of their portfolio in growth investments, preferably stock funds, to help stay ahead of inflation.

   Life-cycle mutual funds offer several guidelines. For example, the Vanguard LifeStrategy Conservative Growth Portfolio (800-662-7447), which targets investors ages 60 to 75, holds about 40% of its assets in stocks. Even Vanguard's LifeStrategy Income Portfolio, designed for people 75 and up, has a normal 23% stake in stocks.

   The Stagecoach Lifepath 2000 Fund, designed for people planning to retire or start withdrawing money for other purposes in 2000, has about 23% of its assets in stocks.

   But that jumps to about 50% for Lifepath 2010, which is appropriate for people with an eye on starting retirement 14 years from now. The Stagecoach funds (800-222-8222) are managed by Wells Fargo Bank of San Francisco.

   One thing to note about retirement planning is that you don't need to move all of your assets from growth to stable investments on the first day you stop working.

Ways you can collect 40% more from a retirement plan:

There's no one magic method to almost double your retirement savings, but there are a combination of strategies which can yield you substantially more on withdrawal.

1. Contribute your own money. A company pension will grow faster if you add your own money--up to 10% of salary--to your employer's contribution. The interest accrued by your voluntary contribution isn't deductible, but is tax-free. And when you do begin withdrawing funds at retirement, the part attributable to your voluntary contributions remains tax-free. (The exact percentage is determined by a complicated formula.)

2. Self-directed pension accounts. Many employers are severely reducing their employee retirement plans--and requiring workers to manage their own pension plans. But you can make this work to your favor. By assuming control of your retirement funds, instead of putting all your funds into fixed-income investments such as CDs, money-market funds or government bonds, you can take advantage of the growth potential offered by quality stocks or mutual funds.

Caution: But don't chase high yields at the risk of losing retirement money. If you lose money in a retirement account, you get no tax deduction from the government. And don't overtrade your self-directed retirement account. Dollars in an IRA, Keogh or 401(k) are worth far more than regular dollars, since earnings are tax deferred.

3. Avoid withdrawal penalties. Under current tax law, if you take possession of your 401(k) or 403(b) funds before depositing them into an individual retirement account, you will be subject to 20% withholding for income tax purposes on the payout. Why? Because the government is assuming you're cashing out of your retirement savings plan and wants its tax payment immediately.

And if you are under age 59 1/2 and redeposit your account proceeds within 60 days into an IRA, you will be forced to dig into your pocket to come up with the 20% that the government withheld or face an early withdrawal penalty of 10% federal and 2.5% California on those funds.

The best way to handle this IRS trap is a lump-sum withdrawal move from either a 401(k) or 403(b) plan is through what is known as a "trustee-to-trustee" transfer, asking your employer--before you actually terminate--to transfer the money directly into an IRA.

4. Fix a target retirement date earlier than your actual retirement date. This bit of self-deception will force you to boost your retirement savings contributions. If circumstances actually force you into early retirement, you'll be prepared. If not, you'll have the option to retire early--or keep working and accumulating even more funds.

You may be able to collect social security now:

Think you have to be 65, or 62, to finally start collecting Social Security? Some do, some don't. Millions of people begin getting their benefits at earlier ages--children, students, widows, working adults. There are other benefit programs that include disability pensions and workers' compensation.

Younger people need fewer credits to be eligible for disability benefits, or for their family members to be eligible for survivors benefits if they should die.

Full-time, unmarried students, age 18-22, can qualify for Social Security benefits to help pay for a college education. To qualify, one of your parents must have died--or worked long enough to qualify to receive retirement or disability benefits.

You can also qualify if you attend a high school, trade school or vocational school for at least 20 hours of study over a 13-week period. Benefits will terminate at age 22, or if you marry, quit school or reduce attendance to part-time basis.

* Disability

If a physical or mental condition prevents a worker from doing substantial, gainful work, and that condition is expected to last at least 12 months (or is terminal), a worker is deemed disabled under federal law.

To prove this, you must show medical evidence of the severity of the disability. It isn't enough to show you can't perform your regular or preferred work. You must demonstrate that your impairment prevents you from doing any substantial, gainful employment.

But the fact that doctors predict your eventual recovery doesn't prevent your getting disability benefits. Social Security will take into account your age, education, training and work experience. Payments are based on earnings level and the age at which you became disabled. Benefits continue as long as you remain disabled and are unable to perform substantial and gainful work.

Disability benefits are also available to your dependents and spouse. Other potential qualifiers are unmarried children under age 18, unmarried adult children of any age who were disabled before age 22, and a spouse of any age who cares for a disabled child under age 16.

* Workers Compensation

If you're injured in connection with your job, you can qualify for cash benefits and medical care via the workers' compensation program. Workers comp also provides survivor benefits to your dependents in the case of your death from a work-related accident.

Most workers' compensation cases involve temporary total disability. This means you're unable to work during recovery, but are expected to recover fully.

Note: Receiving workers compensation may reduce your Social Security disability benefits. This is because, according to the law, the sum of all disability payments can't exceed 80 percent of average earnings over a period of time shortly before you became disabled.

* Supplemental Security Income

SSI, as it's usually called, makes monthly payments to people with low incomes, and who are 65 or older, or blind, or disabled. Children can also qualify for SSI benefits due to blindness or disability.

Payments range from $458 to $470 for an individual, and from $687 to $705 for a couple. That rate is reduced if you live rent- free in another's home, or live in an institution where room and board are subsidized by the state. Other states add money to the basic rate.

Social security benefit age pushed back:

For years, retirees could start collecting reduced Social Security benefits at age 62-- benefits 20 percent less than those who waited until age 65.

But legal changes have extended the age at which people will start getting Social Security payments. The full retirement age will be increased gradually. For example, for those born in 1938, benefits will start at age 65 and two months, and at 65 and four months for those born in 1939. For those born in 1940, it's age 65-and-a-half, 65 and 8 months for those born in 1941, and 65 and 10 months for those born in 1942. Those born between 1943 and 1954 will have to wait until they reach 66. And those born in 1960 won't reach full retirement until age 67!

Working beyond full retirement age can help you get higher Social Security payments by adding higher earnings--since higher lifetime earnings equal higher benefits. On the other hand, working while you're getting Social

Security can lower benefits. If you are 62 to 64 and earn more than $8,040, you could reduce your payments by $1 for every $2 you earn over the limit. If you are 65 to 69 and earn more than $11,160, your benefits are trimmed by $1 for every $3 you earn over the limit.

Thankfully, though, once you hit 70, your benefits can't be cut, though, no matter how much you earn.

The following graph estimates annual Social Security benefits for those who retire at 65. But actual benefits depend on your own earnings history and your spouse's. For a more accurate estimate, you should call the Social Security Administration, 800-772-1213, for form SSA-7004, a "Request for Earnings and Benefit Estimates Statement." Fill it out, mail it back and you'll have your statement in six weeks or less.

Note: After your benefit level has been determined for the first year of eligibility, the amount is recomputed each December to reflect increases in the Consumer Price Index. Best bet: repeat the request-for-benefits process every five years.

Estimated Social Security Benefits
The benefit amount assumes you work steadily over the years and don't reflect automatic cost-of-living adjustments:

Total Annual Working Income	Annual Benefits		
	Single Worker	Worker & nonworking spouse	Worker & working spouse
$0 to $25,000	$ 8,500	$12,750	$12,000
$25,001 to $35,000	$11,000	$16,500	$14,500
$35,001 to $45,000	$12,500	$18,750	$17,000
$45,001 to $62,500	$13,500	$20,250	$20,500
$62,501 or more	$14,500	$21,750	$24,500

Caution: Under current law, income in addition to your Social Security benefits up to 85 percent of your benefits could be included in taxable income. But Congress has been tinkering with the amount subject to taxation, and inevitably will do so again.

Senior jobs a way to keep active:

A growing number of older Americans, many past the traditional retirement age of 65, work part time. There are currently more than 4 million part-time workers 55 or older in the work force, according to the Bureau of Labor Statistics.

The reasons why older employees work part time vary. For many, part-time work allows them to continue to do what they love, but also to enjoy more leisure time.

For others, economics is more important. They worry that their Social Security, pension and savings won't keep pace with inflation or be enough to support them for the rest of their lives. They figure a part-time job could help make up the difference.

Some may be supporting adult children or offspring of second marriages. Others, victims of the current wave of corporate downsizing, would like to work full time, but part-time or temporary work is all that is available. Many Social Security recipients between ages 62 and 69 decide to work part time to avoid forfeiting some or all of their Social Security benefits.

For others, working provides a chance to interact with people and keep their brain active. It also imposes some structure on life, but allows them to move at a slower pace.

And for yet others, working part time gives them the means to travel, to buy fancy presents for children and grandchildren. Having a job keeps others independent.

With many people retiring earlier and living longer, working beyond retirement makes sense. If you retire at age 60, you could live another 30 years. That's a long time to sit on the porch.

However, many senior job hunters often run into age discrimination. Sometimes it's subtle, sometimes not. Even if companies don't openly discriminate (it's prohibited by federal law), many have preconceived ideas about the capabilities of workers in their 50s, 60s and 70s.

Increasingly, corporations are recognizing the value of re-employing their retired workers. Transamerica Occidental Life Company in Los Angeles offers workers a retirement package that includes registering with Second Careers to work for Transamerica or some other company on a temporary basis. A similar program has been in effect at Arco since 1982.

NOTES

_____

_____

_____

_____

_____

_____

_____

_____

_____

_____

_____

_____

_____

Chapter

Legal and Estate Planning

17

How to pick a lawyer:

Wealthy folks usually have an attorney at their beck and call, but the rest of us hope we never need one. And then, when inevitably we do, we're not sure how to find one that won't bleed us dry and give us very little in exchange.

It's not enough to find an lawyer who'll take your case on a contingency basis. As in most things when your money is at stake, you should shop around. Don't say yes to the first lawyer you talk to, or the first contingency percentage offer.

And don't be afraid to negotiate. An attorney may quote you 40% to 50% as his or her acceptable fee. But if your case is strong, many will agree to drop to 30% or even 20%. If an attorney refuses to bargain, keep looking. Maybe you need to find someone a little hungrier. In case you haven't heard, there's an oversupply of attorneys in the marketplace. Which means it's a buyers' market.

There's no penalty for lawyer-shopping, by the way. An initial consultation should always be free.

Don't let a lawyer bleed you dry:

Attorneys may specialize in different areas of the law, but all of them seem to have a mastery of billing. You can chat on the phone with one for 2 minutes, have them spend another five minutes dictating a letter on your behalf, then get hit with a bill the size of a week in Hawaii.

Guess what? You don't have to sit still for that kind of bloodletting. There are firms that audit legal bills to help you avoid ripoffs. These firms aren't free, of course, so you might prefer to do your own auditing. Here are some effective anti- ripoff measures:

1. Demand a Monthly Statement.
This way you'll find out quick if you're getting shafted. And you'll be able to review the charges while the services supposedly provided are fresh in your mind.

If you think you're being overcharged, complain. And do more than that. Ask for copies of all documents prepared for you, and see how the likely difficulty of preparation matches the charges.

You may be surprised to see how quickly specific charges can be reversed, or adjusted downward. But if you find yourself being stonewalled instead, it's time to knock on the door of the local bar associations and ask for a fee-dispute hearing.

2. Watch Out for Bogus Extra Items
Some lawyers generate higher billings by doing more than requested--or claiming to have done more. You don't have to pay for something you didn't ask for--whether it was done or not.

3. Agree Firmly on All Charges in Advance.
You should know before hiring an attorney what his or her hourly rate will be, who will work on your case, and what each person's function will be. You don't want to hire one lawyer, then be billed for two or three, plus several paralegals.

And any agreement should state clearly that clerical work be handled by clerks, and mundane work by paralegals, at lesser hourly rates.

Winning in small claims court:

For disputes involving a relatively small amount of money, small claims court may be the best way to go. a fast and efficient way to settle it.

Most cases are decided within three months, experts note, and most litigants emerge satisfied. Indeed, recent surveys have found that 61% of litigants were satisfied with the court's decision, even though 50% of those surveyed had lost.

Small claims courts are usually divisions of state or municipal court systems that agree to hear fairly small financial disputes. Cases heard in these courts include landlord-tenant disputes over security deposits and customers' disputes with dry cleaners, car mechanics and appliance repair people.

The maximum size of claims is determined by states and counties. In some states you can sue for as much as $5,000; elsewhere, limits range from $1,000 to $15,000.

In most states, small claims cases are heard within two months after papers are filed. In other civil courts, you may have to wait between two and four years to have your case heard.

Plaintiffs can file cases on their own, without the help of an attorney. Court costs boil down to filing fees that generally range between $5 and $20.

If you need help filing, some courts offer small claims advisers to assist you with the paperwork and give tips on what information and documentation needed when you go to court. And interpreters and small claims advisers may be available.

There is little ceremony involved in these "people's courts." Attorneys usually aren't allowed, except when representing themselves. Individuals simply stand at opposing podiums in front of a judge, state what happened and how much they believe is owed them--or why they think they're not obligated to pay. A judgment is usually rendered on the spot.

But the swiftness that makes this process appealing also creates risks for those unprepared in court. You are expected to appear with all the necessary information and documentation--receipts, invoices, photographs, etc. If you don't, you're likely to lose. And in many states, your ability to appeal a judgment is limited.

What you need to know about wills and living trusts:

An amazing statistic is that only about one in three of Americans has a will. Less than one in four have executed "advance directives" to limit aggressive health treatments in cases of terminal illness. Fewer still have taken measures to alleviate tax, probate or funeral costs.

But if we don't do it, someone else--or loved ones--will surely have to. And, aside from putting this burden on them, there's no way of knowing that they'll make the decisions we would prefer. In addition, by not taking action in advance, we may be costing our estate and our survivors a shocking amount of money.

Funeral costs run into thousands upon thousands. Probate costs can wipe out a modest estate. Estate taxes can cause the liquidation of a family-owned business, the sale of the family home. And dying without a will--"intestate"--can cause your assets to fall into the wrong hands, or a minor child to end up in the guardianship of someone other than whom you would have chosen.

Fortunately, many of these issues can be handled easily and inexpensively--if you start now. Here are the issues you need to consider:

* Writing a Will

The simplest solution is a handwritten statement spelling out who you are, what you've got and who should get it. These so-called "holographic" wills are simply signed and dated. Witnesses are unnecessary.

You can also buy fill-in-the-blanks "statutory" wills at virtually any stationery store. You fill out the form, get a few witnesses to sign, and either stick it in your safe deposit box or give it to a trusted friend or relative for safekeeping.

You can also buy a will kit--either in book form or computer software. They're relatively cheap and come with easy instructions.

Attorneys belittle these do-it-yourself wills, saying that people can make mistakes and end up with a will that is invalid. Certainly if you're wealthy or have a complicated family arrangement--such as children from different marriages-- or tricky estate wishes, you might be wise to hire an attorney.

But if your aims are simple and assets modest, do-it-yourself wills may be the way to go. Just be sure to have the will witnessed--but don't have heirs as witnesses. If a witness is also an heir, his or her testimony can be questioned.

* Probate

After death, your assets go into a legal limbo called probate. Your executor hires an attorney who files your will with the local probate court. The court notifies your creditors that you have died and your estate is being settled. The court pays your debts and "proves" the validity of your will.

Once probate is through, creditors can't go after your heirs for payment of a bill. It also settles disputes between heirs. But probate is both time-consuming and expensive.

A simple, uncontested will takes about nine months to a year to clear probate. Where there are disputed creditor's claims or infighting among heirs, probate can take years.

And hiring a probate attorney can be costly. They are paid either by the hour or according to a formula set by state law.

If there are disputed claims or the estate is difficult to probate, a judge can award "extraordinary" probate fees, too. The executor is entitled to the same fees, but executors who are also heirs often don't accept fees. (And it's better to inherit the money tax free than to collect taxable executor's fees.) All these fees easily can consume your assets when you die.

Probate also opens your estate to public view. The curious can look up your case and determine just how much money you had and who got it.

* Living Trusts to Avoid Probate

The most popular anti-probate technique is the living trust.

These are three-part legal documents which, properly executed, set up a formula to handle the financial aspects of death and possible incapacity without the time, expense and disclosure involved in taking these matters through court.

The first part of the living trust deals with the distribution of assets while you are sound of mind and body. This may be as simple as naming yourself trustee and giving yourself the right to distribute your assets as you see fit.

Part two names a successor trustee who can handle your financial affairs if you fall into a coma or are otherwise rendered incapable of handling them yourself.

Part three serves as a will and provides for the distribution of assets and the appointment of guardians for minor children after you're gone.

These documents are revocable, which means you can change or cancel them while you are alive and competent. At your death, however, they become irrevocable.

Disadvantages of living trusts:
They're expensive. An attorney will charge $500 to $2,500 to set up a fairly simple one--but that's still often less costly than probate.

And property in a living trust may be more difficult to sell or refinance, since it's held in the name of the trust. You still may have problems finding a lender willing to make a home loan on real estate owned by a trust.

Since some people don't remember to deed all their assets to the trust, many attorneys advise executing a so-called "pour-over" will, which transfers any forgotten assets into the trust at your death.

While a living trust helps you avoid probate, which is advantageous for your heirs if you live in a state that has burdensome probate laws, it may not be worth the time it takes to set up a living trust--let alone the cost, which runs to hundreds or even thousands of dollars.

Talk with an attorney who can give you an objective opinion about whether you should have a living trust--not an attorney who specializes in living trusts. One alternative to a living trust is a well-crafted will and a durable power of attorney.

Other ways to avoid probate:
All those assets that can't be left in a will--insurance policies, jointly-owned property and the like--automatically skirt probate. You can also name beneficiaries for pension plans, brokerage accounts and bank accounts, leaving little--or nothing--to the probate process.

Estate Tax Planning:
Most people don't worry about estate tax planning, since only estates worth $600,000 or more are subject to inheritance taxes. For the rich, estate tax gambits aimed at

trimming inheritance taxes--which range from 36% to 70%--are plentiful and complex. But for middle-income families with just a shade more than $600,000 in assets, the strategies are fairly simple:

Annual gifts. Before you die, you can give an unlimited number of people up to $10,000 a year without triggering estate or gift taxes. In addition, you can pay for a child or grandchild's health care or education expenses.

Bypass trusts. If you don't like the idea of annual gifts because you're worried about having enough money to last you and your spouse's lifetimes, consider a bypass trust. These devices help married couples leave up to $1.2 million to their heirs without triggering estate taxes.

Life insurance. This involves paying 1% of the value of your estate for a period of years to purchase an insurance policy. The policy is put into an irrevocable life insurance trust, and the proceeds pay estate taxes after you die. Generally, the younger you are, the less you pay, for the simple reason that the insurer is able to use your money for a longer period of time.

* Advance Directives
More and more people are refusing life-prolonging medical treatment by means of "advance directives." These legal documents spell out for your doctor the point at which treatment should stop, either by stating the specific conditions under which you refuse treatment or by designating who can make such decisions for you.

These documents are commonly provided to patients at nursing homes, hospitals, hospices and senior centers for nominal charges or for free. But a simple letter to your doctor stating the conditions under which you'd like to live--and die--should suffice. You should also specifically mention under what circumstances you would want the doctor to withdraw oxygen, food and hydration devices, as these require specific consent in many states.

There is also a financial point to such directives, since life-prolonging treatments are among the most expensive in medicine. This may seem incidental if a procedure saves your life, but not if it keeps you alive in a wretched condition.

* Funeral Planning
Shopping around for funeral arrangements can save hundreds--even thousands--of dollars. Federal law requires funeral directors to provide detailed price information on request.

The biggest cost item is usually the casket. Prices vary from about $250 for an inexpensive wood coffin to as much as $25,000 for a luxury, bronze coffin with adjustable mattress. There are charges for use of the mortuary, services of the funeral director, flowers, music, transportation, preparation of the body, embalming, and obtaining permits and death certificates.

At the burial, the biggest cost is the grave, crypt or "niche" for cremated remains. With in-ground burials, there is often also a charge for an "outer burial container"--typically a cement casement that goes around the casket; fees for opening and closing the grave; a charge for the marker and, possibly, recording fees. For cremations, there's often a fee for the urn and for a container in which the body is cremated.

Determine your preferences and call several mortuaries. The cost of an identical funeral can vary by as much as $2,000 at different funeral homes in the same city, according to an AARP survey.

Sign only one copy of your will:

In most states, if any copy of an executed will is not produced in court for probate, the will is presumed to be revoked. To safeguard against this terrible possibility, you should only sign a single copy of your will, which should then be kept in a safe place--a safe deposit box, or in your attorney's care.

Save taxes on charitable bequests:

Instead of funding a charitable bequest with money from insurance or investments, designate payouts from an IRA. Leaving your Individual Retirement Account to charity, you get to make a charitable contribution deduction for your estate--and you also save your heirs the income tax they would have to pay on those IRA distributions. They will not have to pay taxes on distributions of cash, or proceeds from securities or insurance.

NOTES

_____

_____

_____

_____

_____

_____

_____

_____

_____

_____

_____

_____

_____

Chapter

Insurance Savings

18

A dozen kinds of insurance you don't need:

The insurance industry keeps on trying to peddle marginal policies--and succeeding. Consumer investigators estimate that billions of dollars spent each year on unnecessary policies for life and health, home and car, and travel and entertainment. In many cases, the policies are either redundant or too narrow in scope to be cost-effective.

The point of insurance is to comprehensively cover you against catastrophic dollar losses--to avoid severe financial stress, not inconvenience.

You should be especially wary of policies hooked to a purchase, such as extended-service contracts offered by auto dealers, home warranties from builders, or certain trip-cancellation insurance sold by travel agents, consumer advocates say.

Before making any decisions, consumers should review their current policies to see what is already covered or if any modifications are needed. We all have legitimate insurance needs. But too many of us have costly policies to cover things that simply don't need covering. Here are 11 examples of policies you should avoid buying. And if you already have them, you just might consider canceling:

1. Life insurance if you are single or childless. There's no sound economic reason to purchase life insurance if you have no dependents, or if a working spouse can get by without your income. If you are single, or if nobody relies on you for financial support, life insurance is a waste of money.

2. Life insurance on children. The loss of a child is emotionally catastrophic, but not economically since there are no dependents involved.
Exception: If your child is a movie star.

3. Flight insurance. This is too specialized a policy. Your dependents need protection from the economic consequences of your death from any cause, not just an air crash. You can get comprehensive coverage that comes from a basic life insurance policy. And statistically, you're more likely to slip and fall in the shower than die in a plane crash.

4. Car rental insurance. At around $10 to $12 a day, or $4,000 a year, it is too expensive and usually unnecessary since many credit card companies provide similar coverage anyway. Your own auto insurance also may extend coverage to rental cars.

5. Collision insurance on old cars. Why maintain collision coverage on a car more than 5 years old, or if the collision portion of the premium exceeds 10% of a car's market value? As your car depreciates in value, your comprehensive and collision coverage should also be adjusted downward.

6. Mortgage and credit insurance. They protect your family or estate if you die and make any payments due on a house, car or other major purchase. But a good annual renewable term life policy can do the same thing cheaper, while protecting against all economic consequences of your death, not just outstanding mortgage payments.

7. Hospital indemnity insurance. Many plans promise an extra $100 a day if you are hospitalized. But good health insurance will take care of hospital expenses.

8. Cancer insurance. Again, this is not comprehensive enough. Good life or health policies will cover this and other life- threatening illnesses.

9. Contact lens insurance. According to consumer surveys, the cost of the premium is about equal to the cost of a lens at a discount eye-wear store.

10. Rain or trip-cancellation insurance. Yes, you can actually buy such a policy, which pays if it rains a specific amount during a vacation. While a drenched vacation may leave you emotionally drained, it isn't worth a single premium.

Often, trip-cancellation policies--which cost about $5.50 per $100 in coverage--are filled with fine-print exclusions. For instance, many will not pay out if you cancel because a chronic ailment flares up or if a tour operator defaults.

11. Pet insurance. Health-care costs for sick dogs or cats are not that exorbitant.

12. Lifestyle protection. This is expanded coverage of homeowner's insurance, geared to active two-income families. Among the coverage: up to $1,000 if the day-care center to which you send your children burns down; up to $1,500 if your health or country club goes belly up; up to $1,000 if you get robbed after withdrawing money from an ATM, and up to $20,000 if you are sued while doing volunteer work.

Forget this frivolous coverage and take your own sensible "lifestyle" precautions. Line up backup baby-sitters, check out the track record of any health club before joining, use ATMs inside banks and markets.

Bonus weird coverage to consider: Did you know you can actually buy insurance against UFO abductions. Yes, and it's a real bargain--only about $1 a year. So, if you see flying saucers on a regular basis, think it over.

Most people do need:
* Comprehensive health insurance;
* Life insurance if there are dependents;
* Auto insurance if they have a car;
* Homeowner's or renter's insurance.

Save on homeowner's insurance without reducing coverage:

The easiest way to save on property insurance premiums is to raise your deductible. On a homeowner's policy, the average customer has a $250 deductible (the amount you must pay before the insurer starts reimbursing you.)

If you raised the deductible on the homeowner's policy to $500, your premium would drop about 10%. Raise the deductible to $1,000, and the premium could fall as much as 25%.

Typically, about seventeen events are covered by homeowner's insurance, including theft, fire and windstorm damage. Earthquake or flood-related damage is usually excluded. A special policy would be required, and this could be costly.

Consumers should check their existing policy to make sure they are covered in the event their home is completely destroyed or burglarized. A home should be insured for 100% of the cost of rebuilding it and include an "inflation guard clause" that would automatically adjust the limit when a policy is renewed to reflect costs in your area.

Collect on claims
your health insurance doesn't cover:

Most of us believe our health insurance policy is etched in stone, like the Ten Commandments. If a particular service isn't listed there, or one of our claims is denied, we figure nothing can be done.

Wrong on both counts. Many contractual provisions in insurance policies are negotiable. And many problems in collecting the maximum due on a claim are actually a result of incompetence or negligence on the part of the administrators in your company who handle insurance benefits.

There are effective things you can do to improve your ability to collect:

* **Study** your health insurance contract carefully. And be aware that everything is negotiable. For instance, though your policy may state that only home health care by a registered or practical nurse is covered. And yet, if you're willing to negotiate, an alternate source of home health care could be covered.

* **Ask** your company's insurance broker to help you negotiate with the insurer. After all, this broker makes money from selling your company the policy, and also will have more leverage with the insurer. If this person won't help you, lobby your company to switch to a more cooperative broker.

* **Cultivate** the person in your company in charge of employee claims. This person should have a good working relationship with the insurance company. If a settlement is too low or doesn't cover your needs, your firm's claims person should be able to get you a better settlement.

But if your claims person is uncertain whether you can get more compensation, ask for permission to contact the broker directly. The broker should have an idea of how to get your claim paid (assuming it's legitimate).

* **Talk** to your doctor about making unallowable treatments allowable. For instance, if you want to claim cosmetic surgery necessary for health reasons, your doctor may be able to help. Similarly, some infertility treatments can be billed as a covered gynecological procedure. It's strictly between you and your physician.

Finally, if you find your company policy inadequate, consider taking out a supplemental or coordinating personal policy.

How to slash new car insurance costs:

If you're buying a new car, you're also going to buy a new auto insurance policy. And here's the really scary part: You could pay as much for insurance coverage over the next few years as you pay for your new car.

For a new car costing about $20,000, you'll pay a bit less than $5,000 a year, if it's financed for five years. But in some large cities, a young male driver will pay even more than $5 grand a year to insure that car.

The solution? Shop carefully--both for your wheels and your insurance. If you do, you can save hundreds, even thousands, by taking advantage of discounts and special deals offered by most auto insurers.

This same young driver, for instance, could cut his premium more than $2,000 annually by keeping his grades up, opting for anti-lock brakes and passive restraints--such as air bags or automatic seat belts--and raising his deductible.

And you can save a fortune by buying a station wagon instead of a sports car, or a medium-priced sedan instead of a luxury model. You'll not only qualify for lower basic rates, but for additional discounts that can be worth up to $1,000.

Auto insurance discounts are tricky, however. They vary company to company and by state. Even worse, many insurance agents "forget" to apply the discounts.

Solution: Always ask to have any and all discounts applied to your policies. This means, of course, that you should always ask what discounts your company offers.

Here are some common types:

* **Good driver discounts.** Most insurers will give you a break ranging from 20% to 40% for maintaining a clean driving record. (In some states, a good driver discount is mandatory.)

* **Good students.** Keeping a "B" average or better is likely to win a 10% to 20% premium break.

* **Anti-lock brakes.** Considered an important safety feature, anti-lock brakes can cut your overall premium between 5% and 10%.

* **Passive restraints.** Air bags and automatic seat belts can also cut your premium, although usually by lesser amounts.

* **Multi-car discounts.** If you insure more than one car with the same company, you'll usually score something akin to a volume discount. These discounts can slice between 5% and 20% off your annual bill. Some companies also give you a break on auto rates if you insure your house with them too.

* **Loyalty discounts.** If you've insured with the same company for several years--usually more than three--and have a good driving record, you could get up to 20% off your rate.

* **Defensive driving discounts.** If you're over 55, most insurers will cut your rate 5% to 10% if you complete a defensive driving course. Many states require insurers to offer these discounts.

* Low-mileage discounts. If you drive less than five miles to work each day, you may qualify for another modest break.

* Anti-theft devices. The comprehensive and collision portion of your premium can be trimmed if you buy and use certain anti-theft devices, such as car alarms. These discounts vary widely, depending on where you live, what you drive and the type of anti-theft device purchased.

* Nonsmoker discounts. These are relatively rare, but they can be substantial where offered.

Aside from discounts, you can cut your auto insurance premiums substantially by raising deductibles, limiting comprehensive and collision coverage on older cars and notifying your insurer when driving-age children go off to college.

Auto insurance policies are less standardized, but raising the deductible from $100 to $250 or $500 would generally save between 10% and 40% on comprehensive and collision coverage premiums, which make up about half of average cost of auto coverage.

Shelter your nest egg under insurance umbrella:

Umbrella policies, long favored by the very rich, are appealing to more and more people these days--principally those who wish to guard their assets against civil lawsuits. President Clinton even has one! These relatively inexpensive policies provide broad protection, sheltering the wary from risks they may never have contemplated.

"Umbrellas" are stand-alone insurance policies that extend other liability coverage already purchased on your house, car, boat or other assets--and they cover you for almost any kind of suit. The average umbrella policy adds $1 million in liability insurance on top of any (or all) of these other coverages.

So, if your auto policy offers $300,000 in liability protection and your homeowner's liability limit was $100,000, one umbrella policy would boost your auto liability coverage to $1.3 million and your homeowner's protection to $1.1 million.

Normally, your homeowner's or auto policy will protect you before an umbrella policy is tapped. An umbrella only kicks in when you're sued--for an amount beyond the upper limits of these policies. However, it also can protect you from legal liability-- suits for slander, defamation of character and false imprisonment. And such policies are fairly cheap--from about $100 to $300 a year.

* What's the catch?

Not everyone can get an umbrella policy. If you have numerous tickets, drunk-driving convictions, young drivers, vacation homes or a boat, you may have trouble finding an insurer willing to sell you one.

Most insurers also won't sell them if the underlying liability limits on your homeowner's and auto insurance policies aren't fairly high.

Caution: If you think an umbrella policy might suit you, you should first review coverage limits with a trusted insurance agent or financial adviser.

Are you a savvy insurance shopper:

People may spend weeks or months looking at houses or cars before making up their minds. But these same folks may then buy the first insurance policy they're offered--without carefully reading the contract.

Best advice: Shop around, just like for a car or house. Ask friends, relatives, co-workers. Are they happy with their agent? Have they filed a claim? Were they satisfied?

Don't stop there. Contact three or four agents or company reps. Describe the kind of policy you're looking for. Ask what it costs. Give each person the same basic information so costs can be compared.

Don't be pressured into signing. Tell the agents you're still shopping and aren't ready to make a decision. If an agent doesn't explain something to your satisfaction or respond when needed, try another.

The easiest way to keep costs down is to keep the deductible high enough so you are paying for "affordable" losses yourself. This way, insurance pays for the big losses, the ones you can't afford.

The Insurance Institute also advises consumers to check with insurance rating companies:

 * A.M. Best & Co., available in business libraries, rates insurance companies for financial stability.
 * Standard & Poor's Corp. also rates insurance companies. Its information is available free of charge.
 * Consumer Reports magazine provides an annual survey of insurers.
 * State departments of insurance can tell you whether complaints have been filed against a company.

NOTES

_____
_____
_____
_____
_____
_____
_____
_____

Chapter
_____

Tax-Fighter's Guide

19

A half-dozen often overlooked deductions:

The Republican Congress, through its "Contract With America," promised tax breaks for families, a cut in capital gains taxes and to make tax-favored IRAs available to all. Also promised: the end of the marriage penalty that can cost couples thousands and the Social Security tax that pushes middle-income seniors into a tax bracket that's otherwise reserved for the very rich.

But the bill loaded up with all these ambitious goodies was killed by presidential veto. And prospects for its revival seem dim. But until Washington gets around to giving you a break, there remain ways for the individual filer to make his or her own breaks--and ways to avoid costly mistakes.

Here are six deductions you may have missed:
    1. Nanny taxes. Individuals who hire baby-sitters and other household employees can declare the employee's wages on the employer's 1040. That's a change from past years where you needed to file a whole slew of federal forms to report your worker's wages and pay your half of his

or her employment taxes. All you need to do now is declare the taxes you owe on line 53 of your 1040 and include a Schedule H--"Household Employment Taxes."

But failure to report an employee's income and taxes on your 1040 is considered falsifying your return. If it's done on purpose and you're caught, you could not only be fined, but sent to prison.

2. Deductions for job search expenses. If you were among the millions of people who were "downsized," "outsourced" or otherwise booted out of a corporate job, most of the money you spent looking for work is tax-deductible. That includes travel expenses, resume preparation, mailing, phone calls, fees for employment agencies and career counseling. Even if you didn't find new work during the year, you can still deduct these costs. Medical exams to prove your fitness are also deductible.

However, these miscellaneous itemized deductions can be claimed only when they exceed 2 percent of your adjusted gross income. If you earned, say, $30,000 annually, you can deduct only miscellaneous expenses that exceed $600.

3. Replacement residence reporting. If you sold a house--or lost one through foreclosure--and didn't immediately replace it, you'll probably get an IRS notice asking whether you bought a house of equal or greater value in the 24 months following the sale.

If you didn't, you must pay tax on the difference between the sales price and your tax basis--read "cost"--in the home. And yes, you can have a taxable profit even when you lost your house in foreclosure, simply because your tax basis accounts for any and all gains on previous residences that were rolled into the purchase of your most recent residence. Here's how: if you made a profit of $50,000 on your previous home, rolled that gain into the purchase of a new home, but lost $40,000 when the second home was foreclosed, you would still have a $10,000 taxable gain.

Note: People over 55 can qualify for a one-time capital gains exemption of $125,000.

4. Points. Any points paid to refinance your house are deductible over the life of the loan, though this doesn't usually amount to much. If you refinanced and paid $2,000 in points on a 360-month (30-year) loan, write off $5.55 per month--$67 per year--on your income taxes, for example. However, if you refinance a second time, any unclaimed points are immediately deductible.

Note: An amended tax return must be filed to take advantage of this benefit. Non-deductible expenses include title insurance, loan-application fee, credit report, appraisal fee, service fee, settlement or closing fees, bank attorney's fee, attorney's fee, document preparation fee and recording fees.

5. Health insurance deductions for self-employed workers. If you're self-employed and buy health insurance for yourself and your family, you can write off 30 percent of the cost as a business expense. Previously, only 25 percent of the cost was tax deductible.

6. Charitable deductions. You know you can deduct money given to charity, but do you keep good records? Some people give cash and forget how much they've contributed. Other people give property, such as used furniture and clothing, but fail to keep receipts to back up their deductions. Still others give little in cash, but donate time. You can't claim deductions for the time you spend, but you can claim for mileage at a rate of 12 cents per mile. You can also deduct necessary fees or parking expenses.

Deductions for clothing and personal items should be claimed at an amount equal to what you could receive if you sold them at a garage sale. Meanwhile, even if you forgot to keep records of cash contributions, check with the recipients. Churches usually record cash contributions from parishioners who use envelopes, for example.

Keep the IRS away from investment income:

Savvy investors have figured out ways to significantly reduce the federal tax bite on investment earnings. Here are four smart strategies:

1. Account for trading costs: When you sell a stock, your taxable gain or loss is computed by subtracting the purchase price from the sales price.

But many investors fail to factor their trading costs into the equation. In fact, you should subtract the cost of buying and selling securities--brokerage commissions or fund sales "loads"--from the taxable gain. If you use a full-service broker, these costs can be considerable--and can substantially reduce your taxable gain.

2. Deduct investment interest against investment income: If you paid interest expenses because you borrowed to buy stocks or taxable bonds, you can deduct those costs from your gain as well.

But to do this, you must have paid the debt during the year--if you were billed but didn't pay in the taxable year, the cost isn't deductible--and you can deduct investment interest expenses only to the extent that you have investment income.

Caution: If you borrowed money to buy tax-exempt bonds, your borrowing costs are not tax deductible.

3. Declare miscellaneous expenses: If you buy magazines, newspapers, research reports, newsletters, books or other items in order to make savvier investment decisions--and bigger profits--you can deduct these costs as miscellaneous itemized deductions. However, these deductions--which also include unreimbursed business and job-search expenses, tax-preparation charges and appraisal fees to determine the fair market value of donated property--are deductible only when they exceed 2 percent of your adjusted gross income. So if you earned $50,000 annually, you could only write off miscellaneous itemized deductions that exceed $1,000--2 percent of income.

What about claiming you're in the business of investing, so you could deduct 100 percent of your investment-related expenses-- forgetting the 2 percent floor? Better not try it, unless you are truly in business--buying and selling securities for yourself and others.

4. Don't forget reinvested dividends: When investors automatically plow dividends and interest distributions back into additional shares of the company or mutual fund, they frequently forget to account for them when figuring their capital gains. When you invest in mutual funds, however, your profits are "distributed" and taxed every year--regardless of whether you got them in cash or simply used them to buy a bigger stake in your fund through an automatic dividend reinvestment plan. The same holds true for reinvested dividends in individual stocks. If you fail to account for reinvested dividends, you'll be taxed twice on the same earnings. Be sure to check your records and adjust your cost-basis to reflect all the shares you've purchased.

Final Note: Make sure you keep good records, establishing when you bought, sold or gave away each individual security, tax accountants advise. These records are imperative for executing a savvy strategy, and they'll be worth their weight in gold if you're ever audited.

How to stiff the IRS and get a great suntan:

It's not really recommended, of course, but if you really hate paying Uncle Sam, you can just say no--and leave the country. Of course, you'll have to turn in your passport on the way out, renounce U.S. citizenship and relocate to some Caribbean tax haven.

Particularly tempted by this scheme might be those with large estates, who get the dual benefit of being able to bequeath their assets to relatives, without worrying about U.S. estate taxes that can eat up more than half of a wealthy person's fortune.

There's a catch, though. If you get sick of the Bahamas, say, and try to return to the U.S. in less than a decade, the IRS can "look back" at all the income earned in the years you were gone and tax you on it. Worse still, the Administration and certain members of Congress are talking about a new tax that would essentially impose a toll for leaving on people who hope to take valuable assets with them.

Legal tax-shelter offering fat write-offs:

There is still one real tax shelter left in the U.S. tax code, a shelter that provides write-offs that exceed your investment.

If you buy into a qualified low-income housing deal, you can get roughly $9,500 worth of tax credits each year that go to reducing the federal income taxes you pay dollar-for-dollar.

The catch? While the return in tax benefits can be substantial, the chance of getting your initial investment back is slim, particularly when the housing project is in a state with high land values and high construction costs.

For corporations and a few high-income individuals who materially participate in the real estate industry, the tax breaks may be reward enough. But, for most other people, it may not be the most appropriate investment.

These deals also require you to invest for a minimum of 15 years. If you want out early, you'll have to give back a portion of the tax breaks.

How retirement savings can slash your taxes:

People who really detest paying taxes should consider socking more money away, instead of giving it to Uncle Sam.

For instance, if you earn $50,000 in wages, set aside as much as you legally can--15% of your income, or $7,500--into a 401(k). Now, say, you also have $10,000 in self-employment income, which allows you to contribute another $2,000 into a Keogh plan, a tax-favored retirement plan for the self-employed. Finally, you pop $2,000 into a non-deductible IRA.

All that will get you $9,500 in deductions, as well as assets to generate non-taxable investment income.

You wouldn't be paying any tax on your 401(k), Keogh and IRA investment income. If you can afford to live without the cash, tax-free compounding is a wonderful thing.

Your $60,000 in gross income would sink to $44,100 in taxable income, assuming a standard deduction and one personal exemption. This saves you $2,660 in federal taxes immediately, and defers taxes on any investment income you earn on the retirement plans until you start to pull the money out at retirement.

Caution: If you withdraw your savings before retirement, you get hit with a hefty tax penalty. And, of course, you've got $11,500 less to spend each year.

How to avoid audit triggers:

Tax experts agree that there is one simple way to vastly reduce your chance of getting audited:

Procrastinate.
People who file their returns four months late, say, are far less likely to be singled out for examination by the IRS-

-even when their returns would otherwise have a very high probability of being audited. You can get an automatic four-month extension simply by filling out Form 4868.

Caution: The deadline moves back for filing your return, but doesn't stop interest and possible penalties from accruing if you don't pay any cash owed by April 15.

There are other ways to anticipate and evade a possible tax audit. And those ways do not require you to back away from taking legitimate deductions, so long as you take care to substantiate each claim and maintain the records to prove it.

Obviously, the IRS doesn't have enough time or staff enough to look at every tax return to ferret out cheating. So the agency uses computer searches to look for certain triggers--deductions that are unusually high when compared to income, for instance. IRS auditors then work their way through the returns that are flagged.

Roughly 90% of all audits are triggered by the ratios reported on the Schedule A--"Itemized Deductions"; and the Schedule C--"Profit or Loss from a Business."

The most troublesome form is probably Schedule C, a form filed by those who own their own small companies or who moonlight by operating a small business after work. The IRS suspects that a high percentage of people who run their own businesses either under-report income, exaggerate deductions or misclassify hobbies as profit-making enterprises so that they can write off personal expenses.

However, filing a schedule C alone doesn't put you at risk, insiders report. It's only when the deductions on your Schedule C exceed a certain percentage of your self-employment income-- usually around 52% of income.

And when deductions exceed 63% of income, you can bet you'll be computer tagged for audit.

On the itemized deduction form, the caution point hits when deductions exceed 35% of income, and the critical point is probably around 45%.

If you fall into these deduction percentages, better keep good records, and, when appropriate, provide more information than necessary, so the IRS examiner who looks at your return can easily determine that you're not a cheater.

There's nothing wrong with including an extra sheet of paper that indicates what you bought and how you accounted for the expenditure on your tax return.

Here's a list of common audit triggers:
* Self-employment income. (Reported on Schedule C)
* Barter income (Reported on 1099-B)
* Home office deductions.
* Casualty losses from fire, flood, earthquake, tornado and other disasters.
* Earned income credit, for low-income individuals and families.
* Bad debt deductions--particularly write-offs of uncollectible loans involving a family member.
* Donations of expensive property to charity--including artwork, real estate or other hard-to-value items.

Tactics for dealing with an audit:

Don't panic if the IRS invites you in for a little chat. About one in every 100 returns is audited--and many of those are kicked back by the IRS with demands for more taxes--but only a token number of individuals are prosecuted for fraud. (And as filing time neared in 1996, the IRS announced it was cutting 8,000 jobs nationwide due to federal budget crunch, and was planning to audit 18% fewer returns than the previous year.)

In 1995, 3,573 people were indicted for tax crimes related to 1993 returns, the IRS says. That's an infinitesimal fraction of 1% of the millions of people believed to be cheating.

How To Have It All! 267

Why so few? It's tough to prove intent. In absence of a confession, the IRS must show that a taxpayer's wrongful actions are so methodical that they could not have happened by accident. The agency tends to prosecute only the most egregious cases--situations in which there is a long history of hiding income, falsifying deductions or otherwise underpaying tax.

But if you get the summons, do be prepared. It's probably not a random request. Even if the examiner who shakes your hand may seem like a real friendly or sympathetic type, don't be duped. The agency has probably found something in your return it thinks is suspicious, and it's the examiner's job to squeeze more tax dollars out of you.

Your job, of course, is to show why their proposed changes are incorrect. Do not, however, ramble on too much in response to questions, volunteering extra information. Keep your answers brief but responsive to the point.

For office audits, it may be worth your while to seek help from a tax accountant--especially if there's a lot of money at stake. If you paid someone to prepare your return, that person should be willing to provide guidance. In fact, his or her fee may already include representing you.

And who knows, maybe you'll be that lucky one out of 15 audited taxpayers who actually ends up getting a bigger refund.

Don't let your refund become a dead-letter:

Believe it or not, nearly 100,000 refund checks were returned to the IRS last year by the post office because of outdated or incorrect addresses. How much was an average dead-letter refund? More than $800!

Be sure to notify the IRS of any residential changes on Form 8822. And if you think that your refund might be one of those returned checks, call the IRS toll free at 800-829-1040.

And if you need an IRS form fast, even in the middle of the night, you can get them faxed to you if you dial 703--487-4160 from your fax machine. Otherwise, call 800-829-3676 and have them mailed to you, allowing seven to 15 working days.

Dependents don't have to live with you:

Your kid or a close relative doesn't have to live under your roof for you to claim an exemption. Generally speaking, a dependent must have had less than $2,500 in annual income, though there's no limit for a child under 19 at the end of the taxable year, or under 24 and a full-time student. The tax-exempt Social Security benefits an older dependent gets don't count as income.

But in all cases, you must provide more than half of a dependent's support.

Simplify your business auto expenses:

To avoid the hassle of figuring depreciation and keeping track of actual costs, you can deduct 31 cents a mile for the use of a car on business. And though meals are only 50 percent deductible, taxi fare to the restaurant can be written off in full.

But remember, the deductibility of travel and related entertainment expenses depends on the purpose of the trip and the amount of business conducted, tax experts say.

If you undertake a trip for legitimate business purposes and spend the bulk of your time conducting business, you can write off the cost of travel. However, if you sandwich a business meeting into a personal trip, only the expense of that meeting--not the entire trip--is deductible.

Travel expenses also must be "ordinary and necessary" to the business activity, and your costs must be properly substantiated. And be forewarned: Claiming such expenses is widely believed to be an "audit trigger" that kicks your return out for closer IRS scrutiny.

How to safely take the home-office deduction:

Despite significant limitations on home office deductions, you can still write off portions of your personal residence if you can substantiate the business use, accountants say.

A home office is deductible if it's your main place of business, is where people come to meet you and is dedicated space designed and maintained in a businesslike fashion with the ultimate goal of making money.

Beware: IRS Sleuths lurking in cyberspace:

If you have a back tax bill with the Internal Revenue Service, watch out. The IRS has been searching digital databases for signs of noncompliance as well as electronic records of cars, credit and real estate it can seize from delinquent taxpayers.

IRS agents with computers and modems now scan records filed with the DMV, county tax assessor's offices, credit-reporting companies and the U.S. Bureau of the Census in an effort to find people underreporting business sales, overestimating deductions or trying to hide assets-- or themselves--from federal tax collectors, IRS officials say.

While tax officials have been able to request copies of these records in the past, they generally had to do it by foot- -hoofing it down to county offices and standing in line to get the data they needed to determine whether taxpayers were hiding assets. So they tended to check only taxpayers who appeared likely to be big-money cheats.

Now they can access these same records in a fraction of the time from their government offices. So it's faster and easier for them to ferret out tax fraud, even small-time.

This may seem like a great step forward to the IRS, but it's frightening news for a lot of honest taxpayers. After all, those records are not always right. And the tax agency does not need to inform you that it is searching these records, nor is it required to allow you to correct records that are in error.

So, if you suspect you're under possible IRS scrutiny, it may be a good idea to check your own records for accuracy first.

Let your computer do your taxes:

Need tax preparation help? Don't want to pay an accountant or tax attorney? Why not ask your computer to roll up its sleeves? The machine can't do the whole job, but PC tax preparation programs are not only getting more sophisticated, they're also easier to use.

The two biggies are TurboTax from Intuit and Kiplinger TaxCut from Block Financial Corp. Both are available on CD-ROM as well as diskette.

Both use an "interview process," just like you'd get from a tax preparer. You don't have to fill out forms, just answer the questions. The program fills out the forms for you. And both programs can print out IRS-approved forms that you just sign and mail in.

Both can also prepare data for electronic filing, which gets you a quicker refund. Users of either program can use their modem to send their returns to a service bureau that, for about $20, will file the return for you. (TaxCut users who are also CompuServe subscribers can file with the service for $10.)

Both Kiplinger TaxCut and TurboTax give plenty of help and handholding. Intuit boasts that TurboTax can import data from Quicken, its best-selling personal finance program. But so can TaxCut. Both programs can also import data from Microsoft Money, Managing Your Money and other major personal finance programs.

Of course, no method of doing taxes, including using a CPA, is foolproof. If you complete the same return using different tax programs, you're likely to get slightly different results, but that's also true if you provide the same data to more than one professional tax preparation service.

But if you have a complicated return or need professional advice, you may be better off going to a tax professional.

By the way, if you drop into the IRS site on the World Wide Web (http://www.irs.ustreas.gov), you can download forms, get "tax help and education" and read tax regulations "in plain English."

NOTES

_____

_____

_____

_____

_____

_____

_____

_____

_____

_____

_____

_____

_____

Chapter
_____
Banks, S&L's, and Credit   **20**

Tricks to beat your banker:

Want to match wits with bankers and beat them at their own game? Want to demystify the lending process and increase your chances of getting a loan?

Insiders suggest anyone who applies for a business loan get ready for piles of paperwork, intense financial scrutiny and puzzling delays. Why? Because bankers are pathologically cautious, due to the strict government regulations enacted by Congress in response to the nation's crippling savings and loan industry collapse in the late 1980s--making it tough for business owners to borrow money.

The level of paperwork is ten times what it was five years ago. In addition to voluminous loan applications, many banks now require business owners to submit quarterly, rather than annual, financial statements.

Instead of focusing on whether or not someone is a good credit risk, bankers worry more about whether government regulators will approve of the loans they make.

How do you get around this and get your business loan? Here are some tested tips:

Find out who your bank's real decision maker is. Ninety percent of the time it's not the person sitting in front of the small-business person.

When you want to borrow more than $100,000, your request will probably go to the bank's credit administrator, who wields the real power in a bank. Yet this person rarely speaks one-to-one with the borrower. The trick is to bring that "back-room assassin" into the open.

Another tactic for business owners--by-pass your bank. Open a full-service account at a brokerage house or elsewhere.

How to avoid all those banking fees:

Smart customers figure out ways to cut through the ever-increasing thicket of banking fees and charges. If you don't, banks will squeeze you for every penny they can.

One good tip: Find out how your bank calculates the required Federal Deposit Insurance Corp. charge and what day they actually assess the fee, typically 16 cents per $1,000 on deposit.

Best tactic: Deplete your account on the last working day of the month or quarter. Invest these funds for one day or move them to another instrument to avoid the major cost of this charge.

Other savers:
1. Encode checks so they can be read and processed quickly by computers.

2. Figure out exactly when your money is available after it hits your account.

Another tip: Do some homework, try to gain the financial literacy to talk about their business from the perspective the banker wants to see. Banking insiders say that often a business is financeable, but the entrepreneur doesn't know how to structure the loan package.

3. Take the trouble to balance your checkbook. If you bounce even one check as a result of not balancing your account, the bank generally will ding you with a $10 to $15 fee. And most merchants slap on their own charge for a returned check, which can range from $5 to $25. So, one bounced check could cost you between $15 and $40.

Things your bank doesn't want you to know:

You may get all kinds of mail from your bank, outlining their policies and trying to sell you on extra services. But there are plenty of policies they'd just as soon you didn't know or comprehend. Here are some examples:

* **Checking Accounts:** Your bank may offer you immediate drawing power on all deposited checks, so long as you provide collateral in the form of another account.

But they won't tell you that if the "collateral" account happens to be a six-month certificate of deposit, and the check bounces, they can cash in your CD before maturity. If this happens, you're liable for the interest penalty on early withdrawal.

To make sure this doesn't happen to you, ask for an account that gives you time to cover bounced checks before money is withdrawn from any timed deposit. If your bank won't provide this service, find one that will.

* Savings: Your savings institution publishes the effective annual yields of their savings accounts. They don't, however, tell you that competing money-market funds are only allowed to advertise their simple interest rates, despite the fact that money markets compound interest on a daily basis. So, if a bank and a money-market fund actually pay the same rate, the banks will be able to advertise a higher rate.

* Mortgages: If you make a lump-sum payoff of an old low- interest mortgage, the bank tells you that they'll offer you a "big saving." They won't tell you, however, that the "big saving" doesn't come from interest, but principal, and is therefore taxable income to you.

A better course for you is to take the amount of money the bank is requesting in a lump-sum payment and invest it yourself.

* Other banking "secrets": Your banks won't cash checks dated more than six months previously, no matter how much money is in the issuing account. (U.S. Treasury checks are an exception.)

When sending checks through the mail for deposit, write "For Deposit Only" above your signature on the back. If the letter goes astray, your endorsement cannot be used by someone else to cash the check.

* And if your bank, like so many, changes hands through a takeover or merger, better find out all of the new bank's policies. The new corporation may alter interest rates and costs and fees for various banking services, as well as check-holding policies. If you don't like what you find, it's time to move on--and investigate a mini-bank instead of one of the mega-merger institutions.

Save time and money banking from home PC:

Quicken, the best-selling personal finance software, has now moved into the era of on-line financial services, including banking, investing and personal finance management. Other software is right behind: Microsoft Money, Block Financial Software's Managing Your Money and other personal finance programs. All allow you to track your checking accounts, savings, investments, credit cards, loans, cash and other assets and liabilities. And they provide tax data that can be sent to a tax preparation program and to a printed report, making tax time less taxing.

Designed around a checkbook metaphor, Quicken's program lets you "write checks" and automatically posts changes to any linked account. Use your checking account, for example, to pay a credit card bill, and Quicken automatically takes money out of your checking account and adds it to your credit card account. All of this, of course, is on your computer's hard disk, and in the past, the program never really interfaced with the banks and financial institutions themselves. But now Quicken can also call your bank or credit card company to move money between accounts and compare your data to what the institutions have in their computers.

In fact, the 1996 version of Quicken for Windows and Macintosh is full of on-line financial services. Intuit has formed relationships with a variety of financial institutions, including American Express, Smith Barney and 19 banks, including Wells Fargo, Home Savings, Union Bank, Chase Manhattan Bank and First Interstate Bank. By purchasing Quicken and establishing an account at one or more of these institutions, you can issue checks via modem, review balances, transfer funds between accounts and capture all of your records on-line so they're automatically entered into the appropriate Quicken register.

Each institution sets its own account fees but, in some cases, on-line banking is cheaper than banking the old-fashioned way. That's a pleasant change from a few years ago, when the few banks that offered on-line banking services added a surcharge.

Many of the banks have yet to start their on-line banking services, but most plan to gear up within the next month or two. Wells Fargo, for example, lets you access account information for checking, savings, credit card and many line-of-credit accounts, transfer money between accounts at no charge and automatically download transactions into Quicken to balance your checkbook.

Quicken also comes with a copy of the popular Netscape World Wide Web browser program and, through an arrangement with the Concentric Network Internet service provider, Quicken users who have a modem can go to Intuit's World Wide Web site (http://www.intuit.com) at no charge. If you want to go to other Web sites, you can sign up for Internet service for $1.95 an hour with no sign-up fee and only an hour a month minimum. Users also have the option of paying $9.95 for seven hours a month plus $1.95 for each additional hour, or switching to another Internet provider.

In addition to the other on-line features, the new CD-ROM-based Deluxe version of Quicken now comes with Investor Insight, which provides information about more than 5,000 companies and mutual funds including charts, quotes and news from Dow Jones and other services. You create your own "watch list" to track just the companies and funds that interest you. The service costs $9.95 a month, and the first month is free.

The deluxe program has a number of multimedia financial advisory tools including a tutorial featuring financial gurus Marshall Loeb and Jane Bryant Quinn. The contents of some of those tutorial changes depending upon the data stored in your Quicken registers. It's not exactly the same as having your own personal adviser, but it's a step in that direction.

There have been small improvements to the program's user interface. Instead of having to deal with overlapping windows, the software now displays tabs--such as those on file folders--for each account you're working with. Intuit has also improved the reporting feature, adding "EasyAnswer Reports," which lets you quickly create common reports about your finances. The company has also improved the program's main menu screen to provide easy access to all of its services and has simplified report printing and investment tracking.

Increase your odds of getting a loan:

You might think that filling out a loan application is all you can do, and the rest is up to institutional policy. That's pure myth, however. There are strategies you can follow to increase the chances of that application being stamped "APPROVED." Here are a couple:

* **Draw up a financial statement.** Your loan officer may rank you considerably higher because of this standard document, which shows your income, assets and personal investments. In fact, banks will provide you blank forms for personal financial statements. If you need help filling any part of it out, ask your accountant.

Advice: Don't exaggerate your financial status. You can, however, use high-end estimates for the value of assets like a house and anticipated future income.

* **Cultivate a loan officer.** Any relationship you can develop with bank officers will help you in securing a loan. Bankers routinely bend the rules in favor of applicants they know. Local service organizations are one place to begin meeting these financial movers-and-shakers.

In fact, get to know as many folks in the bank as possible, and in other banks and lending institutions, including your credit union.

If your loan officer still says no:

Bankers seem to have an infuriating policy of turning down loans, unless the applicant can absolutely demonstrate he or she doesn't need the money.

If this keeps happening to you, there's a quick and easy alternative, and one you can get at almost any bank-- a cash advance or line of credit on a Visa or Mastercard.

Just walk into the bank (not necessarily the card-issuing bank), show them your credit card with a second form of ID (usually a driver's license) and fill out a simple cash advance form. You can even do it by mail, by requesting a cash advance form. Fill it out for any amount up to your available credit limit, and use it to pay bills, or deposit it to your savings or checking account.

Caution: Because of high credit-card interest rates, and associated fees, this should only be used as a last resort. And if you must do this, at least compare credit card rates (including annual membership fees).

Dangers of safe-deposit boxes:

Most people think that a safe deposit box is the ultimate risk-free depository. Not so, unfortunately. Theft of these supposedly impregnable bank mini- vaults is on the rise, as robbers grow more sophisticated and bold.

Best bet: Don't keep cash, savings bonds or securities locked on in safe-deposit boxes. If they're stolen, you may have no way of substantiating or recouping your loss. Keep these valuables at home--in your own safe--and only keep copies at the bank to prove ownership.

Borrow cheaply from your credit union:

Unlike banks, credit unions are not out to make a profit. This status allow them to pass savings on to their members in lower-interest loans or higher-deposit interest rates.

Credit unions have long been a favorite place to get low-cost car loans. But more and more credit unions are offering other financial services, including credit cards. If yours does, or you can join one that does, chances are you'll beat the bank rate on credit cards by a hefty margin.

And on unsecured personal loans, credit unions average two- and-a-half points lower than banks, while paying a full point higher than banks on money-market accounts.

Don't drop that crystal vase:

Credit Card Update: As of March 1, 1996, Visa USA canceled one of its premium perks--its gold card purchase-protection policy. This insurance policy allowed a person who used a gold visa to get complete reimbursement for any merchandise subsequently broken or stolen.

Both MasterCard gold and all American Express cards still offered the service as of March 1. And Citicorp also continues to offer purchase protection on its cards--even Visa cards. Visa claims that its research shows that their gold card consumers find this coverage less important than other perks, such as free extended warranties.

Keep a sharp eye on your credit card rate:

Declining interest rates have lulled many card holders into believing credit costs are a problem of the past. As consumer and political pressures rose in recent years, many card issuers did reduce rates, especially for their better customers.

But many card issuers also made another change. They switched from fixed to variable interest rates, meaning that every quarter, or even monthly, they can raise the rates they charge. Issuers of variable-rate credit cards aren't legally required to tell customers.

Holders of variable-rate cards can tell if the rate has changed by looking at the little box at the bottom of the monthly statement, noting the rate and comparing the statement with others from previous months.

Issuers of fixed-rate cards must still notify customers of any rate change and give them a chance to stop using the card. But about 60% of the cards in use now are variable.

What we are seeing is the first spike in rates in two years. There has been a steady decline as rates have worked their way down, but there is good news and bad news: Consumers should be paying much lower rates (from a few years ago), but the bad news is, most of the cards are variable and (consumers) will be feeling (increases) more quickly than in the past.

Variable-rate cards typically are indexed to some general market rate. This is often the prime rate but may be something else. Signet Bank, for example, offers a Visa card indexed to the London Interbank Offered Rate, known as Libor.

If your statement shows your rate has risen, you have alternatives. The business remains very competitive. Some issuers haven't raised rates; others will cut a deal to keep a good customer. Still others, anxious to expand their market share, are offering low introductory rates, typically for a few months but in some cases for as long as a year.

The first step is to call your issuer's customer service line and ask for a lower rate. Say that you will close the account if you don't get one. If you carry a balance of at least $2,000, charge at least $3,000 a year and have a responsible record, you have a great deal of leverage. If the issuer won't deal, you can call local banks or refer to a listing of low-rate cards.

Beware of free cash-advance credit-card checks:

Millions of checks--blank and ready to be filled-in--are pouring into mailboxes all across the country. They are from credit-card issuers, eager for new business in a more competitive market.

The come-ons vary, but all are tempting: Take a vacation. Pay off holiday bills. Get an advance on your tax refund.

But beware--you'll have to pay back these loans, and very likely at a stiff interest rate. It's not always easy to decipher the accompanying promotional material.

Best bet: ignore the bold type and look for the fine print:

Check the interest rate on the "cash advance" checks. Don't assume it will be the same as the one charged on normal credit- card purchases. If you can't find the rate, call the issuing company and ask.

Then make sure you know how long the rate is valid. Some promotional rates click off after a few weeks or months.

Then check the transaction fee. Issuers often charge for a cash advance. Typically these range from $2 to $10. Be particularly alert for transaction fees if the promotion indicates there is no interest charge for a period after you use a check. The deal may look like an interest-free loan, but it probably isn't.

Check the grace period. Many credit cards don't charge interest for 25 days or so if there's no outstanding balance on the card. However, the interest meter starts ticking immediately on most cash advances.

Check on frequent-flier miles. These may not apply to cash advances.

Final caution: If you don't plan to use these checks, destroy them. They're negotiable. If someone forges your signature, you're at least going to have a headache on your hand, getting yourself off the financial hook.

Why you shouldn't have too many credit cards:

Some financial writers have suggested that the more credit cards you get, the better, especially if they have low rates and fees. The argument: You'll always have credit when you need it.

But, while you certainly should trade in a high-rate card for a low-rate card with no annual fee, you shouldn't accept every "pre-approved" credit card that comes in the mail.

Having too many credit cards can actually hamper your ability to get a mortgage or personal loan, because lenders look at all your available credit--the credit limits--when they consider your borrowing ability. If you have tens of thousands of dollars in available credit--regardless of whether or not you've used the cards--you may be deemed overextended.

Best low-rate, rebate and secured credit cards:

Here's a point-by- point matchup of the best credit cards, in terms of annual interest rate charged, rebates offered and those secured by collateral. Because fees and interest rates vary, check before signing up:

Five best low-rate cards:
Wachovia Bank (GA), (800-842-3262), prime rate first year, $18 annual fee, 25-day grace period, $153 annual cost on $1,500 balance.
Arkansas Federal Credit Card, (800-477-3348), 10.75%, $35 annual fee, 25-day grace period, $196 annual cost on $1,500 balance.

Central Carolina Bank (NC), (800-577-1680), 11.5%, $29 annual fee, 25-day grace period, $201 annual cost on $1,500 balance.

AFBA Industrial Bank (CO), (800-776-2265), 11.5%, $35 annual fee, 25-day grace period, $207.50 annual cost on $1,500 balance.

Crestar Bank (VA), (800-368-7700), 9.9%, $20 annual fee, 25- day grace period, $168.50 annual cost on $1,500 balance.

Five largest rebate cards:

AT&T Universal (800-786-3131), 18.9% variable, $20 annual fee, $303 annual cost on $1,500 balance, one point for every dollar on monthly statement.

GM/Household Bank (800-846-2273), 19.4%, no annual fee, $291 annual cost on $1,500 balance, 5% rebate on every dollar up to $500 per year, redeemable on GM autos.

Ford/Citibank (800-934-2788), 18.9%, no annual fee, $283.50 annual cost on $1,500 balance, each purchase earns 5% rebate toward purchase/lease of new Ford.

Smartrate/Discover (800-347-2683), 19.8%, no annual fee, $297 annual cost on $1,500 balance, cash back bonus up to 1% paid yearly based on amount of annual purchases.

GE Rewards/Capital Consumer Card Co. (800-437-3927), 16% to 18%, no annual fee, $240 to $270 annual cost on $1,500 balance, tiered rebate structure; up to 2% cash back on annual purchases up to $10,000.

Five best secured credit cards*:

*Secured cards require holders make a deposit to be held as collateral on which interest is paid. Credit charges usually cannot exceed the limit of that security deposit, and interest rates charged on the card balances tend to be on the high side. Nevertheless, these cards are a good way to establish or reestablishing credit for those with bad or nonexistent histories.

Citibank (SD), (800-933-2484), 18.4%, $20 annual fee, 25-day grace period, $300 minimum deposit, 4% interest paid on deposit.

Federal Savings Bank (AZ), (800-285-9090), 9.75%, $39 annual fee, 25-day grace period, $250 minimum deposit, 2.5% interest paid on deposit.

Orchard Bank (OR), (800-873-7307), 18.9%, no annual fee, 25- day grace period, $400 minimum deposit, 4% interest paid on deposit.

Key Federal (MD), (800-228-2230), 18.9%, $35 annual fee, 25- day grace period, $300 minimum deposit, 4% to 4.5% interest paid on deposit.

Signet Bank (VA), (800-333-7116), 20.8%, $20 annual fee, 25- day grace period, $200 minimum deposit, 5% interest paid on deposit.

Credit card for the very rich:

If you can handle a minimum credit card monthly payment of around $2,000 on a balance of $100,000, you can sign up for MBNA America Bank of Wilmington's "Platinum Plus" Visa or MasterCard. This prestige plastic carries a credit limit of $100,000, the highest in the country. (By the way, if you wonder how long it would take you to clear a $100 grand balance with those $2,000 monthly payments at 16% interest, figure around 43 years.)

Digging out of installment debt:

Red ink isn't only swamping the government, it's at flood tide for far too many individuals and families. If you're in this epidemic category, and find your installment debt growing and growing with seemingly no way out, it's probably time to take drastic action. Here's a list of sometimes painful but always practical remedies:

1. Cut spending to the bone. Some of your growing debt is because of escalating interest, but probably another chunk is because you're still buying stuff you can't pay for. So stop-- cold. Postpone as many purchases as possible, major and minor. Cut luxuries to the max, and monthly maintenance expenses to the minimum. For instance, pull the plug on cable, and watch free TV. Read library books or buy used paperbacks from thrift stores. Wash and iron your own clothes--you'll be surprised at how much you save by eliminating the dry-cleaners. Sounds drastic--but comfortable methods don't work.

2. Cut up your credit cards. Isn't that how you dug yourself into the debt in the first place? If you have to buy something, pay cash. Buying on credit vastly increases the cost. For instance, if you bought a $1,700 big-screen television with your 18% credit card and paid the minimum balance each month, the cost of the television and financing adds up to a whopping $3,673. (Now you tell me!) And if you don't have the cash for something, do without.

3. Put as much money as you can toward paying off debts. The point of austerity savings is to accumulate funds you can then use to pay those humongous bills. Make sure that's where the money goes, or you'll be starting a new cycle of debt.

However, if you're debts are so hefty that you're getting hit with late fees and overdraft charges, you may need even more drastic options, like getting a second job or working overtime. Or asking relatives for a short-term, bail-out loan.

Other possibilities to consider: cut unnecessary coverages on your auto insurance; terminate cash-value insurance and switch to cheaper term insurance; change your W-4s to reduce the withholding tax and increase take-home pay.

4. If you can qualify, seek a home equity loan. Equity credit lines generally run 10 percentage points below the interest charged by credit cards, so it makes sense to switch your debt out of the plastic to this kind of loan. If you qualify, refinancing and home-equity loans may work for you, but both entail significant upfront charges.

One debt-clearing remedy to avoid:
* **Consolidation loans.** These are advertised as the cure-all for those in deep debt. It sounds tempting--combining all your bills, except mortgage and car payments, then getting a loan to pay them all off with maybe cash left over. You only have to make a single monthly payment to the loan company--a payment smaller than the total of all the payments you had before.

The reason the payments are less, though, is because of long- term financing, which means a cumulative increase in total interest charges. And the interest rate will be higher than you'd get from any competitive lender.

Get a free credit report:

According to several recent studies, one in four people who review their credit report finds an error. If you've been denied credit within the past two months, you can check on your report at no charge. Just send a copy of the denial letter to the credit agency along with your request. Any one of the four big credit-reporting agencies can tell you how:

TRW Information Systems: 800-392-1122.
Equifax: 800-685-1111.
CSC Credit Service: 800-392-7816.
Trans Union Corp.: 800-851-2674.

Here's a list of common credit problems and how long they'll show up on your credit report:

* **Late payments**--two years. The definition of "late" can vary from lender to lender. Make sure you are clear on yours.
* **Nonpayment or non-filing** of federal income taxes--10 years.
* **Bankruptcy**--seven or 10 years, depending on how you file.

* **Charge-offs**--seven years.
* **Repossessions**--seven years.
* **Foreclosures**--seven years.
* **Judgments**--Show as "unsatisfied" until you've paid them. Once you have settled them, you must file a "satisfaction of judgment" with the city clerk.
* **Wage garnishment**--as long as your wages are garnished.

Get out of debt without declaring bankruptcy:

Personal bankruptcy filings are on the rise. Not surprising, with consumer installment debt hitting all-time highs. If you're deeply in debt, bankruptcy can seem like an easy way to wipe out many debts, protect you from collection agencies and forestall eviction.

But there's a definite downside to filing for bankruptcy protection:

* It ruins your credit;
* it can hinder your ability to get a job or buy an insurance policy;
* it can wipe out your savings;
* it can cause you to lose control of your financial life.

Most people opt for bankruptcy only because they are threatened with eviction or foreclosure or liens that hinder their ability to buy and sell property. Many are being harassed on a daily basis by creditors and collection agencies.

A bankruptcy filing does legally bar creditors from calling you about your debts, it stops numerous legal proceedings and it can forestall eviction. But because of the long-term scars it leaves on your credit report, it should only be considered a last resort on a continuum of options that you should explore.

For instance:

* Consolidate debts. If your debts are on a dozen high-interest-rate credit cards, you might benefit from consolidating these debts into a single loan--or even from putting them all on a single lower-rate credit card. Those with considerable home equity might consider paying the debts off with a home equity loan. This lets you reduce your interest rate and lower monthly debt payments. And you may be able to deduct the interest from your income taxes.

However, if you consolidate your bills and continue to overspend, you'll put yourself on a collision course with either home foreclosure or bankruptcy.

And pay close attention to the interest rate on your consolidation loan--there's no point in consolidating unless you can get a lower rate--and the security you're offering. Remember that a home equity loan puts your house at risk.

* Negotiate independently. If you lose a job or suffer other unexpected and temporary financial reversal, contact your lenders right away and explain the situation. Most lenders will agree to a temporary payment delay, interest rate relief or stretch out your payments. This can save your credit rating and prove beneficial to creditors as well, because they don't have to write off any of the debts.

* Get help negotiating. If you've spent more than you've earned over a long period of time, you're likely to need help reining in your budget and negotiating with creditors. Call your nearest Consumer Credit Counseling Service and set up an appointment. CCCS is a nonprofit organization that helps the overextended reevaluate or formulate budgets and establish workable payment plans with creditors. Generally speaking, however, CCCS can only help you negotiate with creditors if you can realistically expect to pay off the bulk of your debts within five years.

Those who can't consolidate their debts and have no hope of paying off creditors within that period of time may have no better option than to file for bankruptcy.

What you should know about bankruptcy:

Chapter 7 bankruptcy is for those whose debts far exceed assets and ability to pay. It involves selling all your "nonexempt" assets and using the proceeds to pay creditors. This process is fairly swift. Once it is complete, most unsecured debts are erased, regardless of whether creditors received 10 cents or 100 cents on the dollar.

Chapter 13 is for those who can and will pay off all or a portion of their debts in three to five years. It allows you to keep your property and use your income to pay off certain debts according to a timeline set up by you and the court.

This can forestall a foreclosure and stop interest from accruing on your debts--even if the debt is owed to the IRS. But it's more complicated and costly, and people who are able to pay off most of their debts over time may be able to avoid bankruptcy altogether by working out payment plans with their creditors.

What you can keep:
Even in Chapter 7, you can keep some income and assets. The things you legally can keep are called "exempt" assets.

Generally, you retain all or a portion of personal property, such as clothing and furniture; Social Security and public assistance payments; all or a portion of your pension; and a minimum amount of equity in a car and/or in your personal residence. Luxury items are usually not exempt and may have to be sold to satisfy creditors.

* Nonerasable debts. Most debts owed to the federal government--such as student aid loans and back taxes--are not dischargeable. You can't erase spousal or child support or debts that you agreed to pay in lieu of it. Dues and assessments owed to a condominium or cooperative association are not dischargeable in bankruptcy, nor are criminal fines. In addition, if you buy luxury items or take cash advances against a credit card within three months of a bankruptcy, these debts generally cannot be discharged either.

* **Loss of control.** With a Chapter 13, you retain some control over your financial life during bankruptcy, but if you misrepresent conditions to the court, the judge may hand all control to a trustee. If you break the rules, there can be serious repercussions.

* **Scars.** Bankruptcies remain on your credit record for a decade--longer than the 7 years for most credit problems. Even after the bankruptcy is officially "erased," if you apply for a high-paying job or attempt to take out a large insurance policy, the prospective insurer or employer can see the bankruptcy at any time, and neither must inform you that the bankruptcy was a factor in deciding against you.

NOTES

_____

_____

_____

_____

_____

_____

_____

_____

_____

_____

_____

_____

_____

_____

Chapter
_____   **21**

Keys to Real Estate

Checklist to sell your home fast:

In most urban areas, it's still a home buyer's market. That means there are more homes listed for sale than there are qualified buyers. But thanks to lower mortgage interest rates, houses are selling. If you'd like yours to change hands within 90 days, here are 9 things you should consider doing:

1. Get your home into tip-top condition. Home buyers are lazy. They want to turn the key in the door of their dream home and move in. They don't want to make repairs, do fix-up work or landscaping the seller should have taken care of. They want what is called a "red ribbon deal" home in near-perfect condition.

If your home doesn't meet that ideal, it will appeal to only the very small percentage of prospective home owners who will buy a "fixer-upper." And these folks buy only if they can get an incredible bargain price with attractive terms.

So give your abode a coat of paint inside and outside. Replace tired, worn-out carpet with fresh, stain-resistant carpets in a neutral beige color that goes with any furniture.

If you have hardwood floors, have them cleaned and varnished to show their best. If your kitchen appliances are old, replace them with new top-of-the-line models and include them in the sales price. Kitchen appliances help sell houses.

More important, kitchens and bathrooms sell houses. Make yours especially attractive. But don't do extensive remodeling. Just clean and repair. Make your home look as close as possible to a model home.

According to a report by Remodeling magazine, a bathroom remodeled returns 75% to the owner, a bathroom addition 102% and a master bedroom suite 78%.

And pay attention to the landscaping, especially the front yard, which helps make a favorable first impression.

Other tips:
-- Sweep the sidewalk, mow the lawn, prune the bushes, weed the garden and clean debris from the yard.
-- Clean the windows (both inside and out) and make sure the paint is not chipped or flaking.
-- Be sure that the doorbell works.
-- Clean and make attractive all rooms, furnishings, floors, walls and ceilings. It's especially important that the bathroom and kitchen are spotless.
-- Organize closets.
-- Make sure the basic appliances and fixtures work. Get rid of leaky faucets and frayed cords.
-- Ensure that the house smells good: from an apple pie, cookies baking or spaghetti sauce simmering on the stove. Hide the kitty litter.
-- Put vases of fresh flowers throughout the house.
-- Pleasant background music is a nice touch.

2. Obtain necessary professional inspections--before listing your home for sale. These may include termite inspection, energy audit and city building-code inspection. Make any necessary repairs indicated by these inspections.

In addition, have a professional home inspection. This report will reassure prospective home buyers of your home's condition, even if they want to hire their own inspector. By completing these inspections early, you can take care of necessary and recommended repairs, thus removing potential buyer objections.

3. Interview at least three successful realty agents. The most critical step in selling your home is selecting the best agent. Ask friends, business associates and neighbors for names of successful agents who sell homes in your neighborhood.

Three should be interviewed to cross-check their advice, especially about the asking price. If you interview only one agent, he or she might mislead you.

Incidentally, the primary reason agents succeed where "for sale by owners" fail is the local multiple listing service (MLS). Thanks to the MLS, realty agents can show prospective home buyers hundreds of homes whereas a do-it-yourself seller has only one home to sell.

When interviewing the three (or more) agents you select, have a written list of questions.

Here's a sample:
* Do you have any suggestions to improve the salability of my home?
* What is your specific marketing plan for my home, such as advertising, open houses, printed brochures and information fact sheets for prospects?
* Do you suggest using a lockbox to make my home easy to show to prospects?
* How long have you been selling real estate?
* Do you have any professional designations?
* What is the last real estate education class you completed and when?
* How long should it take you to sell my home?
* How many houses have you sold in the last 12 months,

what are their addresses and the names with phone numbers of the sellers?

* Do you recommend a 90-day listing, or a shorter term? (Be wary of agents who attempt to lock you in to long listings without an unconditional cancellation clause.)

* Is there anything else I should know about you or your firm?

Before signing a listing, be sure to phone their three most recent home sellers. Ask, "Were you in any way unhappy with your agent and would you list your home for sale with the same agent again?" You'll soon know which agent should get your listing.

4. Price your home right, and it is half sold. You could hire a professional appraiser to advise on your home's market value. But the agents you interview should be able to help you arrive at the correct asking price.

However, watch out for any agent who inflates his or her estimated value of your home, hoping to get your listing by estimating the highest sales price.

5. Get rid of any tenants or guests. After you have selected the best agent and signed your listing, make arrangements to have the home ready to show on short notice. If you have tenants or guests in the home, make certain they agree to be completely out of the house when it is shown to prospective buyers. This includes you too.

When a home is shown to prospects, there should be no one in the home except the agent and the buyers. Serious buyers are reluctant to criticize a home with the owner or others present. And until a buyer criticizes a home, the buyer isn't really serious.

6. If your home doesn't sell within a few months, offer seller financing. If you can carry back a first or second mortgage, or sell the home on a lease with option to purchase, this will greatly enhance your sales opportunities.

Easy financing sells houses. Some agents also have lenders "pre-approve" a home so prospective buyers know what financing can be easily obtained subject to buyer qualifications.

7. Beware of offers with unreasonable contingency clauses. When you obtain a purchase offer, whether it's the first day your home is on the market, or several weeks later, read the offer carefully. Virtually all offers contain reasonable contingency clauses for financing and inspections.

But beware of offers with open-ended contingencies without a time deadline. The worst contingency involves sale of the buyer's old home. If you agree, be sure it has a release clause so you can accept a better purchase offer from another buyer.

8. Ask your realty agent to prepare a closing cost estimate. Before accepting a purchase offer, ask your agent to prepare a written statement of closing costs and net sale proceeds. This form will show you how much cash you will receive from your home sale if you accept the offer under consideration.

9. Don't be in a hurry to sell your home. The reality is that home sales take time. If your home is in tip-top condition, you select the best agent and it is priced correctly at market value, it should sell within 90 days.

However, if the local market is very slow, up to 180 days might be required. If it doesn't, the first step is to lower the price. Then go through the house and see if there are cosmetic defects that you missed and can be repaired.

And make sure the home is getting the exposure it deserves through open houses, broker open houses, advertising, good signage and a listing on the Multiple Listing Service. If the property isn't getting that exposure, find another agent.

How to find the best real estate agent:

The best sources of contacts are friends or associates who have bought or sold recently and can recommend agents. Be sure to ask your colleagues if they would use the agent again.

If personal contacts don't generate enough leads, call the managers of reputable local real estate companies and ask for recommendations of agents who specialize in your neighborhood if you're selling. Find out if the agent works full time at real estate and how much experience the agent has.

Should home buyers retain their own agents?:

It can be advantageous for home buyers to have their own agents, but buyers can also be hurt by such agreements--when an agent ties up a buyer without results. If you're a buyer, it's better to have an informal arrangements where you work with a particular agent, but are free to purchase elsewhere if the agent doesn't find you the right home.

House-hunting begins with good credit:

This may seem hard to believe, but many wannabe homeowners have too much credit. Every mortgage lender, realty agent or home builder can tell story after story of otherwise qualified home shoppers knocked out of the market by their credit.

For instance, many first-time buyers have too many credit cards. Lenders look at the total amount of credit that the person has available. Too many cards can be a big negative. First-time buyers should have only three pieces of credit that they carry and pay on time for 12 months.

You should do what you can to correct your credit before you apply for a mortgage. One agency that can help is the Consumer Credit Counseling Service, a nationwide nonprofit group that helps people draw up budgets, negotiates with their creditors, develops repayment plans and educates the public on credit and personal finances. It is funded primarily by credit companies, and its services to consumers are either free or offered at low cost.

There are a number of ways that credit can be wrecked, the experts say. Some of the most common:

* Large unpaid credit card balances.
* Auto loans, school loans and department store charge accounts that are out of whack with the ability to repay them.
* Paying bills late or failing to pay them at all.
* Having a car or furniture repossessed.
* Failing to pay or file federal income taxes.
* Filing for bankruptcy.

Other items that scare lenders include court judgments or liens, garnished wages and charge-offs. A charge-off occurs when creditors realize you'll never pay your bills. They'll take the loss and wipe it off their books, but it stays on your credit history for seven years.

A more basic problem for most house hunters: not paying attention to your credit. Most people haven't seen their credit reports in two or three years. And often credit reports reflect misinformation where an account is duplicated or triplicated or contains information that does not belong to that individual.

Another problem: not paying attention to the smaller bills. Many first-time buyers' credit reports reflect overdue bills to utility companies--where a bill may have arrived after they moved out of an apartment, and they didn't realize it hadn't been paid.

Six steps to reestablish credit:

1. Develop a budget to repay your debts. Although it isn't widely known, many creditors will negotiate with you to settle your debts. CCCS will frequently get creditors to stop charging interest on a debt so that clients can begin to settle it.

2. Design a plan to manage your money. Start recording every cent you spend. Knowing where your money goes will help you put together a budget that will allow you to pay your creditors. That budget will probably include giving up credit cards. Which leads to the next step:

3. Pay for everything with cash. Cancel your credit accounts. Although you may not use your credit cards, even having the accounts tells lenders that you could incur a heavy debt load, especially if you've had high consumer debt in the past.

4. Obtain your credit report. You should also get the credit report of your spouse, partner or anyone else who will be applying with you for a mortgage. The three major national credit reporting bureaus are TRW, Equifax and Trans Union. TRW, (800) 831-5614, will give you one free copy of your credit report each year; Equifax, (770) 612-2585, and Trans Union, (312) 408-1400, will charge a small fee for each report. Get a copy from each, plus one from a local credit reporting agency, because each may have different information.

Always check for errors. Many reports contain factual errors that may be easily corrected. But steer clear of credit repair companies. These "clinics" cannot do anything for you that you can't do yourself, and they charge a lot of money for their services.

Contact your creditors. A credit reporting bureau cannot fix your credit blemishes. Only your creditors can do that. If your credit report contains errors, you must contact the creditor with proof of the mistake.

Countrywide, (800) 577-3732, offers a free booklet on credit repair that includes sample letters you can send to your creditors. You may also write an explanation of up to 100 words (regulations limit the length) explaining your side of the story. This explanation will become part of your credit report.

If your account contains "negatives" or "derogatories," such as an unpaid bill that was eventually charged off, you should work to get them removed, by repaying the debt, even though it had been written off by the creditor.

5. Apply for unsecured credit in a local department store.

6. Apply for secured credit.

More tactics to positively influence mortgage lenders:
   * Pay your bills on time. Few folks have an unblemished credit history. Mortgage lenders, however, are far more interested in how you have recently paid your bills. Once you've corrected your past credit problems, make sure you pay every bill on time. That will go a long way to showing a lender you've cleaned up your act.

   * Don't jump jobs. Lenders like to see a history of job stability. So, at least don't change careers just before you apply for a loan. Lateral moves within your career are fine.

   * Don't buy a car before you apply for a mortgage. When you apply for auto financing, often the dealer will send out a request for funding to many lenders. This can have a negative effect on your credit report. If you must buy a car before you apply for your home loan, ask the dealer to keep the request for funding to one bank. Being turned down for any loan can cause a mortgage lender to reject you.

Determining how much house you can afford:

The biggest mistake that people make is looking for a house before looking for a loan, according to lending professionals. Reason: They don't know how much they can really borrow, so they end up looking at homes that are too expensive.

Figuring how much a borrower can actually afford involves many variables. Generally, lenders will extend a fixed-rate mortgage to a borrower where so-called monthly PITI (principal, interest, taxes and insurance costs associated with the residence) total no more than about 28% of the borrower's gross income.

Additionally, the borrower's total obligations for PITI and other debt--such as a car payment or student loan-- shouldn't exceed about 36% of the borrower's gross income. With a variable-rate loan, all of a borrower's housing and debt-related payments generally should total no more than about 36% to 40% of gross monthly income.

These guidelines aren't carved in stone, though. Lenders will routinely go to higher debt ratios when a borrower exhibits good credit and job security.

The four most important factors that the lender looks at are the borrower's ability to pay, willingness to pay on time, the borrower's equity in the transaction and the security of the underlying property as an investment.

Many borrowers don't realize that other debt to be paid off within 10 to 12 months won't count against them. For example, when a borrower has only a few payments on a car, it won't be considered at loan application time. If a borrower has 15 months to go on a loan, however, it's often worth making a few advance payments to remove it from the mortgage lender's consideration.

Some institutions allow wealthy borrowers to pay more than 40% of their income to PITI since these borrowers still have enough discretionary income left over for other things. That typical borrower has an income of about $250,000 and a loan averaging $500,000. Because of this borrower profile, loan officers use a higher debt ratio than is typical in the lending industry.

Prospective home buyers should also check their credit report and clean up any errors or payment disputes in advance of house hunting. And it's a good idea to get pre-qualified for a period of three to six months.

Borrowers who want to refinance their homes will also get better treatment when they've shown an ability to make their current payments regularly. Borrowers who don't have the income to qualify for a particular fixed-rate loan may be able to qualify for an adjustable-rate mortgage. Not only are lenders generally more flexible, but some will even qualify the borrower based on the low introductory rate instead of the higher adjusted rate, he said.

First-time borrowers should seek out an experienced lender or loan broker. The more experience he or she has, the more creative the lender can be.

Latest advances in reverses:

In 1996 the Federal National Mortgage Association--aka "Fannie Mae"--the nation's largest provider of home loans, began to offer reverse mortgage to eligible older homeowners. The move by the agency vastly expands the scope of this program that allows older Americans to tap the equity in their homes without having to sell them and move out.

Reverse mortgages were designed in the late '70s to help seniors who have accumulated substantial equities in their homes but need to tap that money to meet their normal living expenses. These mortgages allow homeowners to spend that equity without selling their homes.

Here's how they work:

Typically, a lendor offers a loan based on the borrower's age--the minimum ranges from 62 to 65--and the property's appraised value. After taking its fees and points up front, the institution pays the homeowner the loan balance, either in equal monthly installments, in a lump sum or as a line of credit for as long as the borrower continues living in the home.

The loan balance, which is actually the amount dispersed plus interest and loan fees, is repaid when the house is sold by the owner or heirs. If the borrower moves out without the intention to return or moves into a nursing home for a year or more, most of these loans can be called.

Are "reverses" for you?

That depends. If you stay just a brief time, the reverse mortgage proves a costly way to pull equity out because loan fees and points on the full potential loan amount are assessed at the outset. However, if you remain in the house a long time, the lending institution stands to pay out more than the home may be worth.

Because these loans tend to deplete the equity of a home quickly, they are usually best suited to homeowners who are in their late 70s or older with a fairly sizable home equity. Such homeowners are unlikely to outlive the term of the loan, thus offering the lender a measure of protection against the possibility of paying out more than the property is worth. The Fannie Mae program requires borrowers to be at least 62.

For more information about reverse mortgages, contact the American Assn. of Retired Persons. Send a postcard asking for the "Home Equity Conversion Kit," publication No. D-15601, to the AARP, 601 E. St. N.W., Washington, DC 20049.

Fannie Mae, which plans to make about 10,000 reverse mortgages per year through affiliated lenders, also offers free brochures on its program. Call (800) 732-6643.

To refi or not to refi, that's the question:

Mortgage interest rates are down, but homeowners aren't rushing to refinance. As a result, lenders are getting anxious because their loan volume is lower than they want.

Frankly, many lenders are approving applications they would have been rejected a year ago. But before rushing to refinance your home loan because you smell a bargain, here are the five key questions to ask:

1. Is this the right time to refinance my mortgage? The "old rule" was that it pays to refinance if you can reduce your mortgage interest rate at least 2%. Today, however, it can be profitable if your new annual percentage rate is just 1% lower than your current one.

Many lenders now offer so-called no-cost mortgages, meaning that the lender includes the refinancing cost in the loan's interest rate. If that rate is lower than you're now paying, refinancing makes sense. In addition, these lenders let you take tax-free cash from your home equity. Finding the best deal requires shopping among many lenders.

2. Do banks, savings and loan associations, mortgage brokers or mortgage bankers offer the best home loans? Even in today's highly competitive home mortgage market, there can be a vast difference among lenders. But chasing the lowest interest rate often isn't worth the hassle of dealing with an uncooperative or demanding lender.

Portfolio lenders who hold their mortgages "in portfolio" are often more flexible than lenders who sell most of their mortgages in the secondary mortgage market to Fannie Mae and Freddie Mac. The biggest disadvantage of going directly to a regulated bank or S&L is that they offer few loan choices and enforce rigid lending rules. The advantages, however, can include quick loan decisions and local service.

Mortgage brokers act as intermediaries between the borrower and the ultimate lender, whether that's a bank, S&L or mortgage banker. They often perform finance miracles, and their cost is usually no higher than the cost of a bank or S&L.

3. Is a fixed or adjustable rate best? In today's market, about 75% of home loan originations are at fixed rates. Most borrowers who plan to keep their homes more than five years prefer fixed-interest rate mortgages. These loans are now at very attractive low interest rates. Of course, the big advantage is that the monthly payment can never increase.

If you plan to keep your home just a few years, an adjustable rate mortgage with a fixed interest rate for the first three, five or seven years is also very attractive in today's mortgage market.

But ask lots of questions about the mortgage index. Treasury bill, CD and London Inter Bank Offering Rate indexes are far more volatile than the slow-moving 11th District Cost of Funds index. Lenders usually add a 2% or higher margin to the index to determine the mortgage rate.

Also ask what safeguards the adjustable mortgage offers, including the maximum interest rate (called a "cap"), maximum annual increase and maximum payment increase. Find out if the loan has negative amortization. If it does, you could wind up owing more than you borrow.

4. Is a 15-year or 30-year mortgage best? If you can afford monthly payments about 20% higher than for a 30-year mortgage, a 15-year mortgage will save you thousands of interest dollars. More important, the mortgage will be paid off in 15 instead of 30 years.

If you aren't certain you can afford the increased monthly payments of a 15-year mortgage, however, taking a 30-year mortgage but paying it off as if it were a 15-year mortgage is the safest alternative. If you then find it impossible to keep up the increased payments, you can always drop back to the required 30-year payment rate.

5. What mortgage refinance charges should I expect? Most mortgage lenders charge a loan fee, usually called "points." One point equals 1% of the amount borrowed. On refinances, loan fees are tax deductible over the loan's life. In addition, expect to pay refinance costs for such services as title insurance, escrow or attorney fees, appraisal fees and recording charges.

Most lenders now offer so-called "no cost" mortgages that eliminate most of these charges, but the trade-off is a higher mortgage interest rate.

Each lender offers different loan terms and rates. When phoning local lenders listed in the Yellow Pages under "real estate loans," watch out for lenders offering low interest rates but unnecessary "garbage fee" extra profit charges.

Examples of garbage fees include application fees, documentation fees, underwriting charges, warehousing charges and loan administration fees. After you make a written application for a mortgage, the lender must itemize these charges for you. Lenders will often waive these fees if you call their bluff.

Conclusion: Now is an excellent time to refinance a high-interest home loan. But shop carefully because all lenders are not the same. Compare loan terms very carefully. Watch out for lenders that charge unnecessary fees to raise their profits at your expense.

Buying a house with little or nothing down:

Putting down as little as possible on a house and taking a larger mortgage allows buyers to take full advantage of the tax benefits of home ownership. Mortgage interest (and property taxes) are fully deductible from state and federal income taxes.

And, although some experts advise against it, home buyers interested in buying a house with nothing down can do so. It's not easy finding these loans and they can be risky.

Occasionally, a builder will offer nothing-down loans to induce sales in an otherwise slow-moving project. Desperate sellers also may agree to finance the full purchase price to get out from under a property. The VA loan program allows buyers to qualify for a nothing-down loan, as well as a loan program offered through some state employee retirement systems.

* The U.S. Department of Housing and Urban Development (HUD) offers a variety of loan insurance programs through FHA that require about 4% to 5% cash down. The down payment must be the buyer's own money--gift money is not allowed--but buyers can finance all non-recurring closing costs.

HUD-owned properties can be purchased only through a licensed real estate broker. HUD acquires properties from lenders who foreclose on mortgages insured by HUD. These properties are available for sale to both homeowner occupants and investors. HUD pays the broker's commission up to 6% of the sales price.

Buyers should be aware that HUD homes are sold "as is," meaning limited repairs were made but no structural or mechanical warranties implied.

* FHA loan limits vary depending on the county where the property is located. Recently, the FHA loan limit was increased to $151,725, but only in high cost areas. FHA loans are originated and serviced by private lenders.

* VA loans are attractive because in some cases they require no down payment. With the U.S. Department of Veterans Affairs, there is no restriction on the purchase price.

For more information, call the U.S. Department of Veterans Affairs at (800) 827-1000.

* The Community Home Buyers Program is sponsored by Fannie Mae, the Federal National Mortgage Assn., and administered through participating lenders. The program has an income cap of 115% of the area's median income. In addition, the borrower must attend a seminar on home ownership and the home buying process.

The program allows for 95% financing. The borrower may put down as little as 3% of his or her own money, with the remaining 2% coming in the form of a family gift or loan from a government or nonprofit agency.

For a list of participating lenders, call Fannie Mae at (800) 732-6643.

* **Another option:** buying a house with a couple of friends or investors. The "tenants in common" (TIC) way of holding title is becoming more popular, especially among first-time buyers as a way to purchase property collectively with other unrelated individuals. Generally, TIC properties are eligible for many of the same loan programs as homes owned by individuals, but the underwriting standards are more complicated because the lender must consider the financial situation of all the parties who hold an interest in the property.

* **Foreclosure properties:** Notice of foreclosure must be published once a week for three weeks in a newspaper of general circulation in the city where the property is located or in the city nearest the property in the county where a newspaper is published.

For a buyer serious about finding a foreclosure, subscribing to a legal publication may be a first step. Many people don't even know of the existence of these legal papers. Therefore, default and foreclosure notices published in such papers are likely to mean fewer pre-foreclosure buyers as well as fewer bidders than if the notices had been published in a general newspaper.

Also, written notice describing the property and announcing the time and place of sale is posted for 20 days on the property and in a public place in the city where the sale is to occur.

But buying directly at the legal foreclosure sale can be a risky and dangerous business. It is strictly "buyer beware." There is no financing--such purchases require cash and lots of it. The title needs to be checked in some manner before the purchase or the buyer could buy a seriously deficient title.

The property's condition is not well known and generally, an interior inspection of the property is not possible before the sale. In addition, only foreclosure and estate (probate) sales are exempt from some state's disclosure laws. In both cases, the law protects the seller, usually an heir or financial institution who has recently acquired the property through adverse circumstances and may have little or no direct information about it.

Trustee sales: These are advertised in advance and require an all-cash bid. The sale is usually conducted by a lawyer, sheriff or constable acting as trustee. They may or may not be helpful and sometimes downright difficult to work with.

The sale begins when the lender who holds the first loan on the property starts the bidding at the amount of the loan being foreclosed. Keep in mind that sophisticated investors are present, so novices may find themselves among stiff competition for foreclosed property.

The successful bidder at the foreclosure sale can look forward to a trustee's deed, which usually is delivered the following day.

* Distressed properties or fixer-uppers can be found in most communities, even the wealthier neighborhoods.

A distressed property is one that has been poorly maintained and has a lower market value than other houses in the immediate area.

The basic strategy for a fixer-upper is to find the least desirable house in the most desirable neighborhood and then decide if the expenses needed to bring the value of that property up to its full potential market value are within one's budget. Most experts say buyers should avoid run-down houses that need major structural repairs.

Beware of real estate con artists:

Swindles involving some sort of title fraud are particularly popular, say title companies, lawyers and law enforcement officials.

All an enterprising criminal has to do is forge your signature, pretend to be you and get a fake notary seal. If you own a rental property, your tenant can easily call a real estate broker and list the property for sale. Pretending to be you, the tenant can sign over the deed to an innocent buyer and walk away with proceeds of the sale!

Con artists can also pretend to be you and take a loan on your house. Chances are you won't know this has happened until an eviction notice appears at your door. By then, the con artist has defaulted on the loan and your house has just been sold by a lender you have never met.

Owners who can prove they are indeed the true owners, generally won't lose their properties. But it can take months, however, and $5,000 to $10,000 to hire a lawyer to do what's known as quiet title.

Another popular scam is perpetrated by people who somehow acquire title to a property and then get it financed many times over. Even when the crooks are caught, law enforcement authorities can rarely pin down where the fraud and forgeries actually took place--creating a jurisdictional problem.

Most D.A.'s offices don't have enough resources to go after all the real estate scams being perpetrated. It's probably impossible to ensure you won't become a victim, but it helps to be suspicious whenever people start asking you questions about your property ownership.

Don't fall for home-improvement scams:

Unscrupulous contractors demand a large down payment before starting a job, do little or no work and disappear.

How to protect yourself: Put no money down or at most 10% to 30% and pay installments as the work progresses; hold back a final payment until satisfactory completion; check that the contractor is licensed and bonded.

NOTES

_____
_____
_____
_____
_____
_____
_____
_____
_____
_____
_____
_____
_____
_____
_____
_____

Chapter

Career Strategies

22

Why it pays adults to go back to college:

Know what the biggest trend is to hit higher education since rising tuition? It's adults who, for a variety of personal, professional and economic reasons, have decided to go back to college.

In 1993, the most recent year for which government statistics are available, 6.3 million adults over the age of 25 were attending college. Adults, "non-traditional" students, now make up 44% of the college population nationwide--and two out of three adults returning to college are women, education experts say. If current trends continue, adults will outnumber traditional students--those ranging in age between 17 and 23--by the end of the decade.

Adults give various reasons for going back to school, but students and experts alike acknowledge that a good part of the explanation is economic. More and more people understand that if they don't go to college, they're not going to make as much money. The prestige in professions where you don't go to college is just not there anymore.

The average college graduate earns roughly $1 million more over a lifetime than the average high school graduate, according the Census Bureau. And many seasoned high school graduates have real-life experiences that make those statistics real.

Rapid technological change is also driving the back-to-school trend. As much as 80% of the jobs in the future are going to demand high skills in conceptual and technological areas, according to vocational experts. Unless you get a higher education, you are going to see yourself falling farther behind because the gulf between the educated and non-educated is getting much wider.

But adults face unique difficulties when going back to college simply because they have far more financial and physical responsibilities than 18-year-olds who are sent to college with a car and a monthly allowance.

By and large, these are people with children, mortgages, car payments and credit cards, who find themselves forced to cut back or give up paying jobs in order to get their schooling. That requires a lot of planning and sacrifice. Some rely on financial aid and academic scholarships to make it through; others secure student loans.

The 10 fastest-growing professions:

This list, compiled from U.S. Bureau of Labor statistics, doesn't necessarily show where the most jobs are, but where the growth sectors will be for the coming decade.

Profession	Jobs in 1992	New Jobs by 2005	Percent Growth
1. Home Health Aides	475,000	645,000	136%
2. Human Services Workers	189,000	256,000	136%
3. Computer Scientists and Systems Analysts	666,000	737,000	111%
4. Physical Therapists	90,000	79,000	88%

5. Paralegals	95,000	81,000	86%
6. Medical Assistants	181,000	128,000	71%
7. Correction Officers	282,000	197,000	70%
8. Travel Agents	115,000	76,000	66%
9. Preschool Workers	941,000	811,000	65%
10. Radiologic Technologists	162,000	102,000	63%

Bottom 10: jobs that are disappearing:

What occupations are the modern equivalent of the buggywhip-maker or typewriter repairman? Here's a list (again from Bureau of Labor Statistics) of jobs most threatened by technological trends:

Profession	Jobs in 1992	New Jobs by 2005	Percent Growth
1. Telephone Repairers	40,000	20,000	50%
2. Computer & Peripheral Equipment Operators	296,000	122,000	41%
3. Communications Equipment Repairers	108,000	41,000	38%
4. Private Household Workers	869,000	286,000	33%
5. Roustabouts (oil rig workers)	33,000	11,000	33%
6. Telephone Operators	314,000	89,000	28%
7. Shoe & Leather Workers	22,000	4,300	20%
8. Apparel Workers	986,000	183,000	19%
9. Textile Machinery Operators	1,218,000	204,000	17%
10. Farmers	1,218,000	204,000	17%

What to do if you're fired:

The good news is that being fired no longer carries the stigma of years past. Merger mania, downsizing, outsourcing, restructuring have made the concept of the lifetime job just about obsolete. Today most everyone understands that companies are cutting whatever staff they can--often the best- qualified, best-compensated workers are the first to go.

That doesn't mean it won't hurt, and hurt bad, or won't be a shock. But if there were company-wide rumblings, perhaps you weren't blindsided, and will be prepared to embark on your next job--which is finding new employment. But your very first step, after the shock fades, is:

Ask for an explanation of why you were let go. This may not be necessary if you were part of a cost-cutting wave of bodies out the door. But if you were singled out, it will be valuable information to learn why. You'll be more prepared to avoid a similar situation in the future.

Were there clues or warning signs you ignored? Typical examples: poor performance ratings, lack of promotions and raises, being omitted from department projects.

If you think you may be a victim of discrimination, contact an employment lawyer. (Example: If you're being fired for allegedly committing a crime that you're innocent of, and which has not been proven, you definitely have legal recourse.) In fact, even if you're sure you weren't discriminated against, it's not a bad idea to talk with an attorney, to make sure you exit with every benefit you're entitled to. A good idea is to write down exactly what you want from your company, then read the company employee handbook carefully.

Concentrate on your exit strategy. Line up whatever higher-up allies you have in the company to help you leave with your pockets full, rather than empty; these allies can also make sure you walk away with good references. A good idea is to request a letter of reference on your final day. You don't want to be held hostage by your supervisors for that letter.

If the company asks that you leave immediately--and these kinds of demands, unfortunately, are not as rare as they should be--try to get more time. Number one, the longer you stay, the longer you'll be getting paid, and the more time you'll have to launch your new job search. But don't sign any documents until your lawyer reviews them.

Two ways to extend your employment is by offering to train your replacement, or to finish up any projects you're currently working on. This may be refused, but it's the professional thing to do.

Most important, make sure you understand how long your health benefits will last and discuss the tax implications of any severance pay, benefits and pensions. Then ask the company about any outplacement services such as workshops, career counseling, resume writing, etc. You should take advantage of whatever resources the company makes available.

Caution: It's okay to be hurt and angry, but don't give in to revenge, or temptations to denounce anyone you think might have been against you. Be professional and positive- -it will help you put a painful episode behind you, and let you start fresh.

Remember, this too, as the saying goes, will pass, and your life will get back together. It's a crisis, but not a disaster. You'd be surprised to find out how many successful folk have been fired along the way, sometimes more than once.

In fact, it's a good idea, and therapeutic, not to rush frantically around for your next job, with a desperate look in your eyes. And don't jump at the first job you're offered. Be systematic, by all means start networking, but also use this interruption to examine future career options. Check out where the jobs are, not just in the classifieds, but in the library, both by industry and geographical location. Is there something you'd rather pursue, something you'd really enjoy doing? You may be able to turn a negative into a positive, a distressing setback into a wonderful opportunity.

Guide to job-switching and career-changing:

Everybody feels job dissatisfaction from time to time. It takes more than that to justify walking away from employment, especially if you're making good money in not unpleasant circumstances.

How do you know if it's time, if you're ready, to make a big leap (and not just a lateral move)? Or should you even dare consider such a bold risk, during uncertain economic times?

Here are some questions that can help you weigh those hefty matters and hopefully reach that decision:

1. Is your present employment a dead-end, or the road to somewhere? Have others, hired when you were, done better or worse than you? If you've been caught in a trap for a long time, not only should you crave new horizons; you could have cause to worry about your present job security.

2. Are your marketable skills growing, or stultifying? List what new skills you added or improved in the last year or so? Are you working on a degree? Improving computer expertise? Making strides in a second language?

3. Is your present field rewarding? Or are you becoming a chronic complainer? If you answered "no" and then "yes," you should definitely consider some kind of employment shift, if only for your own morale and mental health.

Targeting a new career, of course, is a major undertaking, and can involve several factors, like working conditions, values and geography.

If you're not unhappy with your current specialty, perhaps you could just look to better of these important factors--the people you work with, your surroundings, work schedule. And often this can be accomplished by means of a simple departmental transfer, without throwing your whole life up into the air.

10-step winning strategy for job-hunters:

It's an old adage that the hardest work of all is looking for work. It's easy to burn up energy aimlessly wandering the city jungle, pouring through small- print classifieds, mailing out resumes, going on hit-or-miss interviews, and stewing in your own juices.

There's a better way, however. Any plan is better than no plan, and this 10-step program is a very sound way to pursue your job goal:

1. Assess your skills and abilities.
It's good to set your new goals high, but you need to also take practical inventory of your skills and interests. The ideal match is to find something you're good at and love to do.

So start making lists. What skills and talents do you have? What subjects did you excel at? What do you love, have a passion for? Now look at what you've done well.

The next trick is applying this list to a particular field or industry. Imagination can help you here, as well as a literal mind. Someone who loves sports and yet has an orderly and logical mind, and an ability to negotiate, may suddenly realize he or she is drawn toward a career as a sports agent.

More follow-up questions to ask yourself: What motivates you? What makes you comfortable, or uncomfortable? Would you be a self- starter if you opened your own business, or do you need a corporate wagon to ride in?

The more questions you ask, the better picture you'll develop of your skills and optimum career goals.

2. Explore your options.
Don't lock yourself into a narrow job band, at least not without exploring some alternative career paths. And take a

practical look at which industries and occupations are favorably placed to grow along with new technologies, especially those that mesh with your own goals.

If you're not sure if a particular industry suits you, talk to some people in it, or those knowledgeable about it, and ask them some questions. For instance, what do they like about their work, and what do they dislike? What kind of entry-level positions are there? Ask them to recommend one or more trade publications? Where do they think the industry is heading? Then ask them to recommend someone else for you to contact in the industry.

By doing this, you not only gather valuable information about the field, you establish yourself as someone eagerly interested in it. That word, as it spreads, can only benefit you if jobs open up.

3. Assemble a list of prospective employers.
Depending on the area you want to get into, your list could be as short as five or 10 companies, and as long as 100. Some of these firms will be known to you, others will be recommended, and many may come from industry directories. Before contacting them (step 5), rank each company according to how well it matches your preferred criteria.

The business section of your local library can point you to some of the standard company directories.

4. Do your homework.
When you do get an interview (see Step 9 below), you'll want to exhibit a familiarity with the company's products or services, and its position in the market. Unless you enjoy last-minute cramming, why not begin that research ahead of time? Review trade publications, then call any companies you're scouting and request brochures or media packets.

If you want to go further, send for the company's annual report, or look it up in the business section of your local or college library. The tone and style of this slickly packaged document will tell you volumes about the company's management style. Not only will this help in any subsequent interviews, it will also help you decide whether this firm is a place you really want to spend huge chunks of your life.

5. Write a resume.

There seem to be books about everything these days, even writing resumes. In fact, there are whole shelves full of such books. But you don't need to read them. Basically, there are just two standard formats for this piece of self-advertisement:

* The chronological resume: This lists your experience in date order, beginning with your current or most recent job. This works well if you've had impressive titles and steady upward mobility, with no gaps in your employment history.

Under each position, briefly list responsibilities, scope and job skills. Use action words like "created," "organized," "developed." Leave out salary information.

* The functional resume: This secondary model can conceal gaps in employment while highlighting experience and skills gained while participating in extracurricular activities or volunteer work. Employment dates and job titles can be omitted or listed briefly in chronological order lower down.

The functional resume is preferable for people wanting to change careers or those entering the job market for the first time.

Whichever you choose, your resume should be kept within two pages--one page is even better--and should conclude with a short section listing education (names of your college(s), degree(s) and graduation dates, plus professional credentials or awards. Omit personal information such as hobbies and travel.

Another form of the resume is the electronic one (see online job-hunting below). More and more large firms are accepting electronically e-mailed resumes and scanning in all hard-copy ones, so they can be sorted by keywords.

One advantage of this form is that you can have a longer resume, with room for more keywords. Make sure yours incorporates any skills or requirements requested in the want ad, including any industry buzzwords. Avoid odd type styles and fonts, which may cause problems to scanning software.

Another good tip is to take time to customize your resume for each new job opening, emphasizing experience and qualifications to suit.

What about those resume consultants who advertise in the Yellow Pages, offering to write a winning resume for $150 to $200? Forget them. A much better bet is to xerox your favorite resume models from one of those books in the library, then follow the models. Afterward, do ask friends or colleagues to critique and edit for typos, grammatical errors and misspellings, as well as for general effectiveness.

6. Send out resumes.

You may be tempted to do a mass mailing, but your impact will be much stronger if you target no more than 10 or 20 prospective employers, and tailor your cover letter to each one, attaching the resume.

Follow up the mailing with a phone call and request an interview even if there are no current job openings. Your interest and persistence will be noted--and remembered if employment opportunities appear later on.

If your prospective employer is in the media, it might be appropriate to send a videotape resume.

7. Make multiple applications.

Don't restrict your applications to classified employment ads in mainstream newspapers. The overwhelming majority of new jobs never appear in such ads. So you need a much broader-based outreach strategy.

Also look at trade journals and business-oriented publications. And don't neglect your college or university's alumni placement offices, as well as professional associations and job fairs.

Under more traditional categories of job search, you should include employment agencies, executive marketing or outplacement firms and recruiting firms. Many of these specialize in particular fields--perhaps yours--and top companies often rely on them to screen worthwhile candidates.

Hint: The most reputable firms will not require you to pay any upfront fees, but will charge an employer after you're hired.

Other job-hunting resources are online services, with constantly updated electronic databases of employment openings. A resume placed online can be viewed by a large number of employers, agencies and recruiters.

Finally, don't forget to stop by your local library and ask someone at the reference or research desk. And ask for the "Directory of Executive Recruiters" and the "Encyclopedia of Associations."

8. Network.

Think back about how you found previous jobs. Odds are that a happy chance played an occasional part, or someone knew someone else who knew of an immediate opening. This is why networking is so crucial. Your next job may come as a result of a tip from your sister-in-law's manicurist, or from your tennis coach, as well as well-placed industry source.

Spread your net as widely as possible. Tell everybody. Send each new contact a resume and cover letter, describing your career goals and companies you're interested in working for.

A systematic approach is to ask fifteen of your professional, school and personal contacts to give you the names of three people they know who work in a particular company, industry, occupation, or part of the country you're interested in.

And don't forget to check back with people periodically to see if anything may have opened up in the interval.

9. Interview.

One of the keys to creating a favorable impression is to exhibit knowledge about the job you're applying for, the company itself and the industry as a whole. This information is not hard to come by if you ask questions and do research. But it definitely impresses those who hire--if nothing else, it shows you took the trouble and had the interest. You'd be surprised at how many job candidates sit across the table and ask superficial questions, like what does your company do?

Other fundamental advice is to be well-dressed, polite, mannerly, composed, friendly, positive. For more guidance, check out some of the books on interviewing skills at the library.

10. Negotiate your salary.

Congratulations, you've got the job. It's tempting, after such a harrowing journey, to take whatever you're offered, rather than risk losing it, even if you know it's less than you're worth.

The best advice is to research the field, what comparable jobs are being paid, and also to formulate a negotiating strategy. If you can quantify the value you can bring to the company in real dollars, you'll have a stronger bargaining position.

An alternate strategy is to request an early performance review and subsequent salary. Whether or not it's granted, your new employer will respect your self-confidence in your future performance.

Final note: If the plan doesn't culminate in a job as quickly as you'd like, don't give up. Organized persistence will be rewarded. Research, send out resumes daily, keep networking, opening yourself to new possibilities.

Pound the pavements online:

More and more job-searchers are doing their prowling in cyberspace. That's because more and more companies now list employment opportunities on computer networks and accept resumes via computer. High-tech employment searches also involve videotapes, e-mail and diskettes, replacing or supplementing printed resumes.

Companies are also using computers in the hiring phase, screening online resumes for certain keywords that indicate desired skills, degrees and experience. Resume-scanning software is now used by more than 10 percent of the largest corporations.

Where can you post your resume? All the big online commercial services--CompuServe, American Online, Prodigy--offer posting areas and bulletin boards for exchanging messages with other job hunters. There are also online job banks on the Internet--Help Wanted USA maintains a bank of thousands of white-collar, mostly management jobs. CompuServe's E-Span job database has thousands of openings posted by employers seeking professional and managerial workers. Prodigy offers a smaller service, Online Classified, with hundreds of postings.

Tip: Keep your online resume brief and breezy. And if you don't have a PC, you can still benefit from cyberspace. Just mail your resume to one of the many database services that will try to match your skills with company want ads. One such service, Career Database Inc., (508-487-2238), will hold your resume and a 4-page career profile active for one year for $50.

What they can't ask you in an interview:

In 1994 the Equal Employment Opportunity Commission issued new guidelines on how to conduct job interviews without running afoul of federal disability discrimination laws. In general, any interview question may be illegal if used to discriminate or to judge a candidate in a manner that is not job related.

Here is quick layman's guide to some things you cannot legally be asked. If you feel an interviewer has discriminated against you, call the EEOC at 800-669-4000.

You **can't** be asked:
* to take any medical or psychological test before being offered a job.
* any follow-up questions about a particular disability, even if you volunteer that you took time off from a previous job because of that disability.
* about any addiction you may have.
* the results of tests you've taken to explore your honesty, taste, and habits.
* to take a blood pressure or other medical tests after a general fitness test.

Best ways to get a raise:

The days of hefty annual pay hikes ended with the go-go '80s. These days of corporate downsizing, you'll be lucky to stay even with the cost-of-living. And, unless you're married to the boss's daughter (or son), you can't expect a promotion or raise just for clocking in and out. You're going to have to call attention to yourself and your skills in order to convince management to give you more money.

Here are some proven strategies for doing just that, without hurting yourself in the process.

* First is the obvious point already made: you have to call attention to yourself. Which means you can't be shy, you have to let your boss know who you are, and claim credit for the good things you've done.
* Which leads to the second tactic, doing good things to claim credit for. Put another way, make yourself indispensable. Don't work with blinders on. Spread your talents around.

* Without being a showoff, convince your coworkers of your skills as well as your boss. You want them to support you, not stab you in the back.

* Don't make threats. Which means, don't threaten to quit if you don't get your raise. Your bluff may be called. You can, however, entertain legitimate offers from rival firms, and let that fact be known. It's a strong and standard negotiating tactic.

* Don't compare to a better-paid coworker. The obvious reply may be that your coworker is worth more than you.

* If you're in a dead-end or downsizing business, perhaps your best tactic is look for a better deal elsewhere--with a healthier company in a growing industry. Being the most valuable worker around won't help if the company is sinking.

Maximize your employee benefits:

Every year workers at most U.S. companies can re-evaluate their benefits. But too many fail to do so, or do so carefully. Sadly, most employees don't even know what their benefits are.

This is a big mistake. One key to smart financial planning is to learn about all your employee benefits. Here's what you may be missing:

1. Life and disability insurance: Before you buy life or disability insurance at work, figure how much you need. Even at good rates, unnecessary insurance is a waste of money. The rule of thumb for life insurance:

You need a death benefit equal to 2 to 5 times your annual income. The more small children you have, the greater your insurance needs. If you have a lot of assets, few debts and a working spouse, your need for life insurance is modest.

Determining disability insurance is a bit more complex because it comes in two varieties--long-term and short-term.

You may not need any short-term disability insurance, especially if you have a lot of vacation and sick time and your company automatically offers a short-term policy coordinated with the state program.

The Social Security Administration offers a long-term disability program for people severely disabled and unable to handle any job. Because it pays relatively modest maximum benefits, anyone with more than a poverty-level income would want to consider supplemental coverage--if they thought a long-term disability could leave them financially devastated. Most large companies offer a group plan but rarely subsidize it.

2. Paid time off: Many people take this benefit for granted. Don't underestimate its value. More and more part-time and temporary workers don't get any paid time off. Other companies have added a new twist--expiration dates on all days off, regardless of whether it's for vacation, illness or "personal." Other companies limit how many you can store. Pay attention to the rules, because unless you really hate vacations, you might as well enjoy whatever is offered.

"Use it or lose it" has become a big issue because vacation accrual can get very expensive for companies that allow it. If time off doesn't expire, it accrues--leaving companies with potentially vast unpaid liabilities.

Companies are also simplifying the paid-time-off system with something called time "banking" that eliminates the distinction between sick days and other kinds of time off. Instead of getting a set amount of each, workers get a lump sum--typically 23 to 33 days a year--to use however they like.

Most employers that offer time-off banking also allow workers to cash out unused days at either full or a percentage of their wage value. Accumulated days can serve as a short-term disability plan or an emergency fund in case you lose your job.

3. Health insurance: Rising medical costs make it crucial that workers carefully consider their health choices at work. Adding up a typical year's expenses can help sort out your real cost choices. Consider whether you want an HMO or greater options.

Reminder: Even if you choose an HMO, you can still see doctors outside the system and pay the costs yourself.

4. Tax savers: If you usually have unreimbursed medical expenses or pay child-care costs so that both you and your spouse can work, find out if your employer offers tax-saver accounts and use them if you can.

Tax-saver accounts come in two varieties--medical spending accounts and dependent care accounts. They allow you to save pretax money through employee with-holding, then use that money to pay these necessary expenses. Federal tax authorities act as if you've never earned the money, so the amount you save in these accounts can save you a fortune in tax.

Caution: Any money unused at the end of the year is lost. And, unless you've had a change in family status, you can't adjust your contribution midyear. A few months before the end of the plan year, check how much is left in the account.

If there's more remaining than you expect to spend, you can increase medical appointments or elect to fill your contact lens prescription early. And you can use tax savers for services not necessarily covered by insurance, such as chiropractors and acupuncturists.

5. Retirement plans: Assets in 401(k) plans--accounts that allow workers to save and invest their own money for retirement have quadrupled over the past decade, with more than $400 billion saved. But some people still choose not to contribute.

There's just no sensible reason not to contribute to a 401(k), even if you're already covered by another pension. The argument for contributing--as much as possible--is overwhelming.

Why? Traditional pension plans may not pay enough to make you comfortable in retirement, and they aren't portable. If you leave the company in less than five years, they usually evaporate completely. But your 401(k) goes with you. And they have other attractive features:

* Income tax savings: Contributions are taken out before tax. As far as the IRS is concerned, you never earned the money. (But unlike the tax-saver accounts, the money is taxed for Social Security and Medicare.)

* Employer match: Companies typically match worker contributions of up to 6% of salary.

* Access: The disadvantage to contributing to most types of retirement accounts is that you lose access to the money until you retire, unless you're willing to pay onerous tax penalties. However, many 401(k) plans have a borrowing option, which usually gives you the ability to borrow up to 50% of your account value to a maximum of $50,000, then pay yourself back at a reasonable rate of interest.

But the most compelling argument for contributing to the 401(k) is how fast your money grows. Thanks to contribution matching and tax breaks, many workers are shocked to find their accounts swelling into six figures.

12 steps to set up a business:

There's an increasing number would- be entrepreneurs among us. The temptation to punch your clock instead of XYZ's Corp.'s is pretty irresistible. Unfortunately, many of these hopeful attempts fall apart due to lack of organization or a practical business plan.

Here are ten tested steps to keep your new endeavor from becoming one more dismal statistic:

1. Settle on a basic business identity. What's your service or product? Is it new and unique, or have you come up with a new twist on an existing concept? There's nothing wrong with following in someone else's footsteps. Many successful businesses are improvements of someone else's.

2. Pick a name and logo. You can't effectively market your business without an identity. You want a name that is unique and catchy. Visualize the name on stationery and business cards. It shouldn't be complicated, just one or two syllables your customers can easily remember. A lot of "Copy Express" and "SuperCopy" shops have fallen by the wayside, while "Kinko's" was sweeping the country.

When you get your name, hire an attorney specializing in trademark protection to do a nationwide search--even if you're not thinking of going national. Then file the necessary applications to register it. (And if it ever goes international, you'll have to file trademark applications in every country in which you want to do business.)

3. Determine your break-even gross-dollar budget. How much do you have to make to keep going? To have an acceptable lifestyle? Don't forget to include costs of benefits and some administrative costs. Hint: Multiply your expected salary by 2.25 times to come up with an estimated gross dollar earnings figure.

4. Work up a business plan, at least a rough outline. Where would you like to be two months from now? In six months? In a year? Here are the basic you'll need to include:

* Table of contents.
* Brief overview, describing your company's products or services, and the market niche you intend to fill.
* Statement of purpose: why you believe your business will succeed.
* Biographical sketch of yourself and other key owners or managers. (Only needed if you want to attract investors.)
* Brief summary about your industry, target customer, business location, projected development schedule, sales and marketing plan, competition and what distinguishes your business from the competition.

* Long-term goals, pricing, distribution, growth strategy, marketing and sales strategies, evolution of product line, development schedule and planned growth.

* Financial statement and projection of expenses that details your budget, bottom line, fixed assets, cash flow projections, future plans for expansion, start-up costs, equipment costs, hiring schedule and overhead.

* Additional financing sources for credit or capital.

5. Future business projections. Where will you get new customers after your first phase is achieved? You need to spend some time daily thinking about new business, and ideally generating it. This may include cold or follow-up calls, letters or personal contacts.

6. Sketch in cost-efficient advertising and promotion. We're not talking big media campaigns. More likely a simple letter or press release about your business to local media. Or offer to talk about your company and specialty on radio talk shows. Send notes or memos to companies you deal with, or to those you wish to deal with, to see how you can be of further assistance. You want to get your name out there, as widely as possible.

7. Install basic business accounting and finances. You'll need a business checking account and a separate savings account to accumulate money for all taxes. Advisable: a company credit line. This will give you more stability and recognition. A business credit card is another must. A good idea--even if you think you can't afford it--is hiring a trustworthy accountant who specializes in independent and small businesses.

8. Think about your image. Even if working out of your home, you'll need a business wardrobe for in-person meetings to make a favorable impression.

9. Obtain all necessary business licenses. Check with your local chamber of commerce, county clerk and the local office of the Small Business Administration. Requirements differ for states, counties and cities. Don't leave any jurisdictions uncovered.

10. Buy basic business equipment. A phone-answering machine and a computer are musts. A fax and copy machine are next in line. A separate business-only phone line will not only help, but establish a home-office tax writeoff.

11. Talk to an insurance broker about a basic business coverage. This should include a general umbrella policy to cover your whole operation--liability and property insurance. State regulatory requirements vary. Contact your local chamber of commerce or the small-business office in your city for assistance. And don't forget your own employee benefit package--which means opening an IRA or Keogh account.

12. If you have a spouse and children, you'll need to sit down and talk about the sacrifices that will be required. You're going to need to tackle it as a team, with everyone's support.

What you need to know before buying a franchise:

Conventional wisdom holds that franchising is a low-risk way to start a business. For a hefty investment--up to $600,000 or more for a McDonald's, for example--you get all the training and marketing support you need. Then you just manage your business and collect the revenues.

Unfortunately, that's not exactly the way it shakes out. According to recent tracking studies, 35 percent of new franchises fail, compared with 28 percent of conventional start-ups. Franchisees whose companies survived earned less than $15,000 a year, compared with more than $25,000 for other start-ups.

And yet, franchises average annual sales of more than $500,000, compared to just over $100,000 for non-franchises. They are also better capitalized ($85,000 compared to $30,000). There are three possible reasons for this seeming contradiction:

For one thing, franchisees may be picking already saturated markets, or at least areas with tough competition. For another, perhaps franchisees aren't getting the much-touted management advice and support they need. A final reason: franchisees are less likely to take as many risks of self-starters.

That doesn't mean you should avoid the franchise phenomenon. After all, nearly two-thirds of franchises do survive. But you should practice the old buyer-beware caution. The best way to be fully informed is to contact the Federal Trade Commission (202- 326-2161), which offers a free packet of information that includes the pros and cons of franchising and explanations of information that franchisors are required to disclose by law.

Another good source for future franchisees: The International Franchise Association (202-628-8000).

Tip sheet
for small-biz owners and home-office workers:

There have never been more affordable resources for small-business owners. Hundreds of books, magazines, software programs, seminars, classes and organizations are waiting to lend a hand and valuable expertise.

If you don't belong to a professional society or trade association, join the group that best fits your needs and register to attend the next industry trade show. If you hate meetings, subscribe to the organization's newsletter or magazine.

And most successful entrepreneurs are generous with their time and love to share war stories. A quick cup of coffee or a monthly phone call may be all a busy person can spare. But a veteran business owner can steer you around the biggest potholes.

You can also join a national association such as National Small Business United, the National Federation for Independent Business, the National Assn. for the Self-Employed, Women Inc. or the National Assn. of Women Business Owners. Attend a Chamber of Commerce mixer. Sign up for free counseling at the Small Business Administration's Service Corps of Retired Executives.

Here's a quick resource list:
Organizations:
* The SBA Answer Desk can point you in the right direction for help: (800) 827-5722.
* National Small Business United, a 60,000-member, grass-roots political advocacy group, publishes a great fax newsletter on government issues: (800) 345-NSBU.
* National Federation for Independent Business, the nation's largest small-business organization, with 600,000 members: (800) 634-2669.
* National Assn. for the Self-Employed: (800) 232-6273.
* National Assn. of Women Business Owners: (301) 608-2590.
* Women in Franchising: (800) 222-4943.
* American Business Women's Assn.: (816) 361-6621.
* Women Inc.: (800) 930-3993.
* American Franchise Assn.: (312) 431-0545.
* U.S. Chamber of Commerce: (202) 463-5600.
* Small Business Foundation of America, Export Opportunity Hotline: (800) 243-7232.

Magazines:
* Home Office Computing is an easy-to-read, all-around management guide for small-business owners.
* The U.S. Chamber of Commerce's Nation's Business provides nuts-and-bolts management help for entrepreneurs.
* Entrepreneur magazine is another valuable publication. A revived entry into the magazine market is Entrepreneurial Edge.
* BusinessWeek, Forbes and Fortune are geared toward the corporate world but feature news and trends of interest to small-business owners.

* Success and Inc. are also filled with helpful, inspirational information.

Television:
* CNBC's "How to Succeed in Business," airing Saturday and Sunday mornings, provides lively how-to advice for small-business owners. "Bloomberg Small Business," with its news magazine format, airs Saturday morning on the USA Network.

Radio:
* Home Office Computing contributing editors and monthly columnists Paul and Sarah Edwards cohost the "Home Office Show" on the Business Radio Network each Sunday from 10 to 11 p.m. (Eastern Time). They discuss business opportunities, technology and marketing as well as a host of other important topics relevant to running your business. For more information, call 719-528-7040.

Interns:
* A great source of low-cost help are student interns. Colleges provide opportunities for students to do market research and other projects for business owners.

Books:
On Starting a Business:
* "The New Venture Handbook," by Ronald E. Merrill, $18.95, Amacom.
* "999 Successful Little Known Businesses," by William Carruthers, $15 plus $3 shipping, J.J. Publications. (A quirky book filled with offbeat ideas.)
* "Your New Business," by Charles L. Martin, $15.95, Crisp Publications.
* "Getting Into Business Series" (four volumes), by Dan Kennedy, $29.95, Self-Counsel Press. (Self-Counsel Press has dozens of lively, practical books for business owners.)

On Home-Based Businesses:
* "The Joy of Working From Home," by Jeff Berner, $12.95, Berrett-Koehler Publishers.

* "Working From Home", by Paul and Sarah Edwards, $15.95, the Putnam Berkley Group.

On Getting Organized:
* "Organizing Your Home Office for Success," by Lisa Kanarek, $10, Plume/Penguin Books.
* "You Can Find More Time For Yourself Every Day," by Stephanie Culp, $12.99, Betterway Books.

On Marketing:
* "Guerrilla Marketing Online," by Jay C. Levinson, $12.95, Houghton Mifflin Co.
* "Buying Creative Services," by Bobbi Balderman, $39.95, NTC Publishing.
* "CyberMarketing," by Len Keeler, $24.95, Amacom.

On Financing:
* "Romancing the Business Loan," by Gary Goldstick, $19.95, Lexington Books.
* "Banking Smarter," by Dennis Suchocki, $9.95, BCS & Associates.

On Customer Service:
* "Sustaining Knock Your Socks Off Service," by Thomas Connellan and Ron Zemke, $17.95, Amacom.
* "Crowning the Customer," by Feargal Quinn, $19.95, Acropolis Books Ltd..
* "Customers as Partners," by Chip R. Bell, $24.95, Berrett-Koehler Publishers.

On Retailing:
* "1,001 Ideas to Create Retail Excitement," by Edgar Falk, $19.95, Prentice Hall.
* "Up Against the Wal-Marts," by Taylor/Archer, $21.95, Amacom.

Home-based Work
If you're thinking about working at home, Home Office Computing magazine, an essential resource for home-based workers, has ranked the best U.S. cities for that status.

The rankings are based on proximity to a strong economic community, a positive business environment and reasonable taxes. Gaithersburg, Md., topped the list, followed by Phoenix; Austin, Tex.; Atlanta; Portland, Ore.; Boulder, Colo.; Kansas City, Mo.; Minneapolis-St.Paul, Minn.; Pittsburgh, and St. Petersburg, Fla.

Tips for working at home:
* Set a regular working schedule and ask your family and friends to respect your hours.
* To appear more professional, order a separate phone line for your fax machine and leave the fax on 24 hours a day.
* If your office is in your home, keep children and pets out of your office when you are on the phone.
* To combat isolation, have lunch at least once a week with a client or colleague.
* Boost your productivity by taking advantage of low prices to buy more computers and home office equipment.

Can you afford to work less?:

More and more people (mostly women but a surprising number of men as well) are opting out of the full-time rat race and looking for part-time work to better balance career with the needs of family.

While the decision to work less is often personally rewarding, it's tough financially. Dropping back to part-time work not only cuts take-home pay, it pares--or eliminates--valuable benefits, such as medical coverage and life and disability insurance. It may also have long-term repercussions--such as lowering the employee's eventual Social Security benefit or the amount saved toward retirement. Determining exactly how much shifting to part-time work will cost is not simple.

There are no standard formulas for part-time professional work. Usually part-time arrangements are worked out case by case, usually with the employee making a detailed proposal and the employer accepting, rejecting or modifying it. Some who go part-time lose nothing but a portion of their pay; others lose benefits and promotion opportunities as well.

The onus is on the workers to determine what they want, what they're willing to give up and what they must retain in order to afford the part-time arrangement.

On average, how much you lose in employee benefits is largely determined by how many hours you will work.

For example, 76% of the companies surveyed maintained medical insurance for employees working 30 or more hours a week, but only 62% provided that benefit to those working 20 to 29 hours weekly. Just 25% offered it to those working fewer than 20 hours a week.

It's worth noting that many people can afford to lose some benefits. Two-income married couples, for example, often have overlapping medical coverage through their jobs. If one spouse loses that coverage, it won't hurt an intact family.

However, some families, as well as individuals and unmarried couples, will need the benefits that are put at risk by the part-time arrangement. In these cases, you must consider what the benefit would cost if you were to buy it independently--and whether you would be able to buy it at all. The issues concerning salary and retirement are far more straight forward.

Typically, employers will cut a professional's pay in direct relation to the proposed decrease in hours. Someone who wanted to scale back to 20 hours from 40 would see a 50% drop in pay, while a worker who shaved 10 hours off a 40-hour schedule would face a 25% pay cut.

Retirement contributions--and Social Security benefits--are also directly related to earnings. Workers should anticipate that their retirement income will fall with their income. However, if a part-time work arrangement is temporary, you're likely to be able to make up the loss over time.

Most employee pension plans fall into one of two categories: defined benefit plans and defined contribution plans. With defined benefit plans, your employer promises a set benefit at retirement that's based on your wages and years of service. Typically, if you retire or leave the job after you have become vested, your retirement stipend will equal a set percentage of your earnings over the last three to five years.

If you have been working an abbreviated schedule in one or all of those years, your retirement stipend obviously will be significantly smaller. If you go back to a full-time arrangement before you retire, the part-time years will hurt you less, but they're still likely to have an impact. In effect, they're likely to reduce your years of service counted in calculating your benefit. If you worked 20 hours a week in a company where 40 hours is the norm, for example, it may take you 20 years to accumulate the pension equivalent of 10 years of service. Not all plans work this way, but many do.

Meanwhile, the Social Security Administration will provide you with a fairly good estimate of how a part-time arrangement could affect your future Social Security payments. It's worth mentioning that couples married longer than 10 years have a floor on the amount of that impact. That's because the "stay-at-home spouse" can claim either the benefit he or she earned or 50% of the other spouse's benefit--whichever is higher. In some cases, 50% of the full-time spouse's benefit amounts to substantially more than what a part-time wage earner could draw.

If you wish to have the Social Security Administration estimate your future Social Security benefits, call (800) 772-1213. You'll be sent a form SSA-7004, which you fill out and return.

Are you suited to be your own boss?:

What type of person or personality is best suited to go into business for himself or herself? One way to discover this is to analyze those who have already taken the step. Such studies have been done, and have found that those who hang out their own shingle are most likely to be:

* Immigrants or children of immigrants.
* Previously employed in business of fewer than 100 employees.
* The oldest child in a family.
* College graduates.
* Children of self-employed parents.
* Previously fired from more than one job.
* Realistic, but not high risk-takers.
* Well-organized.

Getting the most from a temp agency:

Whether between jobs, fresh from college or looking for supplemental income, signing up with a temporary-employment firm is one of the fastest ways to get work. But how do you get the best assignments--and quickly? How do you make the most money? How can you turn a temporary job into a permanent one, if that's what you want?

There are no set rules, but specialists agree that some basic guidelines will boost your chances for success.

First, know the limits of temping. It usually won't provide you with job security or full health care benefits. You could get stuck doing all of the onerous tasks left by permanent employees, and you may have to deal with misperceptions or prejudices about temps.

But temping gives you more personal flexibility, an inside view of many industries and companies, a weekly paycheck and generally less stress.

Once you're ready to get started, here's what experts suggest:

* Decide whether a specialty or general temporary service is better for you. Some temp firms specialize in data processing, accounting, technical, legal and medical assignments. With these you are more likely to be placed in jobs that utilize your best skills and get higher pay rates.

If you're not sure about your skills, or just want to get a wide range of experiences, a general temporary service would be more appropriate.

* Investigate before you select a temp firm. One of the best ways to scout out temporary agencies is to ask other temps, who can tell you about how they're treated and the assignments they get, how quickly and for how much. You might also screen each service over the phone, taking note of such things as: How is the phone answered? Do you feel like you're being treated as a valued customer? Drop into the offices unannounced and observe how the offices are managed.

* Register with several agencies simultaneously. If you've never temped at all, start out with at least three to four. That broadens your horizon and is an accepted practice in the temp world, so don't be afraid to be up front about it with your temp counselors.

* Are fringe benefits important to you? While full health care benefits and sick pay are rarely provided, many firms offer vacation and holiday pay, and bonuses for attendance, performance and referrals.

There is no industry standard, and eligibility requirements for benefits vary widely from one company to the next. So shop for the agencies with the best benefits and the easiest eligibility terms.

* Call for an interview and make the most of it. During the interview, ask questions, including: What are the industries you serve and some of your client companies? What are your benefits and bonuses? What is your policy if I accept a permanent job from a client?

* Be available and reachable. Many temporary services have a window of only a few hours to fill an assignment, so if they can't reach you, they'll offer the job to someone else.

* Be flexible. Temp jobs are supposed to give you flexibility. But in order to make temping work effective, you need to be flexible, too. That means not being too rigid in terms of pay or job assignments.

* Strive toward your ultimate goal. If you want a permanent job, use your temporary assignments toward that end. Ask your temp firms for assignments that specify temp-to-perm opportunities. Take advantage of any free training provided by the temporary services, and learn new skills in your jobs. Get complimentary letters when you finish an assignment.

How part-timers can negotiate a benefit package:

One of the biggest drawbacks of working part time is the possible loss of valuable benefits. Part-timers face a dilemma: They gain control and flexibility, but still have to pay the doctor and dentist.

More employers are understanding the advantages of part-time employment. But the sad fact is that most part-time workers still don't have benefits. They just haven't caught up with the 23 million Americans--about 19% of the work force--who work part time. Benefits are largely determined by how many hours an employee works. According to a 1994 survey by Hewitt Associates, a benefits consulting firm, only 28% of employees working fewer than 20 hours a week received paid sick leave, whereas 57% of those working 20 to 29 hours earned the same benefit.

Statutory benefits--Social Security, Medicare, unemployment insurance and workers' compensation--must be paid to all employees, regardless of the number of hours worked.

Supplemental benefits--such as insurance, retirement plans and financial assistance programs--are offered at the employer's discretion. But if an employer provides a retirement plan, it may not exclude eligible part-timers. Under the Employee Retirement Income Security Act, coverage must be provided to all employees 21 or older, with one year of service, who work a minimum of 1,000 hours a year.

Compensatory benefits--paid leaves for vacation, illness, holidays, maternity and paternity--are also the prerogative of the employer. The 1993 Family and Medical Leave Act provides up to 12 weeks of unpaid leave after the birth or adoption of a child, to care for a seriously ill child, spouse, or parent or to recover from one's own serious illness.

But employers can exclude employees who have not worked at least one year and have worked fewer than 1,250 hours in the previous 12 months.

While many firms are shifting work to part-time employees precisely to avoid paying benefits, some have instituted part-time benefits policies as an incentive to keep workers productive.

However, most part-time employees find themselves on their own, having to negotiate for the best benefits package they can get. People often feel grateful for the opportunity to work part time and are hesitant to rock the boat and ask for benefits.

But the fact is, benefits are part of your total compensation and need to be negotiated at the outset. If you don't, it's very hard to go back and renegotiate for them. Here are some practical negotiating tips:

* Determine ahead of time which benefits are essential and what the added costs will be if they are not provided.

* Study the company's benefits policy to learn exactly which items are fair game during negotiations.

* In the absence of a clear-cut corporate policy, find out if any part-time co-workers have managed to retain their benefits. Without such a precedent, bargain for insurance coverage, paid leaves and retirement plans separately.

You can try to negotiate a pay raise to compensate for any loss in benefits. But if that doesn't work, and it seldom does, you may need to go outside to secure those benefits. If you are changing jobs, you need that benefit information to negotiate a new salary. If you are going out on your own, you need to include the added cost of benefits in pricing your own services.

And put your proposals in writing. Some people are visual and won't really hear you until they see the proposal written down. In addition to helping you make your case, writing down responsibilities and desired salary and benefits helps clarify expectations and establishes a basis for evaluating your work.

Timing is everything. You're taking your chances if you nab your boss in the hall and suggest a part-time schedule and benefits. Assess your boss's attitude, the office climate and political environment. The perfect time to submit a business proposal is not in the midst of a merger or acquisition, but after a big successful project when everyone is basking in the glory.

When benefit negotiations fail, part-time employees can seek other insurance options. Some HMOs, such as Health Net, have started offering medical coverage for part-time workers. A number of professional and fraternal organizations like the National Organization for Women, the National Assn. of Women Business Owners, the American Assn. of Retired Persons and Kiwanis and Soroptimist clubs, make group rates available to members.

Even though you may no longer be an actor or a carpenter, for example, you may still be able to reactivate membership in unions or guilds that you belonged to at another time in your life. Health coverage is also available through many churches and alumni organizations. People who go back to school for retraining can also receive health insurance.

Managers often lose another type of benefit: "perks" like window offices, executive dining room privileges and preferred parking spaces. Experts suggest discussing perquisites after the more substantive issues have been agreed upon.

NOTES

_____
_____
_____
_____
_____
_____
_____
_____
_____
_____
_____
_____
_____
_____

Chapter

Consumer Saving

23

Top 10 car-buying mistakes:

There are a lot of wrong ways to go about car-shopping. Unfortunately most of us commit them, to the glee of auto dealers.

It's not too late to repent of our victimhood. Here are the key mistakes to avoid next time out:

1. Not knowing the dealer's price

This is the last thing a dealer wants you to know--his actual cost. Yet it should be the starting point of any price negotiation. Most often, that cost bears no relation to the sticker price on the window.

How do you learn the dealer's price? There are two prime sources: The Kelly Blue Book or a service, such as Consumer Reports' New Car Price Service.

The Blue Book is comprehensive and can be found in any public library. You can check the invoice prices of several cars at once--for free. The Consumer Reports service, on the other hand, costs about $10 a car. (The price drops if you order reports on several cars.)

This service also offers tips on dealing with the dealers and information on factory rebates. These rebates, which can range from a few hundred dollars to several thousand, in effect lower the dealer's cost below his invoice price. The Consumer Reports package also includes information about the costs and advisability of various factory options and option packages. The service can be reached at (800) 933-5555.

A number of organizations, such as auto clubs and credit unions, offer similar services, but they may be available only to members.

There's a final source for getting an MSRP and/or a dealer's invoice costs--online services. (See item below)

2. Getting pushed into a lease
A lease is great for someone who drives only late-model cars, doesn't drive a lot and is good at math. If you drive cars until they expire, drive more than 15,000 miles a year and don't have a present-value calculator--or a clue as to how one works--leasing could cost you a fortune.

And leasing companies often require you to buy high-coverage auto insurance, which can add hundreds of dollars to the annual cost of the car.

If you plan to buy, don't get sidetracked into a lease. If you plan to lease, brush up on your algebra. You'll need it. For more information, see item after next: "Painless, Dealer-Free CarShopping."

3. Negotiating car price and financing in one package
Most of us--unless we have a wheelbarrow full of cash--need to finance the car, either through the dealer or a financial institution. Shopping for auto loan rates isn't hard, but sadly many people fail to do it before they car-shop.

Result: they get taken to the cleaners. The dealer promises to drop the sticker price and give them a lower monthly payment by extending the contract. The dealer skips over the loan rate, which is higher than the buyer could get elsewhere with his or her credit rating.

Don't fall for this flim-flam. Shop for the car you want at the best price, but shop for your financing elsewhere. Wrapping them together can obscure the price of one or the other, and that can cost you.

4. Shopping in the showroom
It's fine to visit dealerships and look at new models of your favorite make. But that's not the best way.

You should first check out Consumer Reports' current car-buying issue or its annual Car Buying Guide, both available in public libraries. And while you're in the library, consult newspaper files or on-line services for articles reporting J.D. Power's customer satisfaction ratings for various makes and models.

This will show you which makes and models have good track records, reasonable repair and maintenance costs and hold up well in a crash. Your research will also help you decide what kind of car you really need.

After you choose a few likely models is the time to head to the showroom for a test drive.

5. Falling in love with a car
Sales sharks can see that desire in your eye for a shiny hunk of metal. And they'll make you pay for it.

They'll flatter your taste, tell you you'd look great in the car, how it will upgrade your image--even your sex life.

That's the time to walk away. Off the lot. Think it over. Let your passion cool. If you don't trust yourself, take along a friend and make him promise to pull you away.

6. Forgetting insurance costs

Don't forget what it will cost to insure those new wheels-- and how much more for an expensive model. It can be a lot--a thousand dollars or more--depending on your age and driving record. If you are young with a bad driving history or poor grades, the difference can be a lot more.

And in case of car leases, the leasing company may require more insurance, with lower deductibles. Companies don't want to take the chance you'll get in an accident and not have the money to pay for repairs.

That higher coverage will cost more. You could spend $200 to $1,000 more on insurance each year if you lease rather than buy.

7. Buying off the lot

Car dealers will pressure you to buy right off the lot. This reduces their inventory, which cuts their costs. And immediate sales mean an immediate commission.

But buying off the lot is usually not a good idea for you. You probably will not find the exact car you want in the right color with the right options. You can have missing options added, but the warranty may not cover a dealer-added option. And you'll have to pay for all options--even those you didn't really want.

If you don't see what you want, go elsewhere--or order it.

8. Getting a car "fully loaded"

The cost of a car can rise as much as 50% when "fully loaded" over a stripped-down model.

options--automatic transmission, for example, or three-point seat restraints--are well worth it for reasons of safety, resale value and insurance costs.

But upgraded sound systems, special seats, alloy wheels, tinted glass and special coatings on the paint or seats usually don't pay off.

Best bet: make a list of options you really want and things you'd add on only if the price is right. Then stick to the list.

9. Buying extended warranties

Cars should come with a good factory warranty that will fix free anything that goes wrong during the first year or two.

Extended warranties, which cost $200 a year or more, are usually a waste of money. They usually cover things that statistically don't go wrong. They force you to get service at a particular location. They often become invalid if you fail to maintain regular maintenance. And if the company that provided the warranty disappears or goes bankrupt, there are few, if any, ways to enforce the contract.

10. Forgetting the mechanical check

A new car doesn't need a mechanical check because it comes with a warranty. But all used cars need to be checked. You can't trust the seller's assurances that the car is in good condition. They are routinely "doctored" for a quick sale in ways that a good mechanic can detect in a flash.

Another trick with used cars is odometer tampering-- when the mileage meter is turned back to indicate the car has been driven, say, 40,000 miles when the real mileage is approaching 100,000.

Odometer tampering can be hard to detect, but a good mechanic can give you an estimate as to how accurate the reading seems to be.

Lowdown on auto leasing:

One of the biggest draws in auto leasing is that monthly payments tend to be lower than those for a purchase. But consumers don't build up equity with their monthly lease payments--they're essentially renting the car for the term of the contract. At the end of the lease period--typically between 24 and 48 months--they either buy the car or turn it in.

Many consumers simply don't realize how much a lease differs from a purchase. As a result, they find themselves paying too much for a car--or facing steep charges at the end of the lease that they had not anticipated.

This amounts to a scam: Shoppers are lured in with promise of low monthly payments but find it's impossible to compare the cost of buying outright to leasing.

Tips: Look before you lease and concentrate on the contract, which can be loaded with hidden charges; (such as "excess wear and tear"); remember that low monthly payments almost always mean a high payment at one end of the lease.

And look for other restrictions in the lease contract. For example, the contract usually allows you to drive between 12,000 and 15,000 miles per year. You're charged for any additional miles at a rate of, for example, 15 cents per mile. In other words, if your two-year lease allowed for 30,000 miles and you drove 35,000 miles, you would owe $750 in mileage charges at the end of the lease period.

Or, if you want to get out of the lease in less time than the contract states, you can expect to be on the hook for an early-termination fee that can amount to as much as the total remaining payments left under the lease contract.

Nevertheless, leases can be advantageous for people who like to drive late-model cars and who rarely drive great distances.

And now that auto companies are finally responding to pressure to simplify leasing contracts, consumers have a better chance of negotiating a reasonable deal.

Consumer Checklist: What you should know before leasing:

* Total cost of the car--i.e., the manufacturer's suggested retail price plus the price paid for any optional equipment like power steering, air conditioning and tape decks.

* Acquisition fees and other upfront costs, such as security deposit, taxes and license fees. In some cases, you'll also make a down payment--often termed "capitalized cost reduction"--which serves to lower monthly payments.

* Financing cost: Because you're not buying, borrowing costs are called something else--often "money factor" or "lease factor." It's not an annual percentage rate, but you should demand that it be translated into one.

* Residual value: This is the car's estimated value at the end of the lease term. In a closed-end lease, it can also be the amount you'd have to pay to purchase the car at the end of the lease term.

* Monthly payments: The amount you pay each month to lease the car.

Painless, dealer-free car shopping:

Do you rank buying a car from a high-pressure dealer in the same "fun" category as going to the dentist or shopping for funeral services? Don't worry. You're in the overwhelming majority.

Everybody hates those obnoxious, high-pressure showroom tactics, and the follow-up torture-sessions in the sales manager's office when you're given one of those undecipherable, take-it-or-leave-it offers.

Get ready for good news. You can stay away from those lots. There are alternatives, more and more of them every day--high- tech, painless, even buyer-friendly, finally reinventing the ways cars are peddled.

You can take your pick from:
1. Auto superstores (for both new and used), and;
2. Online auto information providers and retailers.

Auto Superstores

These are what might be called Wal-Mart-like vehicle super-centers, where all the new makes and models-- Fords, Hondas, Chevys--are displayed side by side like TV's at an electronics outlet. Consumers will find these high-tech showcases arguably easier, faster and more pleasant than traditional brand dealerships.

Currently leading the superstore revolution:

* CarMax. Circuit City, a Richmond-based retailer of electronics and appliances, has 375 super-stores nation-wide. It has now moved into the car market. In October 1993, Circuit City opened its first CarMax superstore in Richmond. It has since opened several more outlets.

CarMax has borrowed ideas from Saturn Corp., GM's highly touted small-car division, but pushed the concept further. It offers customers a state-of-the-art, touch-screen computer system that allows them to search its huge inventory by price, make and other parameters, allowing them to compare brands side by side.

It also offers a large selection--500 to 1,000 vehicles, or up to 10 times the number carried by other dealers.

CarMax does not negotiate price. It mostly carries vehicles less than 5 years old with fewer than 70,000 miles. All cars are inspected and given a 30-day warranty. Buyers also can obtain financing and insurance quickly. In independent surveys, CarMax gets remarkably high customer satisfaction ratings.

CarMax is moving into new cars, and has been granted a new-car franchise by Chrysler. It is the first dealership awarded by a major U.S. auto maker to a giant, publicly owned retailer.

* AutoNation USA. This new superstore entrant is opening stores in Florida and Texas and is looking for possible expansion into the nation's 25 top metro areas.

AutoNation's chief backers are two wealthy entrepreneurs: H. Wayne Huizenga, the Florida pro-sports magnate who built Blockbuster Entertainment, and Jim Moran, the nation's largest Toyota distributor.

* United Auto Group Inc., another megadealer financial group, has become one of the nation's largest dealership operators. It now owns 41 dealerships and has annual revenues of more than $1 billion.

Car Shopping in Cyberspace
For the computer types among us, on-line services are not only a good source of information about car shopping, increasingly they are getting into selling and leasing.

Here's a quick tour of electronic showrooms.

* Auto-By-Tel, a California auto information service, has lined up a nationwide network of dealers willing to quote prices and sell cars on the Internet. Dealers fielded 50,000 requests in the first nine months, completing a sale 70% of the time, according to Auto-by-Tel's president.
You can purchase or lease directly from a subscribing Auto- By-Tel dealer near you. There is no charge to use the Auto-By-Tel, no fees to pay, no clubs to join. And Auto-By-Tel claims dealers do not mark up vehicles prices. Customers get the ABT Dealer's Wholesale Price on a vehicle up front. Auto-By-Tel charges dealers a low annual subscription fee and a lower monthly fee to be marketed on our service. And dealers save on sales commissions as well as on inventory costs, interest and storage fees.

Leasing: Auto-By-Tel dealers will give you wholesale price on a lease as well as purchase.

Financing: Subscribing dealers will finance new vehicles at wholesale rates (on approved credit), generally no more than 1/2 point above the subscribing dealer's cost of money.

But Auto-By-Tel is not an information provider or shopping service to get pricing on multiple vehicles. It will only accept a request for the one vehicle you decide to purchase. And the company does not deal in used cars.

How to contact: Auto-By-Tel is available on the Internet (http://www.autobytel.com), as well as on America On-Line, CompuServe and Prodigy.

* AutoNet, also available on CompuServe, Prodigy and AOL, offers up-to-date dealer cost and specifications on almost any car for $4 per report. The information you request is downloaded into your personal computer, with the fee charged to your online account.

New vehicle reports include information on warranty, specs, standard features, optional equipment with MSRP & dealer invoice.

Used car information includes book value of the car you're looking to buy as well as book value for your 1984-1995 vehicle. Company also offers a guidebook on buying and selling a used car.

* AutoVantage provides a comparable service. Memberships are available for $49 a year; non-members can order a report for $11. AutoVantage accepts Visa and MasterCard only and will not bill your online account.

For further information, check out AutoVantage on CompuServe, Prodigy or AOL, or call (800) 843-7777.

* Auto Info Center
This is available only CompuServe. For $14.95, you get:

1. A list of over 50 buying services.
2. Free, a printout of dealer cost on the car of your choice. List of buying service contacts and free report will be delivered via CompuServe Mail within 24 hours of order.

Also available: valuation reports for used cars from 1970-1992, providing the current wholesale and retail market price ranges and including adjustments for major optional accessories and information about the normal mileage for the car.

These reports cost $5.95 each, and are also delivered by CompuServe Mail within 24 hours of the order. You can also get a Buyer's Guide, with tips and information on: How to check out a used car before you buy; how to determine how much you should pay for the car; how to deal with car dealers; how to buy from private parties; helpful information sources.

Used-car buying checklist:

It's not just blind bad luck if you buy a used car that turns into a lemon instead of a peach. There are certain things you absolutely must check.

If you don't trust your own automotive expertise, then by all means give your mechanic $50 to check out the car for you. It's a sound investment. Ask him to drive the car, put it up on a rack to inspect the underbelly, check engine compression, test electrical systems and emission levels.

If you go back to the seller with a written estimate for needed repairs, you'll have improved your bargaining position, if nothing else. (If you don't have a mechanic you trust, look up an auto diagnostic center in the Yellow Pages).

But whether it's you or a mechanic doing the diagnosis, here is a handy checklist:

1. FLUIDS. If there are any problems with seals, there'll be oil spots on the ground. Be sure to look for leaks around the seals in the rear end, and underneath for stains. Also look for oil residue on the block, hoses or elsewhere in the engine compartment.

2. BODY CONDITION. Rust, especially in the rocker panels under the doors, in the trunk or around the wheels, is bad news. If paint is blistered, rust underneath could be the cause. Check the underbody for fresh welds--a dead giveaway of a major accident.

Other possible accident evidence: new undercoating on an old car, uneven or differently colored bodywork. Also check for sheet metal with visible imperfections--doors that don't quite fit and welds that have been redone.

3. TIRES AND WHEELS. If the wear is wavy or uneven with high and low spots in the tires, you have bad shocks, which need to be looked at. If you have wear on the sides, you have front-alignment problems.

Bounce the car by pushing down each corner. If the car keeps bouncing, you'll need to replace shocks or struts. If a front tire can be noticeably lifted by pulling on the top of the tire with both hands, you may have bad bearings or suspension joints.

Original tires should be good for 25,000 miles. A car with lower mileage but new tires may have had its odometer wound back. Also check tires for mismatched brands.

Front and rear wheels should be in line. Have someone check this from behind. A car that veers to the side may only need a wheel alignment, but may have a bent frame. Get a mechanic's opinion.

4. SUSPENSION AND RIDE. Look for rust around all suspension parts. A lot of old cars rust at the top mounting plates from the top of the shocks--especially in the front, where it's evident once you lift the hood and look past the engine at the plates. The struts may actually push through the metal.

Getting bounced around badly may indicate a need for suspension work. Other problem indicators: excessive sway and ominous noises over bumps.

5. INTERIOR. If the vinyl or any part of the interior console is cracked, you can be sure it's been outside a lot. Also, resale value as well as comfort will be affected by seats and carpets that look shabby or smell musty. And beware of worn-down pedals when the odometer shows low mileage. The car may be more used than advertised. Are seatbelts in good working order?

Check the trunk for lid alignment, make sure the spare, jack and lug wrench are present, and that the wrench fits the lug nuts.

6. UNDER THE HOOD. If engine is cold, open the radiator cap. Coolant shouldn't be rusty. A shiny film on the water may indicate oil. Fire up the engine and check the transmission dipstick. Fluid shouldn't smell burned or contain particles of metal. Transmission fluid should be pink.

Check the battery's cleanliness and charge level. Look for wear and cracks in hoses and belts. Check air filter for cleanliness. Oil and fuel filters shouldn't look too old. Is wiring complete, unfrayed, with tight connections?

7. STEERING. You can check this to some extent even before turning the key. Too much play shows a lot of hard wear and indicates the steering system will probably need to be replaced. If there are two inches of play and the tires aren't turning, watch out--the problems go beyond the steering system.

8. EXHAUST. A car that has high mileage is going to show a lot of rust in the exhaust system. You don't want to get an exhaust system that has been spot-welded. The muffler might not leak while you're test-driving it, but a couple miles down the road, it could just fall off.

The best way to check for a rusted-out muffler is to get underneath the car and grab the muffler. When exhaust systems start to go, you can actually crush them with your hands.

More obvious: A tailpipe belching blue smoke means an oil burner. Excess white exhaust clouds are another bad smoke signal-- water in the engine.

9. ENGINE. The car should start and accelerate smoothly. Pings and knocks may or may not be serious. Passing should be smooth and responsive.

10. TRANSMISSION. Automatics shouldn't lurch or slip from gear to gear, manuals shouldn't grab or buck or grind, the clutch shouldn't slip or chatter. Check reverse, including backing uphill as well as on the level.

11. BRAKES. They should stop the car quickly, without veering. Test brakes several times on an empty road. Then press brake firmly for 30 seconds. If pedal sinks to the fire-wall, you could have a fluid leak. Before driving, check pads for wear. A hard-driven car is going to show. Check the rotors for scars. People buying used cars often have to have their rotors ground because they're so rough.

Final Advice: Check Consumer Reports to see if your model has ever been recalled, or get the same information free from the National Highway Traffic Safety Administration (800-424-9393).

Slam the door on auto repair rip-offs:

You know the auto-repair horror story. You go in with a simple problem and wind up with a bill twice your car's Blue Book value.

Some repair shops always pad estimates, but especially when they suspect a customer (like most of us) knows little or nothing about cars. Which is a good reason why you should learn the basics of your vehicle. Some auto-repair operations, unfortunately, are more interested in meeting high billing quotas than in meeting their customers' needs.

How to spot dishonest shops:

1. If you're given an estimate that seems way too high. Too many motorists let themselves be fleeced by fast-talking con artists and meekly surrender the keys. Later, after writing an inflated check, they drive home wondering why they didn't show more backbone.

Don't let it happen again. Tell the shop you're going to get a second opinion. If the estimate guy gets angry or refuses, that should tell you something--namely, to leave and never come back.

The Yellow Pages have ads for mechanics who provide second opinions. These free-lancers will inspect your car for a flat fee, without making the repairs themselves or even recommending anyone. So they have no reason to inflate or deflate their estimate.

Auto inspections are a good idea, by the way, before you buy a used car, before and after any major repair job, or before a warranty expires.

You can take this flat-fee inspector's estimate to any repair shop for comparison. But, before turning over your car, insist on signing and approving a written work order and cost estimate.

2. Avoid repair facilities that don't display:
--The red, white and blue sign of the ASA (Automotive Service Association), or
--The AAA (Approved Auto Repair), or
--The NIASE (National Institute of Auto Service Excellence).

Also drive out of any facility that doesn't have a mechanic factory-certified for your make and model.

Final test: See how the new garage handles a simple oil change before you sign your car up for major surgery.

How to find a trustworthy mechanic:

Word-of-mouth is best. Ask around--among family, friends and colleagues--for a recommendation of a reputable mechanic. True-blue grease monkeys are out there, and somebody will know of one--and usually be happy to sing his praises. Be sure to tell the mechanic who recommended him.

When you find a good shop, keep coming back. The mechanic will learn more about your car's idiosyncrasies over time--and value you as a long-term customer.

No-cost auto repairs beyond the warranty:

Dealers don't advertise this, but there are ways to get a recurring car problem fixed at zero cost, even after the warranty has expired:

1. Informal warranties. Some mechanical troubles occur frequently enough with a specific model that dealers are informed the automaker will cover the cost of repairs--even though the problem may not be covered in the original warranty, or the warranty has expired.

Catch: Unlike recalls, where manufacturers notify owners to bring cars in for repair, neither maker nor dealer has to publicly announce an informal warranty. It's up to owners to ask the dealer's service manager if the problem is be covered by an informal warranty. If the answer is no, double check by writing to the Center for Auto Safety, which keeps files on models with problems that might fall under informal warranties. (Address: 2001 S St. NW, Ste. 410, Washington, DC 20009.) Enclose specifics about make and model, details about the problem and include stamped, self-addressed envelope.

If your car is covered by an informal warranty, but the dealer refuses to make the repair, contact the automaker's regional manager and ask a factory rep to review the case. If that doesn't work, contact the local Better Business Bureau or the state Consumer Affairs office. As a last resort, take the dealer to court. (See legal option below.)

2. Pre-existing conditions. If your problem was first reported while the warranty was in effect, but wasn't satisfactorily repaired, the original warranty provisions still apply and the dealer must honor them. That, at least, is the interpretation of most state consumer-protection laws. If your dealer refuses, follow the same steps outlined above.

Legal option: If the dealer refuses to fix your lemon-mobile before the warranty is up, open to the Yellow Pages' Attorney listings. In most cities, you'll discover firms that specialize in auto consumer complaints. These legal eagles love to take on less- than-honorable dealers and manufacturers. Often they'll not only get you satisfaction, but settlement in the process.

Don't be a victim of auto rental ripoffs:

Beware of sneaky add-on fees that can nearly double the cost of renting a car.

Many rental car companies charge an average of $9 a day for a collision damage waiver, a fee consumers pay to protect themselves from liability for damage to the car. According to consumer surveys, these fees increase car rental costs by an average of 42%!

These collision damage waivers are not only expensive, but almost always superfluous. Consumers are being pressured to buy protection they may already have. Many personal auto insurance policies cover damage to rental cars. In addition, American Express and "gold" versions of many MasterCard and Visa credit cards provide insurance for rental cars.

If you call a rental car company, you'll have to ask about liability for damage, because otherwise agents won't even mention this add-on. If you do ask, agents will quote the fee, but you can bet they won't advise you that you may already be covered by your own insurance or credit cards.

This means you'll arrive at the rental counter without having had an opportunity to determine if you need such coverage. Which makes you a perfect sucker for this worthless and hidden add-on, sold in a deceptive manner.

Good news: In Illinois and New York, consumer pressure has forced collision damage waivers to be banned.

Save over $500 a year at the supermarket:

The secret isn't collecting shopping-bags full of coupons, though that will save you considerably. But the real money-saving trick is not falling for all the tricks and ripoffs that supermarkets use against unwary shoppers. Here are some of their favorites:

1. Inflated "economy" or "club-store" sizes. In order to compete with warehouse and club stores, "supers" have taken to packaging items in giant containers or shrink-wrapped multi packs. Don't fall for the "bigger is always cheaper" ruse.

Turning the tables: Take the trouble to read the fine print and do the rough math. You may find the per-ounce cost actually higher on these "economy" sizes. Then ask yourself this obvious question: "How can I be saving money if I'm buying ten times more than I need?"

2. Scanner scams. Those electronic scanner-blips that ring up your purchases are not infallible. Just because a checker isn't punching a cash register doesn't mean errors aren't made. Checkout-scanners can be programmed incorrectly, so prices scanned from the item's bar code are not those lower advertised specials. Inspections of super-markets confirm that most scanner "errors" are made in favor of the market. Of course, the market can just claim "computer error."

Turning the tables: Take a moment afterward, in the car or back home, to compare advertised prices against your register tape. Over the course of a year, by bringing these discrepancies to the store manager's attention, you may end up netting hundreds of dollars in refunds or credits.

3. Coupon mania. No, coupons are not a scam. But, just as with giant-size packaging, you're not saving money by being lured into purchasing products you don't really need.

Turning the tables: Use coupons only for items you would normally buy.

4. Eye-level lures. Supermarkets, like other retailers, stack higher-profit items at or just below shopper's eye level, in easy reach. Cheaper brands, with less mark-up, are relegated to top or bottom shelves. Supers also dangle toys and TV-advertised products where little fingers can grab them.

Turning the tables: Don't get hypnotized by eye-level displays. Focus on price and value, not packaging and placement.

Tip: Go to the department manager (produce, bakery or whatever) with complaints about any grocery practices or products. Then, if not satisfied, talk to the store manager. And check the product packaging to see if there's an 800 number you can call.

Sevenfold savings at the supers:

Since we spend so much of our weekly budget at the local market, it's one of the best places to recoup savings. Here are seven more cost-cutting tips:

1. Shop after you eat. Empty-stomach marketing is asking for trouble. You'll wheel out a cart crammed with goodies you don't really need.

2. Make a list and follow it. Impulse shopping is another way to fill your basket and empty your wallet. Stray from your list only if you spot a good sale item or can't get what you want for a good price.

3. Comparison-shop markets. It takes time to pick up items here and there, but savings will be worth it.

4. Choose off-brands or plain-wraps and save 10% to 15% over brand-name rivals. In most cases, except for the lower total on your register tape, you won't be able to tell the difference.

5. Use coupons judiciously. Like comparison shopping, collecting and redeeming coupons isn't for everyone. But the savings can be dramatic. Check Sunday paper inserts or the junk mail. Or join a club to swap unneeded coupons. (See below for more coupon-clipping tips.)

6. Patronize street markets. Many towns and cities host weekly street markets offering home-grown produce and fruits. Not only do they beat the "supers" in quality and freshness, but generally in price. Another tip: Stop at roadside stands.

7. Don't buy packaging. Mashed-potato mixes or potato chips are mostly air and packaging, offering minimal nutrition at maximum cost. A sack of potatoes will feed you well for a long time for relatively very little.

Capitalize on coupons:

Practical advice for coupon-clippers who want to maximize savings and minimize hassle:

1. Don't overlook sources. Check market ads, newspaper inserts, junk mail preprints, product labels, cartons, store displays.

2. Don't clip coupons for things you don't need--unless you join a coupon-exchange club, where members mail in unwanted rebates and get back those they do want. In-store coupon-exchange bins also allow customers to swap for coupons they want.

3. Develop coupon-brand loyalty.

4. Organize coupons. Sort by category. Then, before going to the market, select those that match your shopping list. As you go through aisles, sort again in checkout-line order.

5. Cash in on coupon-plus savings. Some store ads offer items discounted by both coupons and sale prices, or with bonus mail-in rebates. To check current rebates, subscribe to the Refund Bundle, Box 141, Centuck Station, Yonkers, NY 10710. Price: $9 for six issues.

Prescriptions filled free or half-off:

Prescription medicine costs outpace many salaries and most pension incomes. Some retirees are even forced to do without needed drugs to meet food, shelter and heating budgets. But there are ways for anyone to slash drug company markups, and even eliminate prescription costs altogether.

Here are 6 secrets:

1. Always ask for samples. Most physicians have drawers full of their most commonly prescribed items in sample sizes and will be glad to hand you a few tubes or pill-packets.

2. Buy generics. No-name drugs are identical to brand-names, but cost less because pharmaceutical companies don't have to recoup heavy development and advertising costs. Drugstores love that huge markup more for name brand, over-the-counter painkillers.

3. Avail yourself of senior discounts and/or volume-buying plans.

4. Check to see if your health-insurance contains a preferred-provider arrangement with a specific pharmaceutical firm. If so, you may be able to enjoy a substantial discount.

5. Take advantage of discount offers. Some auto clubs and consumer clubs offer members prescription discounts of 50% or more. Members of British Petroleum's Horizon

Club, for instance, can save up to 60% on most common medications. (For information, call BP Customer Service at 1-800-321-9555.)

6. Buy mail-order pharmaceuticals. These volume discounters offer a full line of products and many fill prescriptions overnight--and for substantially less than drugstores. (See next item for more information.)

Save big with mail-order medicine:

Smart shoppers bypass their local pharmacy--and high pharmacy markups--by ordering prescriptions at a discount via mail-order. Here are 2 of the most popular sources:

* Action Mail Order Drugs, P.O. Box 787, Watersville, ME 04903-0787 (800-452-1976 or 207-873-6226). You can get a quote over the phone, with prices guaranteed for 30 days. Their catalog comes with a $5 coupon good for the first order. Accepts all major credit cards.

* Medi-Mail Home Pharmacy, P.O. Box 1288, Mt. Pleasant, SC 29465-1288 (800-922-3444). Phone for current prices. Free medical ID tag given with new orders. Accepts Visa and MasterCard.

Don't reach for pastel poisons:

Some chemical dyes used to color toilet paper can irritate--and even infect--sensitive mucous membranes. Other chemicals have been known to cause or aggravate nagging yeast infections in women. Plain white is still the best "color" choice for bathroom tissue. It's both safer and cheaper.

New furniture at discount:

One popular way to beat the soaring cost of home furnishings is to go to one of those European- inspired warehouses where you take your dining room set home in a big box and screw it together yourself.

An even cheaper way, of course, is to decorate your digs out of thrift shops and garage sales. But maybe you don't want to surround yourself with someone else's castoffs, or with those sterile, home-assembly modules. What can you do? Paying inflated pricers at big-brand retail outlets?

No.
There's another alternative. You can buy direct from manufacturers or from catalog outlets that purchase manufacturers overrun then sell by mail. Here's a list:

* Ellenburg's Furniture is a catalog firm offering many lines, including C.R. Laine, National Mt. Airy, Henry Link, Link- Taylor, Pulaski, Hooker and Lexington. Catalog costs $6 and is available by calling 800-841-1420.

* Cherry Hill has been selling hundreds of major home furnishings brands for half-off, and doing so for 5 decades. They also provide nationwide delivery. For price quotes or a free brochure, write Cherry Hill Furniture, Box 7405, Furnitureland Station, C1, High Point, NC 27264 or phone 800-328-0933.

* Designer Secrets sells bedspreads, window coverings, drapes, fabrics and furniture at 75% discounts. Firm also offers a special "design-a-room" service. Their $2 catalog is available by writing Box 529, Fremont, NE 68025 or phoning 800-955-2559.

Bargains: going, going, gone:

You may think auctions are only for country-clubbers who arrive in Rolls-Royces. That image does fit a small percentage of bid-and-buy events--fine art and antique offerings from Sotheby's, say, or sales of vintage automobiles.

But all kinds of bargains are going under the gavel these days, from private auctioneers and government agencies. The trick is finding them, since the best deals are found at auctions not widely promoted, and thus attended by fewer bidders.

Here's how to track them down, then how to play the bidding game for the biggest savings.

* Government Auctions:
1. Department of Defense. Everyone's heard about Pentagon boondoggles--$500 toilets seats, $50 hammers. But you can find many household items among military surplus--VCRs, stereos, even used cars--at bargain-basement prices. Auctions are generally held monthly. Check your local military base's Defense Reutilization Marketing Office for information.
2. U.S. Trustees Bankruptcy Auctions. You'll find these in your local paper's classifieds. There's no way of predicting what sort of stuff you'll find, but prices should be inviting.
3. RTC. The Resolution Trust Corporation "FF&E" and Real Estate Auctions not only offer significant discounts on real estate, but on other items, such as furniture and fixtures.
4. City, county and state auctions. Agencies at every level-- from motor-vehicle departments to utilities to law-enforcement-- put surplus merchandise on the block, including impounded or confiscated vehicles. To find those nearby, call the individual department or agency.

Auctions to avoid: U.S. Marshals Service Auctions and U.S. Customs Auctions are both hugely popular and well advertised. So chances of getting a good deal are the proverbial slim and none. IRS auctions and those held by the General Services Administration also fall into the over-bid, overpriced category. Likewise, big estate sales tend to be well publicized and well attended.

Auctiongoer's 101:

* Don't get auction fever. Study the catalogue and decide what you'll bid on before you go--and settle on your top figure. You can and should talk to appraisers about value, but stick to what the item is worth to you.

* Know in advance the "conditions of sale"--what kind of payment is acceptable, cash on the barrel or credit terms (if any).

* Arrange to take home your purchase. Auctioneers are not responsible for delivering a car to your doorstep, for instance. If you're bidding on a vehicle, bring your driver's license or make towing arrangements.

Don't buy fool's gold:

"Lowest prices in gold jewelry," "best deals in town." Such ads almost sound like sidewalk vendors, the kind who whisper, "Wanna buy a necklace, 24 karats?" How can you make sure a gold chain, say, is actually the advertised 18 karats, not 14K or 10K? (Note: 14-karat gold, the usual grade sold in U.S. stores, is 14 parts gold and 10 parts base metal. 18-karat gold is more common in Europe.)

Fact is, even an expert jeweler's eye can be fooled. Most stores rely on the reputation of the manufacturers or wholesalers. And so should you. Which means don't buy from street-corner or swapmeet vendors, who don't have to stand behind what they sell. You may be purchasing gold electro-plate--a thin layer of gold, 10K or more, over base metal.

Better yet: Go to a reputable store, then check the item's karat content mark and the manufacturer's registered trade-mark. Always get a detailed receipt, including a description, the fineness of gold in karats, plus a statement of the retail-er's return or exchange policy.

Caution: A 14K mark on the clasp of a necklace only applies to the clasp. Look for the karat mark on a loop or tab attached to the chain. If you don't see it, don't buy the item.

Check workmanship, looking for flaws, patchy gold color, crude detail work, bad soldering. Best bet: Ask to use the jeweler's loupe or bring your own.

Mail-order outlets and TV shopping channels offer competitive prices and easy ordering, but refunds and exchanges will cost you money and time.

And never buy gold jewelry as an investment or inflation hedge. Unless it's an antique with artistic value, the resell market is dismal--you'll be lucky to get less a fifth of what you paid. Better gold investments are newly minted bullion coins, such as Canadian Maple Leafs, Kruggerands or American Eagles.

Never pay full price:

You don't have to go to a foreign country and visit an exotic bazaar in order to bargain. Dickering over price is alive and well in the U.S.--and right on your favorite shopping street.

Most merchants are willing to negotiate price, to take a smaller profit rather than miss a sale. The missing ingredient is your willingness to question the number on the pricetag.

That doesn't mean your local shopkeeper will enjoy prolonged haggling or an elaborate back-and-forth ritual like some Turkish carpet seller. Best bet is to be discreet and show that you're a serious shopper with serious money to spend.

Then, in a friendly and non-confrontational voice, tell him or her how much you're prepared to pay. If you have a flexible range, ask if the store can "do better on this price?" Ironically, if you're prepared to walk out without the item, you may walk out with it for 20% to 40% off the original price.

Don't get burned by soldering-iron bandits:

Last year American consumers spent around $30 billion on new home electronics--TVs, VCRs, camcorders, CD players, etc. And another few billion, according to electronic industry statistics, were spent on repairs to keep those gizmos working.

Unfortunately, millions of that went for fraudulent repairs. Some went to out-and-out shysters, and some to bunglers, whose slipshod work can convert your refrigerator into a sauna.

In either case--incompetence or malfeasance--you need to take precautions. Here are the basic Do's and Don'ts:

1. Don't pick the shop with the biggest Yellow Page ad. Sure, it's a temptation to call the outfit that promises the fastest service in the biggest, boldest type. But a lot of these ads are misleading. And once they know you're desperate to get that VCR working, they can--and will--make you pay through the nose.

2. Do consult product manufacturers for referrals to an approved repair technician. Most are better-trained than workers at mom-and-pop businesses. While there are many reputable small repair shops, larger businesses that pay technicians an hourly salary have less incentive for dishonesty than smaller owner-operated concerns.

3. Don't be in a hurry. Visit a repair shop minus the broken item to get a feel of a technician's knowledge of a particular problem. Ask questions and look over the operation for signs of slipshod habits.

4. Do budget ahead of time for repairs. These can run into big bucks, even when handled by honest servicemen. Some large- screen TV tubes cost well over a thousand dollars.

5. Don't respond to flyers and come-ons guaranteeing rock-bottom prices. You're asking to get zapped for a phony fix-it job.

6. Do take your case, if you've been cheated, to a Better Business Bureau or your state's Bureau of Electronic and Appliance Repair.

Don't fall for extended warranty traps:

In the excitement of making a big-ticket purchase--like a new TV or refrigerator--you may nod "okay" when the salesman says, "I assume you'll want to get our extended warranty, it's really a terrific deal--covers you for repairs and defects up to five years."

What you should say is "No"--and firmly. If it was such a good deal, they wouldn't be slipping it in as an after-thought. The fact is, extended-service guarantees are only good deals for the stores and manufacturers, who regard them as pure profit. Here's why:

* Most big-ticket items already come with a manufac-turer's warranty, which usually covers you for the first three years. So in most cases you're buying duplicate coverage. Also: many credit cards double manufacturer's warranties. (To file a claim, mail a copy of the warranty to your credit card company with store receipts.)
* Defects in electronics usually show up during the six- months' burn-in period. So odds are great that anyone who falls for these warranties will never use them.

Protect your privacy:

The Privacy Rights Clearinghouse, a nonprofit con-sumer organization, has released a "Privacy Survival Guide" to help consumers take control of personal infor-mation circulated about them. For a free coy, call the clear-inghouse at 800-773-7748. Among the tips:

* Find out what is in your credit report. To protect your-self from being harmed from incorrect information, order your credit report once a year and make sure it is accurate.
* Find out if information about your medical history is stored in the Medical Information Bureau, the insurance industry data base.

* Avoid entering sweepstakes and other contests if you want to stay off mailing and telemarketing lists aimed at "opportunity seekers."

* Be especially protective of your Social Security number. Your credit report, bank account and other financial records are usually linked to it.

* Think twice before joining a "buyer's club" or using a debit, credit or check-cashing card when paying for groceries. Your name and address can be linked to the list of the purchases created when your groceries are "read" by the price scanner.

NOTES

_____

_____

_____

_____

_____

_____

_____

_____

_____

_____

_____

_____

_____

_____

Chapter

Cheap and Free!

24

Freebies for the asking:

Many companies give away samples and items for promotional purposes. The federal government, of course, gives things away for its own reasons. These 25 giveaways have a little something for everyone (though it's possible some offers have been discontinued). Request products by name, include any postage fee or self-addressed, stamped envelope requested and allow 4 to 6 weeks for delivery.

1. EDMUND SCIENTIFIC CATALOG - Edmund Scientific,101 E. Gloucester Pike, Barrington, NJ 08007.
2. FREE DOG BOOKLETS for a self-addressed, stamped envelope, from Gaines Obedience Lists, Box 1007, Kankakee, IL 60901.
3. FREE GOLF PAMPHLETS from Golf Digest, 495 Westport Ave., Norwalk, CT 06856.
4. RECIPE BOOKS - Ann Pillsbury Kitchens, Pillsbury Co., Minneapolis, MN 55402; and fromNestle Test Kitchen, 100 Bloomingdale Rd., White Plains, NY 10605.

5. FREE BOOKLET - 'WHAT EVERY WOMAN
SHOULD KNOW BEFORE BUYING A CAR' - from
Ford Motor Co., Marketing Programs,
P.O. Box 2959, Detroit MI 48202.
6. FREE TOURIST INFORMATION -
from Australian Information Bureau,
636 5th Ave., New York, NY 10020;
Austrian National Tourist Office,
500 Fifth Avenue, New York, NY 10110;
Belgian National Tourist Office,
745 Fifth Avenue, New York, NY 10150;
Bermuda Department of Tourism,
630 5th Avenue, New York, NY 10021;
British Tourist Authority,
40 W. 57th Street, New York, NY 10019;
Canadian Consulate General,
1251 Avenue of the Americas, New York, NY 10020;
Danish Tourist Board,
655 Third Avenue, 18th floor, New York, NY 10017;
Finnish Tourist Board,
655 Third Avenue, New York, NY 10017;
French Government Tourist Office,
610 Fifth Avenue, New York, NY 10020;
German National Tourist Office,
747 Third Avenue, New York, NY 10017;
Greek National Tourist Organization,
645 Fifth Avenue, New York, NY 10022;
Irish Tourist Board,
757 Third Avenue, New York, NY 10017;
Italian Government Tourist Office,
630 Fifth Avenue, Suite 1565, New York, NY 10111;
Luxembourg National Tourist Office,
801 Second Avenue, New York, NY 10017;
Netherlands Boards of Tourism,
355 Lexington Avenue, New York, NY 10017;
Norwegian Tourist Board,
655 Third Avenue, New York, NY 10017;
Portuguese National Tourist Office,
590 Fifth Avenue, New York, NY 10036;

National Tourist Office of Spain,
666 Fifth Avenue, New York, NY 10022;
Swedish Tourist Board,
655 Third Avenue, New York, NY 10017;
Swiss National Tourist Office, Swiss Center,
608 Fifth Avenue, New York, NY 10020;
Turkish General Consulate Information Office,
821 United Nations Plaza, New York, NY 10017.

7. FREE TICKETS TO TV SHOWS - from ABC, Guest Relations, 7 West 66th St., New York NY 10023, or ABC, 4151 Prospect Ave., Hollywood, CA 90027.

8. FREE BABY CARE AND NUTRITIONAL BOOKLETS - from Gerber Products,445 State St., Fremont, MI 49412.

9. FREE RETIREMENT MONEY GUIDE - 42-page booklet, from American Assn. of Retired Persons, 215 Long Beach Blvd., Long Beach, CA 90801.

10. HOW TO DETECT COUNTERFEIT MONEY - from Research Dept., Federal Reserve Bank of Atlanta, Box 1731, Atlanta, GA 30301.

11. INTRODUCTION TO MODEL RAILROADING - 29 cents postage - from Model Railroader Magazine, 1027 N. 7th St., Milwaukee, WI 53233.

12. FREE BOOKLETS FROM U.S. GOVERNMENT (hundreds available) - write Consumer Information Catalog, Dept. B., Pueblo, CO 81009.

13. FIRST AID CHART - from Health and Welfare Division, Metropolitan Life Insurance, One Madison Avenue, New York, NY 10010.

14. BOOKLET "AUTHOR IN SEARCH OF A PUBLISHER" - 40 pages from Vantage Press, 516 W. 34th St., New York, NY 10001.

15. SKY AND TELESCOPE MAGAZINE - free copy from Sky Publishing, 49 Bay St. Road, Cambridge, MA 02138.

16. FREE SOFTWARE - can be downloaded from many BBS (computer bulletin boards) using your computer and modem.

17. OFFICIAL SOFTBALL RULES - send 29 cents postage to Hillerich & Bradsby Promotions, Box 18177, Louisville, KY 40218.

18. BOOKLET "KAMPGROUNDS OF AMERICA" - lists 800 campsites - send first-class stamp to KOA Handbook, Box 30558, Billings, MT 59114.

19. CHESS LIFE AND REVIEW - one free magazine from U.S. Chess Federation,186 Rt. 9W, New Windsor, NY 12550.

20. MOVING WITH CHILDREN BOOKLET - from Consumers Services Dept., United Van Lines, United Drive, Fenton, MO 63026.

21. TRAVELING WITH YOUR PET BOOKLET - Alpo Pet Center, Box 4000, Allentown, PA 18001.

22. AMERICAN BABY MAGAZINE - 3 issues for $1 postage, from American Baby Magazine, 352 Evelyn Street, Paramus, NJ 07652.

23. HOW TO ESTABLISH CREDIT - booklet from American Express Company, Consumer Department, American Express Plaza, New York, NY 10004.

24. HOW TO GIVE UP CIGARETTES GUIDE - from American Cancer Society, Distribution Department, 4 West 35th Street, New York, NY 10001.

25. STAMP COLLECTING FOR FUN - booklet from U.S. Postal Service Advertising Director, 475 L'Enfant Plaza West S.W., Washington DC 20260.

Scents for pennies:

If you want to pay top-dollar for colognes and perfumes, then patronize the fancy boutique counters at local department stores. If you want to get the same scents for a lot fewer bucks, check out mail-order perfume houses. And consider their plain-wrap brands--the same chemical make-up, the exact fragrance of prestige labels, minus trademarks and sexy packaging, for drastically fewer dollars. For catalog and samples, send $1 to Paris Perfumes - samples - $1 postage, Paris Perfumes, 25 Aladdin Avenue, Dumont NJ 07628

Consumer goodies from cyberspace:

Shoppers who can navigate the Internet can land on some great bargains. On the World Wide Web check out Consumer World and find updated sections for discount shopping in everything from autos to zircons. Just point your web browser to:

http://www.consumerworld.org/edgar/pages/bargains.htm

Other freebie-finders are on Internet Newsgroups-- consumer- oriented bulletin boards with hundreds of daily postings offering freebies, cheapies and cost-cutting tips. Here are three of the most popular, which you can visit or subscribe to:

alt.consumers.free-stuff
misc.consumers.frugal-living
misc.consumers.house

One recent promotional giveaway was a free mousepad from AT&T. The offer may still be in effect, or AT&T may have other freebies. Check it out at the phone company's World Wide Web site:

http://www.att.com/hotquiz/

Browser Beware: Because there's no censorship on Internet postings, these newsgroups may contain a certain percent- age of come-ons masquerading as legitimate bargains.

Free phone cards:

FREE PHONE CARDS--Here are two phone-card give- aways from the alt.consumers.free-stuff newsgroup:

1. Free 5-minute long-distance phone card from the FX cable network, call: 1-800-FXFXFX1 and press "2" at the first prompt, "1" at the second, and "3" at the trivia ques- tion prompt. You also can order a free Do-It-Yourself FX logo from the same #.

2. Free discount calling card. With the ATN (American Travel Network) Discount Calling card, you pay no surcharge and a low per-minute rate. Typical rates for Big Three (AT&T, MCI and Sprint) cards are 25-30 cents per minute plus the 80 cent surcharge per call. Send for a free brochure/application, return the application and in 10-14 days you'll get your card. Send SASE to: POWER COMMUNICATIONS, 234 Tennis Villas, St. Helena, SC 29920.

Cashless craze: barter-mania:

More people are using barter as an alternative to paying with scarce cash. This ancient system of doing business is gaining popularity around the country, as more and more people are discovering old-fashioned swapping as an alternative to paying with hard currency.

These days, the practice once referred to as horse trading--now called bartering--is usually done via computer.

Bartering groups are one way to go. These trade groups generally have a membership cost and receive a commission on all transactions. Most members are small-business owners, but many are individuals with a specific service to offer--such as giving massages or manicures--or people who have a onetime big-ticket item, such as real estate, to exchange.

Example: a hotel operator barters room nights (which would otherwise go empty) for new upholstery and a resurfaced parking lot to printing services for brochures--without paying a penny. Bonus: the hotel also gets repeat clientele.

Example: A woman, married to a businessman, who was a member of a local trade exchange, barters with her obstetrician for the delivery of her daughter. The doctor agrees to the arrangement after he learns a local pet store owner is also in the trade exchange. The doctor's payment for his medical services? Alaskan malamute puppies.

An estimated 550 trade exchanges with about 250,000 members swap about $1.8 billion of goods and services a year, says the National Assn. of Trade Exchanges. Another trade group, the International Reciprocal Trade Assn., estimates that since 1990 barter has grown 10% a year.

Members of bartering clubs have a bit more flexibility. Rather than trade their products or services directly for someone else's, members build up credits--sometimes called "barter bucks" issued in coupon form--which can be exchanged for anything offered by another barter group member.

Even if a desired product or service isn't offered by a barter club member, sometimes it's possible to persuade the person to join the system. In many cases, that is accomplished by simply pointing out the alternative.

Drawbacks: You can't always spend credits the way you'd like to, and it can be difficult to determine what services are really worth. And some people still feel it's somewhat shady, but the IRS has recognized bartering as a legitimate way to do business--provided the barter bucks are treated as real dollars when it comes to paying taxes.

Bartering groups should **provide** members with account statements and a year-end 1099-B form that lets the government know how many trade dollars exchanged hands. Sales tax on all items and services also must be paid by members up front and in cash.

Prospective members should learn whether members are charging manufacturers' suggested retail prices or what the item goes for in the market. They should also ask for a list of the exchange's members to see if the group offers goods and service they want, and ask current members whether they're happy with the exchange and ask the Better Business Bureau whether it's had complaints.

* Barter groups are listed in the Yellow Pages under "Barter & Trade Exchanges" for those interested in joining.

Chapter

Holiday and Travel

25

Free upgrades from coach to first:

f you fly 25,000 miles during a calendar year on a single frequent-flier plan, in most cases you'll receive "elite-level" status for the following year. Aside from the fancy name, this has some very tangible rewards:

* You'll earn more miles for the same flights--often 25% to 50% more.
* You'll also qualify for free upgrades from coach to first class, without using earned miles. So great is this deal that if you're short a thousand miles of 25,000 near year's end, you should buy another ticket just to reach the coveted level.
* Two More Ways to Wrangle Free Luxury Upgrades:
1. Passengers bumped from reserved coach seats are sometimes offered immediate space in first class. Other airline inducements and ways to maximize your chances of getting bumped are listed below.
2. Check your ticket codes. A "Y" on your ticket in the box marked "fare basis" usually means your ticket is full-fare coach, which may allow you to upgrade to first class for free (or a nominal charge).

Get bumped and go to the bank:

Travelers who are "involuntarily" bumped from a flight are usually offered a ticket voucher for a later flight. If this happens to you, here's a little-known secret: You don't have to accept the voucher. According to Department of Transportation regulations, you're entitled to cash instead of a ticket voucher.

And if getting bumped causes you to be more than an hour late, the airline owes you up to $200 or the value of your one-way ticket--whichever is less. If the inconvenience means you'll be more than two hours late, those amounts are doubled.

What if you volunteer to be bumped? In that case, hold out for the best deal you can make. Airline officials may offer a free standby ticket to a domestic location. Instead request a confirmed ticket anywhere the airline flies.

You can take this one step farther: Get yourself bumped "accidentally on purpose" to qualify for the cash or voucher. It's not that difficult. Reserve a heavily trafficked flight and reach the gate after boarding has been complet-ed. Once on the plane, stall to make sure your seat will be taken. Then, at the last minute, collar a flight attendant with your boarding pass and an anxious expression--and get ready to deal.

Get bumped, sue the airlines and win!:

One tenacious passenger actually sued an airline for being bumped. In 1986, William West got bumped from a flight from Great Falls, Montana. He declined the airline's offer of "denied-boarding compensation," claiming his business loss in missing his flight was far greater. He sued for $10,000 and won. The airline claimed he had no right to sue. The case went to the U.S. Supreme Court, which refused to hear the airlines' appeal.

Best times for riding the bumps:

One seasoned bumper goes to the airport on the busiest day of the year--the day before Thanksgiving--with no other purpose than to get bumped from flight after flight.

The resulting handout makes frequent flier plans look pretty measly. For a few hours' inconvenience, a passenger can get credit toward a round-trip ticket and possibly negotiate for much more.

"If it works with my schedule, I'll definitely go out of my way to try to get bumped," says Michael McColl, author of "The Worldwide Guide to Cheap Airfares."

And with fewer empty seats on many flights and carriers, airlines are likely to face more oversold flights and to be looking for more volunteers to give up their seats.

If volunteers are scarce, passengers willing to wait for the next flight can frequently bargain for more than the $150 to $200 first offer from an airline. Some boast of getting as much as $1,000 in free tickets for giving up their seats.

When and where are the best chances of getting bumped?
--Flights between an airline's two hubs generate heavy traffic and provide flights often enough that a wait for the next one shouldn't be too long.
-- Friday afternoons, when business travelers are trying to get home.
-- Sunday flights, when vacationers head home after staying the required Saturday night for a discount ticket.
-- Monday mornings.
-- Holidays--even better than Fridays, Sundays or Mondays. The Wednesday before Thanksgiving, the Sunday after, the days around Christmas and New Year's can be the best times to get bumped.

Airlines intentionally sell too many tickets for some flights, assuming some passengers will never show up. But last summer, when airlines set records for full cabins, bumping increased 14% from the summer before. Airplanes are expected to be even more cramped this summer.

If you're bumped, you still get to use your ticket and, depending on the delay, you should be able to get meal and hotel money from the airline.

Cut your airfare in half: fly courier-class:

Among seasoned travelers, signing on with a courier service has long been known as an entree to travel bargains, with fares often 50% or more below normal ticket prices. You learn to travel alone, pack light and fit your itinerary into someone else's corporate schedule. In return for accompanying a package or documents--usually on both portions of a round-trip flight--you get a great price.

And business is booming. The International Assn. of Air Travel Couriers estimates that 25,000-35,000 flights yearly leave the United States with a courier aboard. That figure is rising--because international commerce continues to increase, and because it takes more time and money to send materials unaccompanied than to match them with a passenger.

The result is an opportunity for international air travelers willing to accompany time-sensitive original documents and other entirely legal materials. And though New York remains the capital of U.S. courier travel, West Coast firms send couriers to a dozen cities around the world, particularly along the Pacific Rim.

"Let's say you were going to Bangkok," says the international director for a Los Angeles-based courier firm. "You sign an agreement saying you'd go on such-and-such date and return such-and-such date. You put up a security deposit to insure you'll come back when you're supposed to come back. Then you report to the airport."

A traveler usually needs to be 21 years of age and have a passport. Depending on the country of destination, a visa may also be required.

Since courier companies only need one seat per flight, the traveler usually must be willing to go alone or have companions pay full fares. Seats can usually be reserved up to three months in advance.

The traveler must pay the courier company well in advance, usually with cash, a cashier's check or a money order, to hold his or her seat. (Courier companies, which have contracts with airlines that allow them to buy tickets at deep discounts, usually buy seats in travelers' names, and hold tickets until handing them over at the airport on the day of departure.) Often the courier firm asks the traveler to put up a refundable deposit of $100-$500, which might be a personal check or a credit card number. (Would-be couriers who cancel, forfeit a portion of their fare, the amount growing larger as departure date draws nearer. Couriers who fail to arrive on the proper return flight lose their deposits.)

Since the courier service is using the traveler's checked baggage allotment, the traveler usually must be ready to fit all he or she needs into a single carry-on bag, small enough to fit in an overhead bin or under a seat.

Travelers are usually asked to appear at the airport two or more hours before departure time. Only then do they receive their ticket from a courier company representative. Usually, the traveler receives only tickets and a manifest, and never sees the baggage that is nominally his or hers.

Many first-timers are wary about what exactly they'll be accompanying. Don't worry. The cargo is usually paper-work--business papers, legal papers, blueprints and so on--

-and occasionally small objects such as computer parts. The materials usually have little value except to the sending and receiving parties.

U.S. Customs officials in New York and Los Angeles say they've had no problems with contraband associated with courier companies. Still, one Customs spokesman urges that travelers make sure they check out the company, and that everything's kosher. One way is to ask how long the company has been doing business and what airlines its contracts are with. For more reassurance, offer to make your advance payment in person at the courier company's offices. They may appreciate the chance to have an advance look at you, too.

After clearing immigration overseas, couriers usually hand off their folders to a company representative in the customs area. (Many companies give travelers pouches with logos on them, so couriers can be recognized when they arrive.) Some couriers never even see a baggage-claim room; others spend a few aggravating hours waiting for their cargo to clear. Once through customs, travelers are on their own until their return flight.

Often, travelers are asked to pledge they won't drink any alcohol on their flight. (Courier companies don't like the idea of drunks carrying their logo around.) Shorts and suggestive T-shirts are often forbidden, as are jeans or sneakers. Backpacks are often discouraged because they are thought to attract extra attention from customs inspectors. When an inspection lasts longer, precious time is lost.

Anyone serious about flying as a courier can get details of the trade and listing of courier companies and offerings in "The Insiders Guide to Courier Travel: How to Travel World-wide for Next to Nothing" ($14.95; published by The Intrepid Traveler, P.O. Box 438, New York 10034). Though the book is frequently updated, readers should note that courier company destinations, schedules and prices change frequently.

Other information sources:

* "Airfare Secrets Uncovered: The Insiders Guide to Huge Discounts on Air Travel" by Sharon Tyler and Matthew Wunder ($14.95, published by the Universal Information Corp., distributed by ProStar Publications, P.O. Box 67571, Los Angeles 90067; 310-287-2833).

* International Assn. of Air Travel Couriers (P.O. Box 1349, Lake Worth, Fla. 33460; 407-582-8320). For a $35 annual fee, the association sends members "The Shoestring Traveler," a 6-times-a-year newsletter that includes updates on courier offerings and other discount travel opportunities.

* Air Courier Association: 303-278-8810.

More airfare-reducing tips:

Your travel agent may assure you a certain fare is rock-bottom. However, that may not always be true. There may be lower fares under conditions which your agent might overlook or simply not mention unless you ask specifically.

Always make a point of inquiring if there are lower rates:

-- at designated off-peak times?

-- if you agree to an earlier departure date, or fly on a different day, or week or month--or even time of day?

-- if you wait for a seasonal or promotional fare?

Safer seating aloft:

There's no absolute answer on where to sit in an airplane to maximize your survival chances in case of a crash. It depends on the nature of the disaster. But the best bet, for those who reserve a seat in economy class, is sit in an exit row. At least you'll have a chance to get out quick, if necessary.

Caution: Airlines often require passengers in exit rows to demonstrate an ability to move quickly and open the exit hatch in case of emergency.

Other considerations: Seats over wings may provide a smoother flight, and seats all the way forward a quieter one. Those up front (especially first-class) also breathe slightly fresher air with less carbon dioxide. Farther back, recirculated air tends to be more stale, which can cause headaches, dizziness and drowsiness.

Seats facing interior dividers separating classes offer more leg room, but may present hazards. According to statistics from the National Institute of Aviation Research (at Wichita State University in Kansas), head injuries suffered by people sitting behind dividers--hurt during sudden stops or turbulence--are the top noncrash injury concern aboard airliners.

Note: Boeing 777s are the only aircraft in compliance with the latest FAA regulations dealing with interior walls.

The Bright Side: If you look at actual airline-safety statistics, you'll find plenty of reassuring news. Statistically, you stand a better chance of winning a state lottery jackpot (1 in 4 million) than of being killed in an airplane crash (1 in 4.6 million). Pretty terrific odds--so keep flying.

Which frequent-fliers fly highest?:

According to a recent issue of InsideFlyer magazine, United Mileage Plus has the best frequent-mileage plan. United was named as the top choice by 22% of the magazine's readers. Delta SkyMiles, at 19%, and American's Advantage program, at 17%, were close behind.

Less close was the voting on the best hotel program--Hilton's Honors was voted best by 45% of the readers, with Marriott Honored Guest Awards a distant second at 26%.

The awards reflect preferences of very frequent fliers--the average person casting a vote has almost 1 million miles or points, according to InsideFlyer.

New frequent-flier strategies:

Most of us are aware airlines have upped frequent-flier mileage-total requirements for free tickets from 20,000 to 25,000. So what's the best way to reach that higher target? Here are three strategies:

1. Get a list of your mileage plan's partners and patronize them. You don't have to leave the ground to rack up frequent-flier mileage. All plans have formed partnerships with hotel chains, car-rental agencies, long-distance telephone carriers, restaurants, florists, credit-card companies, and so on. On residential long-distance calls, for instance, you can get five miles for every $1 spent. And you rack up extra miles by using mileage-plan plastic for expenses you wouldn't normally charge-- things like your insurance or mortgage.

Caution: Don't inflate your credit card bill with such charges unless you clear your balance every month. Otherwise you'll run up high interest charges.

2. If you're an "infrequent" flier, stick with one airline. Totals will accumulate more quickly than using different carriers.

Caution: Some plans expire earned miles at the end of the third calendar year after they're earned. Check your monthly statement for such a provision.

But softer expiration rules may be on the horizon. Alaska Airlines recently became the first carrier to go back on its expiration policy, changing it so that miles no longer expire after three years.

Mileage on most carriers expires after that period, with the notable exceptions of Continental Airlines, USAir and Trans World Airlines--all carriers that have been troubled or faced severe competitive pressures in recent years. Delta Air Lines adds a wrinkle: You keep your miles as long as you fly Delta once every three years.

The best part of Alaska's change may be for travelers who make heavy use of its partners around the country and the world. Miles earned on Alaska's partners--including Horizon Air, SAS, TWA, Northwest Airlines, British Airways and Qantas Airways--and credited to an Alaska account will also no longer be subject to a three-year expiration.

Airline expiration policies differ. America West, for example, automatically issues mileage certificates once an account reaches 20,000 miles. Those mileage certificates expire three years from the date of issue. The mileage is not subject to expiration while it is accruing in the account, however.

American Airlines, United Airlines and Northwest Airlines, on the other hand, bank miles for three years at a time by calendar year. Any miles earned in 1993, for example, will expire at the end of 1996, regardless of whether they were earned at the beginning or the end of 1993.

If no combination of miles is enough to get you a free ticket award, you can still get some benefit from your expiring miles by donating them to charity. American, for example, has a Miles for Kids program that uses donated miles for charities. United also allows you to sign miles over to a charity of your choice.

3. Don't redeem miles at the last minute. Spur-of-the-moment plans to cash in your credit may run afoul of heavy airline traffic. Some carriers charge service fees up to $100 if given less than a month's notice when redeeming miles. Airlines usually only reserve about 7 percent of seats for frequent fliers. If those seats are gone when you ask, you're out of luck.

Six to eight months in advance is the optimum advance time to make your reservations. With this early start, you've got a good chance of getting into that chosen 7 percent.

4. Always study your mileage plan's newsletter. These often contain special offers and changes to their programs and mileage awards.

Fare-reducing trick to avoid:

Airlines are cracking down on "back- to-back" ticketing, a common technique for reducing air fares. A typical back-to-back ticketing situation involves buying two round-trip discounted tickets, one originating in the city from which the traveler departs and the other originating at the traveler's destination. By using half of each ticket for a single trip, the traveler can sometimes save hundreds of dollars over the price of full-fare.

It's attractive to business travelers because it sidesteps Saturday-night stay-over rules, created specifically to encourage leisure travelers to take trips they might not otherwise take over a weekend. Business travelers who plan ahead could even use both tickets for two separate midweek business trips. Using both tickets is called "nesting," because one round trip is "nested" inside of the other round trip.

But now such methods may backfire. Northwest Airlines, for instance, has amended its rules to cancel any reservation or confiscate any ticket on the spot if it even appears to be a back-to-back ticketing arrangement.

The rule changes make it possible for reservation or gate agents to decide if someone appears to be using two tickets to get around the rules. The agent can act if he or she even thinks a passenger is breaking the rule.

Currently, Alaska Airlines, American Airlines, America West Airlines, Trans World Airlines and USAir have specific rule language prohibiting back-to-back ticketing. United, Delta and Continental do not have specific language to prevent it, but do have rules that may cover this situation, namely that the airline will charge people full fare if they are discovered in violation of Saturday-night stay requirements.

For some travelers, however, the issue comes down to basic consumer rights. "They can't stop people from buying two fares," one advocate says. "They don't have a right. If they don't like the way people buy tickets, then change the fares."

Another popular but unethical strategy is "hidden-city" ticketing, invariably prohibited by the airlines. "Hidden-city" ticketing is used when a flight to a city beyond the stopover or hub city is cheaper than flying to the hub itself. Travelers buy a ticket to the distant point but get off at the hub. However, airlines now detect that the connecting ticket was not used and increasingly will bar a return flight when the traveler tries to return home from the hub.

Fly cheap with ticket consolidators:

Airline consolidators buy up airlines' excess ticket inventory at discounts, then resell tickets to individuals and travel agents. You can ask your travel agent about consolidators' tickets at reduced rates.

Caution: Always pay for such tickets with a credit card in case problems occur. And be aware that consolidators' tickets may not be changeable or refundable.

Airfare scam alert:

Some ticket "discounters" trumpet rock-bottom airline fares, but then when you call or show up, there are no seats available at those prices.

Tips: Don't be talked into a higher fare when the advertised one is unavailable; use travel agents or reputable airline ticket wholesalers.

How to pick a travel agent:

The best savings come to those willing to bargain directly with airlines and hotels. But if you lack the time or inclination, find a travel agent you trust. A good one can save you hundreds of dollars on even a short jaunt.

Caution: While there are many topnotch agents, there are also many who know little about geography and are more interested in booking you with cruise lines, airlines and hotels that kick back the highest commissions.

Most reliable agents are accredited by the Airline Reporting Corp. (ARC) and belong to the American Society of Travel Agents (ASTA). Many have taken courses to become certified travel counselors (CTC) through the Institute of Certified Travel Agents.

Best way to find a good agent is just like locating an honest auto mechanic: ask friends, co-workers and relatives.

Specialty travel savings:

Keeping tabs on travel savings can be a full-time job, especially with so many mileage programs, airline discounts and promotional tie-ins from rental car companies, hotels, restaurants and credit card issuers.

Solution: Along with the multiplication of programs has come a mini-boom in travel newsletters geared toward helping weary road warriors sort it all out. Here are 5 of the best:

* The Affordable Caribbean features tips on how to find budget hotels, restaurants and other attractions in the area (12 issues per year, $39.95; write to The Affordable Caribbean, Department MTG, P.O. Box 3000, Denville, NJ 07834).

* Travel Alert Bulletin warns readers about trouble spots, ranging from airport construction to pending airline strikes to security issues (10 issues for 5 months, $39; write to Travel Alert Bulletin, Nationwide Network Inc., P.O. Box 1922-M, Saginaw, MI 48605). Nationwide Network Inc. also issues a weekly Fax Travel Bulletin, with updates on everything from airfare wars to short-term airline or hotel discounts that could affect your travel plans.

* Best Fares is a monthly magazine on discount travel, which also tracks the latest travel promotions. ($78 for corporate edition, $58 for consumer edition; write to Best Fares Inc., 1111 W. Arkansas Lane, Suite C, Arlington, TX 76013).

* Frequent Flyer magazine, published by Official Airline Guides, contains news and features of interest to frequent travelers (12 issues per year, $24; write to OAG Travel Magazines, 2000 Clearwater Drive, Oak Brook, IL 60521).

* The Consumer Reports Travel Letter (12 issues per year, $39; call 800-234-1970) includes information useful for business travelers, but its primary focus is the leisure traveler.

Better rooms at lower rates:

You may think you'll get the best room rate by calling the hotel chain's national reservation number. Fact: Local hotels can adjust room rates in response to demand or seasonal factors that don't apply on a nationwide basis. So you may get substantial savings by making reservation directly with the hotel where you want to stay.

Call both the local hotel reservation desk and the chain's nationwide toll-free reservation line, then reserve through whichever quotes the best rate.

Two more hotel strategies:

1. You may be able to save as much as 35% on your hotel expenses just by asking for the corporate rate. Don't expect this to work at a popular resort area, but it's a good tactic in any major city that has stiff competition among hotels.

Conditions: Usually you'll have to reserve in advance to receive the special rate, and may have to stay a minimum number of nights each year. But some hotels offer the corporate rate to anyone who writes or faxes for reservations on company letterhead stationery.

2. Reception clerks may just stick you into a basic room, even when your nightly rate entitles you to a better one. Make it standard policy to utter these seven magic words: "Got a nicer room at this rate?" More times than not, you'll get upgraded. And if you're not pleased, go back and ask again.

Overlooked hotel savings:

A lot of folks are members of AAA, but lose benefits by failing to mention their membership when they check into a hotel. AAA has negotiated member discounts from 5% to 25% at thousands of hotels nationwide. Always take out your card and show it to the hotel clerk.

Getaways for gratis:

Some folks with a limited budget and unlimited wanderlust travel the globe for nothing--or close to nothing. The trick is to fit your vocational or avocational skills with the wide world of travel opportunities. Here are some free passes to global adventure:

* Travel agents enjoy hefty travel discounts and freebies. Not surprisingly, many people become agents for no other reason than to take advantage of this bonus.

For information on starting your own home-travel agency (or even a full-service office) contact the Independent Travel Agencies of America Association (ITAA) in Rochester, NY. Call: 800-947-4822.

* You don't have to be a travel agent to get a free get-away. Other travel-related businesses have similar opportunities: car rental, hotels, etc. Cruise ships, in particular, hire people with experience in everything from food service to entertainment.

For information on travel-industry opportunities, call 800- 929-7447, and order "Jobs for People Who Love To Travel" ($12.95) or "The Complete Guide to International Jobs & Careers" ($13.95), both by Ronald and Caryl Krannich.

* Tour escort or planner opportunities. Round up enough friends or family for a vacation on the same plane, and you may be able to fly free. Some airlines require a group of 10, others 15. Free seats may be available for organizing ski trips and cruises.

Of course, you can't just show up at the airport with your group and ask for your free ticket. You must cut your deal in advance with a travel agent.

Tip: For bringing in extra business, you might also request a percentage of agency commissions. If you do this sort of thing often enough, you're in the travel business and your trip expenses are deductible.

* RV delivery. Many retirees and others are getting paid to take RV vacations. Here's how it works: Makers or dealers need people to deliver brand-new recreational vehicles to new owners-- which could be anywhere in the U.S. or Canada. You get paid--some people earn up to $50,000 a year. You can usually pick your own route, so long as you reach the destination in a week or so. And you sleep free in the RV. It may even be possible, with a few phone calls, to arrange another delivery job to get you home--and get paid both ways!

To qualify, you must be between 18 and 88 with a driver's license, though some companies do prefer retirees because of their maturity. No special training or license is required, since RVs aren't trucks. To find these deals, check your Yellow Pages under "Motor Homes" or "Recreational Vehicles."

* The U.S. government "speakers program" pays experts to travel abroad and take part in symposiums and seminars. The program includes many subjects: economics, international political relations, U.S. social and political processes, arts and humanities, science and technology.

For more information, contact: U.S. Speakers, Office of Program Coordination and Development, U.S. Information Agency, 301 4th St., SW, Room 550, Washington DC 20547. Or call: 202-619- 4764.

* Travel free with a laptop and an idea. The angle here is to learn to write about your holidays and make somebody pay you for it. You also get to deduct your expenses.

It's not easy, of course. Many magazines and newspapers are downsizing and cutting back on such jobs. But there are still openings for freelance writers (and photographers), who can enjoy many promotional freebies offered by travel companies and resort destinations.

Do you have to be a Pulitzer Prize writer? No. Editors are always looking for unique travel experiences and alternative viewpoints. Contact your local paper, ask for the travel editor and tell him or her about any interesting travel plans (the more exotic the better), then inquire about submitting an article when you return. The answer will likely be yes (without a commitment to publish, of course).

Next step: Contact the PR department of the resort (or nearest tourist bureau), explain your "tentative assignment" to do an article about them and ask for any cooperation they might be able to extend. You may be surprised at the lavish response. Even if you're not offered discount airfares or lodging (in exchange for a favorable story), you may get VIP handling. And you'll be establishing your journalistic credentials in the process.

Note: Free-lance writers who incorporate locales in non-fiction or fictional works can legitimately deduct travel expenses.

Travelwise tips:

Some travel hassles, especially those you encounter on foreign jaunts, can be reduced or even eliminated by simple practices. Here are four secrets of savvy travelers:

1. When going abroad, always take along a xerox of your passport and tickets and keep the xeroxes separate from the originals, in case they're lost or stolen. You should also keep a separate record of your travelers' checks numbers. It's also smart to carry two extra passport-size photos so a replacement passport can be made up for you at the nearest U.S. consulate or embassy.

2. Keep an inventory of valuable luggage items for insurance purposes should any bags be lost. Again, keep this list elsewhere than in your luggage.

3. When leaving the U.S., always have proof of purchase of any valuables you're taking with you. On your return you will be able to show U.S. Customs officers the item in question was not purchased out of the country and that therefore no duty is owed.

4. To foil airline-baggage bandits, wrap luggage with bright electrical tape. Crooked luggage-handlers will think twice about breaking the seal and getting caught. Even if they do, you'll know about it on the spot and can report the theft immediately.

Tips for thrifty travelers:

Some budget-busting aspects of travel blind-side you. An example are hotel add-ons like minibar and phone charges. Some veteran business travelers have figured out ways to trim these expensive little extras. Here are four such secrets:

1. Cut long-distance charges from your hotel room. To avoid the hotel's per-call surcharge (around $2), don't hang up between calls. Just hit the pound sign (#) to get a new dial tone.

2. Don't get hit with inflated minibar charges. Buy snacks and soft drinks elsewhere and bring 'em in. If you must succumb to one of those overpriced sodas or wine coolers, replace them with the same item bought in a local store. If you don't know when your hotel restocks the minibar, replace items by the next morning.

3. Instead of paying for business or first class, fly coach and wrangle extra leg-room by reserving an exit-row seat.

4. Upgrade rental cars and hotel rooms. On the same principle as flying coach and getting business-class perks, make a basic booking at a car rental or hotel, then ask for an upgrade. It works more often than you'd think.

Sightseeing secrets:

Ever pull up to a popular spot--like Old Faithful or the Lincoln Memorial--and find yourself lost in hordes of bused-in tourists? You probably couldn't wait to get away from the very spot you'd dreamed of seeing. Maybe you figured there was no way around it. But most tour buses arrive according to known schedules. With one advance call to the attraction or nearest tourist office, you can discover the best hours to arrive without being overrun by bus passengers.

Early cruise-bookers get the savings:

Cruise lines used to offer deep last-minute discounts. But these days early-bookers get the best deals. Most lines announce schedules a year or two in advance, and offer discounts from 15% to 40% to those who book first. Prices gradually increase up to the sailing date. Not surprisingly, you must put down a deposit a year before sailing.

If you're well informed, you can still catch a few last-minute sales. This happens when a particular cruise is badly undersold. But those who book early can participate as well, by getting a price-protection plan which guarantees any last-minute price cuts will be passed along to them as well.

Catch: It's up to those customers to notice any late-breaking discount and ask for the rebate.

Picking the best cabin on your cruise:

Nothing can spoil an idyllic cruise like lousy accommodations. A berth next to the engines, underneath the jogging track or the disco, for instance, can ruin your night if you're a light sleeper.

But you don't need to reserve the most deluxe stateroom to rest in comfort. Here's what you really need to know when selecting a cabin:

* **Size:** Cabins costing the same can differ in size, particularly on older ships. Cabins amidship on older vessels are usually the largest, but ask your travel agent to supply you with the dimensions of several cabins within the class you want. Don't be fooled by the photos in brochures; compare them with the deck plans to get an idea of the actual size.

* **Location:** On some of the larger ships, the cabins can be quite a distance from the nearest elevator. Also, party animals may want to be close to the disco, but party poopers will want to avoid it and other clearly noisy night spots. Study the deck plan carefully before choosing.

* **Price:** Booking far in advance also puts you in line for an upgrade if an unsold higher-priced cabin becomes available at the price you paid. (Make sure your travel agent has you on the upgrade list.) Don't count on last-minute bargains--there are fewer of them than there used to be.

* **Bargain Cabins:** Outside cabins with views that are blocked by lifeboats or other obstructions often are discounted. Cabins that accommodate four people are, of course, cheaper per person than the standard room. Also, if you don't intend to spend much time in your cabin, consider one with no view at all.

* **Deck by Deck:** The aft end heaves less than the bow, but engine noise can be a problem. The bridge deck houses expensive, spacious luxury cabins and penthouse suites. At this height, though, there can be more pitch and roll, particularly in the bow and stern. Cabins often have large outside windows, verandas or balconies. The Boat or Upper Promenade deck has more expensive accommodations than lower decks, but the view is sometimes partly blocked by lifeboats.

The Promenade or "Prom" Deck is also usually the "entertainment" deck, near bars and restaurants. It can be noisy. Some cabins even look out on a public deck. The Main Deck can also be noisy, especially beneath the entertainment areas on the Prom above, but it usually has the most horizontal stability. Try to pick a cabin that doesn't connect internally with another. Lower Decks (usually designated alphabetically) have cheaper cabins, but they can be affected by noise, especially amidships, close to engine and near the stern.

NOTES

_____

_____

_____

_____

_____

_____

_____

_____

Chapter
_____ **26**

Leisure Deals

Secrets of getting fine restaurant service:

Though the '90s have been called the Decade of the Customer by business management gurus, bad or indifferent service at many restaurants is still the order of the day.

You know the nightmare: You're stuck in a corner next to the kitchen door or the busboy's tray. You wait 15 minutes for a waiter or waitress to notice you, 30 more to get a meal that should take 10 minutes, then you're lucky if the server ever visits again to see what else you might need, or even to refill your coffee cup.

But this doesn't happen to everyone. Some people always get good tables, prompt service, hovering attention. And they get it wherever they go, at roadside diners as well as big-ticket restaurants.

What's the secret? The most obvious trick is that these diners don't accept bad treatment, don't take whatever table they're given, don't suffer in silence. They know squeaky wheels get oiled. They ask for what they want-- and expect to get it.

"Do you have a better table available?" These seven simple words nearly always work--if delivered with a smile and an expectation of being obliged. Or be specific: "Could I please be moved to that table by the window?"

Enquire how long a particular dish will take to be served. This places the server on notice, and he or she will remember--if he or she wants a tip. If you've got theater tickets and a deadline, let them know in advance. After your food is delivered, request the server "please check back in a few minutes."

Final tip: Don't make unreasonable demands. Don't ask that the music be changed or turned off, or bombard the waiter with dietary requirements and expect the chef to prepare a special meal.

If, in spite of every precaution, you still get rude service, contact the manager later and let him or her know your problem. You may get invited back for a complimentary meal.

Half-off discounts a hotels and restaurants:

There are many hotel and restaurant discounts available. Some are great, some are scams, but the right booklet can easily pay for itself with the first reservation you make.

Here's how most programs work. Once you buy an annual book (with an ID card valid for one year), you get a 50% discount at selected hotels and restaurants. Most programs offer further discounts, such as special offers from cruise lines and airlines and discounts of 10% at chain hotels.

Cautions: The discount is calculated from the hotel's advertised "rack rate," much higher than most shrewd travelers pay, and the discount offer is based on availability, so if your chosen hotel expects to be 80% full on the night of your stay, it probably won't be willing to rent any rooms at half-off. And these programs are designed for travelers who book their own trips. There's no financial incentive for a travel agent to recommend them.

The biggest discount-book company is Entertainment Publications Inc. (40 Oakview Drive, Trumbull, Conn. 06611; 800-445-4137), which publishes more than 125 different discount books. Consumer Report's editors recently evaluated 10 discount book programs and pronounced Entertainment their favorite "for extensive coverage and diversity."

Most Entertainment books are keyed to specific North American cities, from Fresno to Toronto, cost $28-$48, and offer discounts on hotels, restaurants and various leisure activities. The company also publishes a National Dining and Hotel Directory (50% off at more than 2,800 hotels, and 20% off at 2,000 restaurants, for $37.95) and an Entertainment Europe book (more than 700 hotels in 35 nations for $48). And the Entertainment people are starting to market discount books based on specific areas within Europe.

Another popular program is Encore Marketing International (4501 Forbes Blvd., Lanham, Md. 20706; 800-638-0930). Members get directories and cards; participating hotels offer 50% off or a second night free (guests must stay two nights before they can capitalize on their membership). Members are also told of special package travel offers, rental car deals and other potential bargains. A year's Encore membership costs $49. The directory includes 4,000 U.S. hotels, another 1,000 foreign properties and several hundred restaurants, which offer discounts varying from 20% off to second meals for free.

Other programs:
      * America at 50% Discount (1031 Cromwell Ridge Road, Baltimore, Md. 21286; 800-248-2783). Includes roughly 1,300 hotels in the United States and Caribbean

with half-off offers. Membership cost is ordinarily $49.95, but in a special promotion, callers who mention "Money" magazine are quoted a discount rate of $19.95.

* Carte Royale (131 N. State St., Suite J, Lake Oswego, Ore. 97034; 800-847-7002). A relatively new program that specializes in more upscale properties. Includes about 800 hotels, the vast majority of them in the U.S. Membership runs $71 for a year, or $131 for two years. (Life membership runs $301.)

* Great American Traveler (P.O. Box 27965, Salt Lake City, Utah 84127; 800-548-2812). Includes about four foreign hotels and 2,000 in the United States. No restaurants. Usual membership rate is $49.95, but a current special is being offered at $29.95.

* ITC-50 (6001 N. Clark St., Chicago, Ill. 60660; 800-342-0558). Includes about 2,700 hotels worldwide at 50% off, along with 300 restaurants with discounts of some kind. Cost: $36 yearly.

Get the best seats every time:

There's something you really want to see--a big concert, a sporting event, a musical. So you call early, ask for great seats, pay top dollar. Then you show up and find you need binoculars to find the stage. You wonder:

Who are those people up front? How do they rate? Who do they know? One thing you can be sure of: Those ringsiders didn't go the sucker route like you did.

Here are 3 secrets for getting "up close and personal":

1. Ask at the last-minute. Often you can get the best seats available--front row, box seats at concerts--the night of the show. What happens is this: Season subscribers to some series events can't come every night. So they call the box office and let them sell the seats (a tax-deductible donation for the subscriber). You appear at the ticket window an hour before showtime and ask if box seats are available. If they are, you can "trade up" by paying the difference between your ticket and the price of a box seat.

These kinds of priviledges will never be available for those who book in advance.

2. Ask about "meal tickets." At some concert venues, the best seats in the house--that is, the front third of the auditorium--are reserved for those willing to fork over $20 or more for an entree, a beer and a tip. That's in addition to the concert ticket charge. The food may be mediocre at best, but the location may be well worth the surcharge. Diners often have the opportunity to buy a better seat, and the theater, by selling food, gets to exact a premium on those seats.

3. VIP programs. Some of us pay top dollar and still end up in the cheap seats. If you're willing to pay the freight, you can guarantee results by buying series or VIP tickets. These premium programs usually include preferred parking and other amenities.

Catch: Such tickets are usually marketed first to companies and well-to-do individuals. If you're not in this category, try and make a friend who is--and get invited down-front on a regular basis.

Where to get those hard-to-find videos:

The big video chainstores, like Blockbuster and Wherehouse, concentrate their inventory on the current popular titles. So if you're looking for an older movie or a foreign flick or any offbeat titles, you're probably out of luck. Unless, however, you tap into the fantastic video mail-order world. Here are some of the outfits that specialize in harder-to-find films. Some rent and sell only through membership deals, while others are happy to deal with one-time customers:

* Alternative Videos, P.O. Box 270797, Dallas, TX 75227, 214-823- 6030. Specializes in films for those of African descent. The catalog is free, but there's a $25 basic membership charge before you can rent or purchase.

* The Brauer Beta Catalog, 26 Emery Lane, Woodcliff Lake, NJ 07675; 800-962-7722. For those who still insist on clinging to the old Beta machine. There's a free catalog, and they sell packs of blank tapes.
* Columbia House, 1400 N. Fruitridge Avenue, Terre Haute, IN 47811; 800-262-2001. Good deals at first, but read the agreement and respond to your mail--monthly selections are sent unless you say in advance that you don't want them. Free catalog.
* Critics' Choice Video, P.O. Box 749, Itsaca IL 60143; 800-367- 7765. The free catalog of 2,500 titles is just the tip of the iceberg; some of the unlisted titles are available via another special 900 number. Call for information.
* Dave's Video, the Laser Place, 12114 Ventura Blvd., Studio City, CA 91604; 800-736-1659. Ten percent discount on all discs. Dave's insists it can and will find any title currently available on the laser disc format. Catalog available on request.
* Festival Films, 2841 Irving Avenue S., Minneapolis, MN 55408; 612-870-4744. Specializes in foreign titles at lower-than-average prices. The price of the $2 catalog is applied to your first purchase.
* Filmic Archives, The Cinema Center, Botsford, CT 06404; 800-366- 1920. One of the few mail-order houses that only sells to teachers. Three free catalogs: one each for teachers of English, history and kindergarten through 8th grade.
* Ken Crane's Laser Disc Superstore, 1521 Beach Blvd., Westminster, CA 92683; 800-624-3078. The superstore claims to have over 100,000 titles available--with an updated list every week. Every purchase is automatically discounted by 10 percent.
* Mondo Movies, 255 W. 26th Street, New York, NY 10001; 212-929- 2560. The avant-garde specialists, from raunchy B-movies to hard- to-find, experimental art-shorts. Free catalog.
* Science Fiction Continuum, P.O. Box 154, Colonia, NJ 07067; 800- 232-6002. The name says it all. The catalog costs $1.
* Whole Toon Catalog, P.O. Box 369, Department LM, Issaquah, WA 98027; 206-391-8747. A treasure trove for animation lovers. The $2 catalog also specializes in imports.

The best mail-order music sources:

Just like videos, most music chainstores stock only titles from the big record companies. To get a good selection from the hundreds and hundreds of smaller labels, you need to check out mail-order catalogs. And you'll discover a wealth of new titles, as well as some of the greatest names in blues, jazz, rock, country and classical.

* Bomp!! Rare Records, P.O. Box 7112, Burbank, CA 91510. The Bomp!! catalog doesn't look like much from the outside, but it contains lots of hard-to-find music available at reasonable prices. The catalog isn't available by phone, so you'll have to send a written request to their Burbank address.
* Cadence, the Review of Jazz & Blues, Cadence Building, Redwood, NY 13679; 315-287-2852. Cadence is both a catalog and a magazine. Every month it dedicates about 100 pages to jazz. But it's the 40 pages of rare albums for sale that really makes Cadence special. Over 9,000 titles are indexed and alphabetized by record label. Cadence can be ordered for $3 at the phone number above. A year's subscription is $30.
* Double Time Jazz Records, 1211 Aebersold Drive, New Albany, IN 47150. Another well-organized jazz outlet, it offers nearly 5,000 titles. All eras of jazz are represented, but Double Time is especially good at locating out-of-print items. Write to receive a free catalog.
* Music in the Mail, P.O. Box 1, Brightwaters, NY 11718. Music in the Mail is for serious classical collectors only. Several hundred classical labels are represented in their catalog. They offer a wide variety of hard-to-find new and used CDs, plus LPs. Prices are reasonable, and requests are shipped once a month. The catalog costs $1.
* Rhino Catalog, 10635 Santa Monica Blvd., Los Angeles, CA 90025; 800-357-4466. The label bills itself as the top archival record label in the country; the extensive catalog bears out that claim. It covers music from the '50s to the '90s, with a great selection of funk anthologies and rock compilation albums. The catalog is free. Requests are handled at the 800 number.

* Rounder Records, One Camp Street, Cambridge, MA 02140; 617-354- 0700. A small label with a lot of character. Rounder releases a consumer catalog about once every eight weeks, filled with eclectic zydeco, blues and world music titles.

* Time Warner & Sony Sound Exchange, 45 N. Industry Court, Deer Park, NY 11729; 800-521-0042. Sound Exchange is a catalog released seasonally by entertainment mega-corps Sony and Time Warner. There's an artist index across from the order form that allows you to quickly scan for what you want, and there are several pages of $7.98 CDs. Catalogs and orders are facilitated through the 800 number.

Get tickets to attend your favorite TV show:

A favorite place for vacationers to New York, LA or Chicago is to attend the taping of a network or syndicated TV show. Here's how to arrange it:

In New York:
* The Late Show With David Letterman, Ed Sullivan Theater, 1697 Broadway, New York, NY 10019; 212-975-4321. Despite the show's name and airtime, taping starts at 5:30 p.m., Monday through Friday. Stand-by tickets are given out each weekday at the Ed Sullivan Theater box office, starting at noon are limited to one per person. You must be 16 or older to make the cut.
* Saturday Night Live, 30 Rockefeller Plaza, Room 1719, New York, NY 10012; 212-664-4444. Hard to get, so plan ahead. Taping is at 11:30 p.m., with an open dress rehearsal earlier in the day. Reserved tickets for both are distributed by lottery; get standby tickets at 9:15 Saturday morning in front of the GE Theater. You must be at least 12 to attend.

In Chicago:
* Oprah Winfrey Show; 312-591-9595. All you have to do is call one month in advance to reserve a free seat. You

will be asked to give your name and phone number, and someone will call you to confirm if they have a seat on the day you'd like.

In Los Angeles:
    * The Tonight Show With Jay Leno, 300 Alameda Avenue, Burbank, CA 91523; 818-840-2222. Write at least three weeks in advance. You will receive your tickets 10 days before you are scheduled to be on the air, provided you are at least 16 years old. The tickets say you should be at the taping by 4 p.m., but those who know say it's best to be there by 3 p.m.

Best and cheapest places to buy your computer:

Computer shopping is taking over car shopping as a debated topic in some circles. Not only do people argue over what's the best kind of computer to buy--there are too many variables to answer--but where to buy. Everybody's seen those computer superstore ads in the paper. But that's just the top of the list. There are also the mom-and-pop stores, secondhand dealers and mail-order houses, all claiming to be the outlet of choice for discerning and cost-conscious PC shoppers.

Here's an annotated rundown:
    * Discount warehouses. These computer supermarkets carry most of advertised brands at bargain prices. This works well for those who already know what they want before the walk in.

The downside is you aren't likely to get the kind of service that you will from smaller retailers. But since most computers come with all the software and manuals you need to get up and running, lack of sales support may not pose a major problem.

    * Stereo and home electronics shops. TV, stereo and appliance retailers are making more and more shelf space available for computers these days. You can certainly find a

bargain there, but stick to well-known brands. And don't put much credence into anything the sales staff tells you. These folks may know woofers and tweeters and video equipment, but probably can only give you dangerously misleading information about computers.

* Mail-order houses. Some of the biggest computer manufacturers established themselves by selling directly to customers via mail order. Dell is the prime example, with Gateway right behind. Pick up any computer magazine and you'll find mail-order ads for these and other makers. They offer computers at great prices, and also the option of a machine custom-built to your specs. Products are delivered usually via UPS within a couple weeks.

Downside: You obviously can't drop by a mail-order house to get your monitor fixed if it breaks down. So check with friends who've ordered from a particular mail-order house to see if they were satisfied. And also enquire about any gripes in regard to technical support phonelines.

* Used machines. Budget-conscious shoppers can save big by foregoing the latest souped-up models and buying from the aftermarket. Of course, they also have to do without any kind of warranty. This may not be as risky as it sounds, since once a computer's chips are "burned in," they may go years without any significant problem. For further information, check out the adds in local computer papers or call the American Computer Exchange (800-786-0717), which matches computer buyers and sellers.

Mail Order Computer Firms:
* Dell Computer Corp., 9505 Aboretum Blvd., Austin, TX 78759 (800-289-3355).
* Gateway 2000 Inc., 610 Gateway Drive, North Sioux City, SD 57049 (800-846-2000).
* Tangent Computer Inc., 197 Airport Blvd., Burlingame, CA 94010 (800-800-5550).

Kindergarten guide to the World Wide Web:

The biggest buzzwords these days are Internet and World Wide Web. Some say they're revolutionizing the world; others claim they're overhyped. But millions of people don't really know what they are--or how to go about checking them out to see what all the excitement is about.

The fact is, browsing the web is as simple as remote-surfing your TV. Here's all you need to know to get started:

* What is the Internet?
It's really a network of networks--a mass of computer networks linked globally. It was originally started about 20 years ago by universities and the military, to share information computer to computer. It's growth in the last few years, however, has been explosive. The Library of Congress is now on the Internet, as are most government departments and most university libraries in the U.S., and many abroad. You can exchange information with people from around the world.

No one runs the Internet. It's a massive, community-maintained-system, created by the people who participate in it. While there are no governing bodies or censorship (a topic for heated debate these days), there is something called "Netiquette"- -a mode of decorum favored by experienced net users. For instance: Don't type e-mail or bulletin-board messages in ALL CAPITALS (considered equivalent to shouting); don't barge in on others' bulletin-board conversation, or resort to insulting or profane language ("flaming").

* What is the World Wide Web
The World Wide Web, often abbreviated as WWW, is a way to access the resources of the global Internet in an attractive, easy-to-use graphical format. World Wide Web documents are creating using a hypertext language called HTML (more on this later). When you enter the Web, you may feel as though you are in the middle of a magazine.

* How to get on. All three major online commercial services-- America Online, CompuServe and Prodigy--now offer World Wide Web browsers. There are also many mom-and-pop Internet providers. And recently AT&T entered the business, offering 5 free hours a month of Internet access to its phone customers. This may be the easiest way for newcomers to get involved.

* Once you have access, what do you do? Or how do you find anything amid the vast and growing array of Web offerings? The truth is, Web navigation is really pretty easy; that's sort of the point of the Web. The Web itself contains all the indexing, pointers and assistance you're likely to need, as long as you know where to look.

Each time you tell your browser to plug into the World Wide Web, it will in all likelihood pull up a "home page" first. The most popular browser, Netscape, pulls up the Netscape home page, for instance.

Many home pages contain links to Web searching tools. Some browsers even have built-in buttons to take you to a sort of front-end that pulls together access to various Web resource databases. It's really important to know about these places on the Web; they can serve as a terrific gateway to everything else out there in Web-land.

One favorite organizing site is the Yahoo Page, accessible at http://www.yahoo.com. (This cyberspace address starting with "http" is known as a Universal Resource Locator, or URL for short. Each specific site or file on the Internet has its own unique URL.) Established by a couple of Stanford University graduate students, Yahoo has grown into a huge and wonderful index of much that is worth seeing and doing on the Web. Resources on Yahoo are organized by subject, but you can also search Yahoo's index for whatever you're after, and it will generate a custom menu for you.

Another World Wide Web starting point is Global Network Navigator, at http://gnn.com/. Like an increasing number of really good Web sites, this one asks you to register, but there is no charge. Once you're in, you'll find all kinds of goodies, including the Whole Internet Catalog, which brilliantly organizes Internet resources for you, even offering a preview before you go. And let's not forget http://www.cern.ch/, the Web's original home, in Switzerland.

Probably the best-known Web search tools are Lycos at Carnegie-Mellon University (http://lycos.cs.cmu.edu) and WebCrawler at Washington University (http://webcrawler.cs. washington.edu/WebCrawler/).

Generally, you will be asked to type in a word or phrase, and the search tool you've chosen will look for Web page addresses or descriptions that contain your search term.

So now you know how to find Web resources on baseball, for instance, or astronomy. The fun of the Web, of course, is in finding what you aren't looking for. Remember to use your browsers' bookmark function when you find a place you like.

For instance, quite a few museums are reachable through the Web, which is an ideal medium for this sort of thing. Perhaps the best-known site of this kind is an entirely virtual institution, Nicolas Pioch's WebMuseum at http://www.emf.net/louvre/. This incomparable resource offers a host of great paintings from many museums, including the Mona Lisa.

For those interested in Internet commerce, visit http://www.commerce.net. There are also lot of places to go shopping, such as the Internet Shopping Network at http://www.internet.net/.

A good way to find government resources on the Web pages is http://www.fie.com/www/us--gov.htm. And you can find the Prez at http://www.whitehouse.gov, or the Library of Congress, at http://lcweb.loc.gov/homepage/lchp.html.

For less lofty fare, visit http://www.cbs.com, where you can search an archive of David Letterman's top 10 lists.

* Serious Web Searching

If you're really serious about searching for stuff on the World Wide Web, not to mention elsewhere on the Internet, you might want to consider InfoSeek, a fee-based Internet searching system.

Why pay when there are free alternatives? It depends on how seriously you're searching. Free search engines are sometimes busy, for instance, or index only keywords and not the full text of the data to which they refer.

InfoSeek offers deeper searching, scouring a vast database of World Wide Web information, or the entire body of more than 10,000 Usenet newsgroups, or various computer magazines and news services, depending on your choice. InfoSeek is at http://www.infoseek.com.

* More About Home Pages & HTML

One of the nice things about the World Wide Web is that anybody can set up a home page. The tool for creating a Web page is something called Hypertext Markup Language, or HTML.

Creating the most rudimentary home page is easy. Prodigy users, for instance, can jump WWW to invoke the service's Web browser, and then click the hotlink on Prodigy's home page for creating a home page of your own. All you have to do is fill out the form. These pages really are rudimentary, though, and can't even accommodate a photo. CompuServe and America Online also offer subscribers a chance to set up home pages, as do a number of Internet access providers.

The reason creating a basic page is so easy is that WWW pages are really just text files that contain some relatively simple HTML codes. These codes tell browsers such as Netscape and Mosaic to interpret the text in a certain way. The codes make it relatively easy to show bold-face, different headline sizes, and hypertext links to other pages, files, etc.

HTML may sound complicated, but it really is no big deal. Mostly it consists of simple symbols at the beginning and the end of lines to indicate boldface, italics, new para-graphs and the like. Since these are just text files, you can do the whole thing with a tool as simple as Windows Notepad.

You can get some basic instruction in using HTML from several sites on the Web, including http://www.ncsa.uiuc.edu/General/Internet/WWW/HTMLPrimer.html.

There is also a good deal of software designed to make HTML page creation easy. One very simple program called Web Wizard lets you fill out a form and then gener-ates a basic page--including, if you wish, a graphic. Web Wizard, by David Geller, is available at http://www.halcy-on.com/webwizard. Or you can download another excellent piece of freeware known as HTML Writer, created by Kris Nosack at Brigham Young University.

This program, which you can obtain at http://lal.cs.byu.edu/people/nosack/, makes HTML point-and-click easy, even when you have no real idea of what you're doing. The program makes it just as easy to make your e-mail address, for example, into a hypertext link that brings up a "mailto" form. And it includes a sort of sample template that contains handy HTML codes you can put at the beginning and end of your file. To preview your work, it will launch your browser. Then you toggle back and forth between HTML Writer and the browser, reloading the page off your hard drive each time you change it.

Your home page will probably reside in a sub-directo-ry of your home directory on your Internet provider's com-puter. Links on your home page can refer to sub-pages by their file name (if the sub-pages reside in the same sub-directory) or by their full URL.

One way to get some insight into all of this is to fire up your browser and visit some personal Web pages. When you see one you like, use Netscape's View Source command (or the equivalent on other browsers). This will show you the page as text, with all HTML codes revealed. You can even save this to a file and, replacing the creator's information with your own, make a page that looks the same (be a sport and make some changes so that yours isn't an exact duplicate).

When you've got your page ready, you'll have to upload it to your Internet provider's computer and set the permissions so that everyone can access it. Your provider should have information on such housekeeping matters, which can vary.

* Where to Look

For access to a large index of personal home pages, try pointing your Web browser at http://web.city.ac.uk/citylive/pages.html, where you'll find "Who's Who on the Internet." It's often busy, but when it works, it is a fine place to see what people are doing on their pages. You can even register your own.

What you need to get started on the Web:

Obviously the first item you need to connect to the brave new world of cyberspace is a computer. Specifically:

* A computer with graphical interface, such as those running Windows, Windows 95, OS/2 or a Macintosh. Then you'll need:
* A high-speed modem: Since it can take awhile for graphics to be delivered over phone lines, you're best off with a modem that can process quickly--14.4 bps or faster. The new standard is becoming 28.8 bps, and it'll go higher.
* An Internet account. To access the Web, you need a special, turbo-powered type of Internet account. These cost more than regular accounts (usually about $10-$15 more

per month). Tell your Internet provider you'd like to add SLIP (Serial Line Internet Protocol) or PPP (Point to Point Protocol) to your account.

A cheaper and more popular alternative: a dial-up connection. Your modem dials up the computer of a service provider that has a permanent connection. It's kind of twice-removed connection to the Internet--you're connected to a computer that's connected to a network that's connected to the Internet.

These are called access or service providers. Most universities, and more and more companies, have connections to one of these access providers. If you're a student or an employee at fair-sized company, just call up the internal computer services department and get them to give you an Internet account. Often these are free.

If you are a single user, you can get an account with a dial- up provider--there are hundreds of these around the country. They usually charge a flat rate of about $20 per month with unlimited online time. Or you may get a cheaper rate geared to maximum monthly usage. They will give you an account, which lets your modem dial up their computer, which is already connected to the Internet.

The third and probably the best way for beginners is to access the Internet through a gateway on one of the big online services, such as America Online, CompuServe or Prodigy. (AT&T and other communications giants are now barging into this market with attractive deals.) You can generally download the necessary software from them, and most offer a free trial period, which gives you time to explore what the Net or the Web has to offer.

* Web browser. This is special software than lets you access, view and search for sites on the Web. Browsers are available as shareware--meaning that they can downloaded for a nominal charge from the Internet.

* Decompression and viewer/player programs. It's a good idea for Windows users to have an unZIPping utility, because most of the shareware you'll download will be compressed using the ZIP method. You'll also see audio and video files, such as WAVs and AVIs, that will require separate utilities to be heard or viewed. Fortunately, player and decompression programs for Windows (such as VFD and WinZIP 5.6) and Macintosh can be found on the Internet.

NOTES

_____
_____
_____
_____
_____
_____
_____
_____
_____
_____
_____
_____
_____

Chapter

_____

Big Gaming Secrets   **27**

Sweepstakes winners share their secrets:

Most of us never win lotteries or sweepstakes, the kind that promise big prizes or exotic vacations. But some folks do. In fact, some win again and again, on mail-in sweepstakes and giveaway game shows--and it's not just luck. These people are persistent, but they also know the tricks of the game. For them, sweepstakes are no contest.

It's a booming pastime. Aficionados subscribe to newsletters and gather in computer online "chat rooms" to discuss the hottest contests. Some hard-core entrants spend hours printing their names on index cards and drive for miles to drop off ballots. All perfectly legal, since, in most retail contests, multiple winnings are not against the rules.

One savvy sweepstaker counsels beginners to avoid contests that ask for a processing fee or require a 900 call. "If it's free, it's safe," she says. "But if they ask for money, forget it."

Another contest veteran uses brightly colored and larger-than-normal envelopes if the rules don't spell out a preference. That way, he figures, when entries are dumped into a bag, his ballot may be more likely to be picked. He also sticks pictures of animals on the envelopes and writes lucky messages and sayings.

Others claim money spent on stickers should go for postage, and that there's no way to know if decorations help, but the Post Office definitely doesn't like stickers that may detach.

One multiple-winner says brightly colored, larger envelopes don't help, but multiple numbers of entries can. But she does write cheery messages on the outside of her envelopes, if only to bring a smile to the person pulling out the ballots.

All agree that now is an especially good time to enter contests, as recent postal rate increases have discouraged many people from doing so.

Winners also agree on other jackpot-winning tactics. Here's their list:
* Enter the most obscure and least-known contests.
* Watch for contests in stores and malls.
* Look in newspapers and magazines for ballots.
* Read the fine print for all the rules.
* Enter as many times as you can.
* Write neatly and legibly.
* Use self-adhesive stamps or a blotter to avoid too much licking.
* Stagger entries over time (a few entries each week).
* If only one entry is allowed per household, use friends' addresses (but let them know in case they're called).
* Use colored envelopes.
* Write positive, happy sayings on the envelope.
* Fill ballots out by hand, not with pre-addressed labels.

* Be aware that taxes must be paid on big prizes.
* Make sure your No. 10 envelope (if a contest specifies that) is 4 1/8 by 9 1/2 inches, not 4 1/2 by 9 1/2 inches.
* Subscribe to the Contest News-Letter Deluxe, P.O. Box 3618, Danbury, CT 06813, for contest listings. $25.97 for 24 issues a year or $15 for 12 issues a year.

More sweepstakes newsletters:

Here are some other publications that specialize in giving out the latest info on contests and sweepstakes: The Winning Advantage!-SO, P.O. Box 385, Bloomington, CA 92316-0385; $weepstakes $ecrets, P.O. Box 17885, Indianapolis, IN 46217-0885; RTR-ONLINE, PO BOX 891, NH 03038-0891; Smith Publications, 1011 Boren Avenue #805, Seattle, WA 98104; The "Dreamers" Newsletter, P.O. Box 1244, Naugatuck, CT 06770.

More hints on submitting sweepstakes entries:

Contest pros also point out a little-known secret for increase your chances of winning certain kinds of sweepstakes or lotteries. When winners are going to be picked from a revolving drum, fold your entries diagonally, or pleated accordion-wise. It may sound nonsensical, but there's logic to it. These folds increase surface area, giving the selector more room to grasp it. It's the same reason some entrants use oversized envelopes--if that isn't against contest rules.

Other tips:
1. Print entries clearly in dark ink. Avoid handwriting, calligraphy and peculiar shades of ink. Addresses written with felt-tip pens can smear in the rain.
2. Follow all instructions and rules. You may be disqualified if you don't copy the address exactly as shown.

3. Never accept COD prizes. If you're asked to pay on delivery for some "prize," it's a scam. Refuse it.

4. Beware of phony sweepstakes with entry fees. By law, sponsors may not demand a fee to enter a sweepstakes contest. If you receive such a demand, notify your postal inspector.

Get sweepstakes updates online:

The Internet is fast-becoming the quickest and cheapest resource for those who want to keep current with the latest sweepstakes--and sweepstake scams. If you're a web surfer, check out the Sweepstake Contest Home Page (http://www.sweepsonline.com/). It features daily updates on dozens and dozens of local, regional and national contests. The Home Page publishes complete entry and prize information, as well as addresses of sweepstakes clubs and newsletters.

Further information and bulletin board postings from sweepstakes aficionados can be found in a new Internet Newsgroup: alt.consumers.sweepstakes.

Don't fall prey to sweepstake scams:

Americans lose more than $40 billion a year to direct-mail enticements because they neglect to read the fine print, want something for nothing or simply don't know their rights, according to the director of U.S. Consumer Affairs.

You've seen those official-looking envelopes, bearing promises of riches and exciting awards: "[Your name] is guaranteed to receive a new Chrysler Park Avenue or $20,000 cash!" But did you also notice the tiny print that adds the catch: "If you submit the pre-selected grand prize winning number...?"

Recipients are told to call a 900 number, which costs $3.98 per minute for an average of seven minutes, giving them a bill of almost $30. At the end of the automated conversation, the "winner" often learns the prize is only $1.

Other consumers receive in their mailbox what appears to be a check for $10,000, say. In tiny letters in the lower left-hand corner of the check are the words "not valid."

Others use threats rather than lures to try to snare the consumer. "STOP PAYMENT ORDER" reads the type on an entry form. "BE ADVISED," it continues, "if you do not claim your award check before the current period deadline, we will be forced to issue a stop payment order to the disbursements division."

Such direct-mail and telemarketing gambits have exploded, law-enforcement experts say, and are moving into their next frontier: cyberspace. But even in their current form, such mailbox temptations are spreading like crabgrass, and law enforcement agencies are trying to catch up and crack down.

Company officials mail out hundreds of millions of offerings a year and 60% of those who respond do so by calling the 900 number rather than sending a postcard-- which costs only as much as a stamp. The odds of winning a lavish prize? About 5 million to one.

Most companies will refund the money of any customer who gets a telephone bill and is upset over how much he or she is being billed in 900 calls. Legally you cannot have your local phone service cut off for failure to pay a 900 bill. But the 900 company can sue you, and failure to pay a 900 charge usually results in the customer not being able to call 900 numbers at any point in the future.

If a gift sounds too good to be true, it probably is. Investigators have two simple rules for avoiding scams: Throw away all flyers and mailers using this come-on language and politely hang up on telephone solicitors. Other ways to avoid questionable prize giveaways:

* Beware of huge returns promised for a small investment.
* Never give money to telephone or door-to-door solicitors without verifying their tax-exempt number, solicitor's name, business name, phone number and business address.
* Never send cash, check or a money order to solicitors; ask to pick up your prize in person.
* Be wary of responding to mailers, especially if they require you to call a 900 number to claim a prize. These numbers usually cost $3 per minute.
* If a prize is to be claimed with an 800 number, beware of punching in a code, as it typically crosses over to a 900 number.
* Read all contractual paperwork carefully; then inform solicitors of your intent to have an attorney read all paperwork.
* Be wary of responding to giveaways through on-line computer services such as Prodigy, CompuServe or America Online.

If you get stung, here's what to do:
* Call the police to report what happened. Have available any information you have about the solicitor: name, company name, address and phone number, etc.

To file a complaint, or for more information, contact:
* Your county district attorney's office, consumer protection unit.
* Or the National Fraud Information Center Hotline: (800) 876-7060

Beating one-arm bandits:

The odds at winning at slot machines are not more unfavorable than at most casino games--craps or blackjack or roulette. But all slots are not equally bad. Some pay better than others--and are programmed to do so.

That means they are going through a "pay cycle" rather than a "down cycle." During pay cycles, slots can give back far more than they're fed--and may keep being generous for many yanks or spins. But down cycles can last just as long--and empty your wallet or pocketbook in the process. The trick is to know where the "hot slots" are. Amazingly, that information is available!

* In order to lure people inside, casinos often will program slots near entrances to pay out more frequently. The cascading coins sing a siren song to passers-by.

For a similar reason, machines near gaming tables may be engineered to entice wives watching husbands play. In other areas slots generally have a lesser percentage of jackpots.

* Brand-new machines may be set to pay off more frequently for a few days to attract more business later. Obviously, to take advantage of this, you need to know a new one-arm bandit from an old one, or see it being taken out of its wrappings and set up.

* A third way to find hot slots is to ask a change clerk. Employees are aware of where payoffs are occurring, and casinos actually encourage them to pass the information along. If the information works, give the clerk a tip. If the machines seem cold, however, move on.

How much to play: Most gaming authorities, inside and outside the industry, agree that payoff odds are better when you play the maximum number of coins the machine allows.

Common-sense casino survival guide:

Casinos--whether in Vegas or Atlantic City--are built on two universal truths: The house has the edge, and people like to gamble.

So if gambling is a compulsion with you, you should get help. But if, like most people, you do it for fun, why not try and make your fan last--and improve your chances of winning? By following a few basic rules and strategies, you can.

Basic Money Management Strategy:

   * For each day's wagering, set aside a gambling stake equal to about 40 times your usual minimum bet. Divide that daily stake into two parts. If you're going to be playing on $5 tables, you'll probably need at least $100 per gambling session. (If you find $2 or $3 tables, use a smaller stake.)

   * Don't touch the next session's stake. If you blow the $100, walk away. If you're on a tight budget, stop playing if you lose half your stake.

   * If you double your stake, pick up half your chips. From then on you'll be playing with the house's money. Keep removing chips each time you reach a predetermined winning plateau. If your luck turns bad, walk away when you've lost half what you're playing with.

   * If you're ahead at the end of a predetermined time, walk away. This, of course, isn't easy, and casino owners know it. But it can be done--and you'll feel wonderful back home!

Basic Blackjack:

   The object of blackjack is to have a hand with a point value higher than the dealer's. You must do this without going over 21 points, which is why the game is also known as Twenty-one. A player or dealer with 22 points or more has busted and automatically loses the hand. All numbered cards are worth their face value; picture cards (Jacks, Queens and Kings) are worth 10 points each; and Aces are worth either 1 or 11--which the player gets to determine. Suits and coloreds are disregarded in the game.

   Before each deal, all players make their bets, if you're playing at a casino. Two cards are then dealt to everybody, including the dealer, who is dealt one card face down. A player whose first two cards add up to 21 (i.e., an Ace and a Queen) has a Blackjack and is immediately paid 3-2, unless the dealer also has a Blackjack. Whenever a dealer and player tie, it is known as a push, and neither one wins the hand.

Once everyone has been dealt, players have several options to choose from. The best move depends both on what you have been dealt and on the one exposed card of the dealer's hand. A player can:

* **Hit:** Take an additional card.
* **Stand:** Take no additional cards.
* **Double Down:** Double the original bet and take only one additional card.
* **Split:** When a player has been dealt two cards of identical value (i.e., two 9s), he can choose to double the original bet and play the two cards as two separate hands.
* **Claim Insurance:** When a dealer is showing an Ace, players are invited to claim insurance that the next dealer's card will be worth 10 (and thus Blackjack). Insurance involves risking half the amount of the original bet and pays off at two to one, if the dealer has Blackjack.
* **Surrender:** Forfeit the hand and lose half of the original bet. (Not an option in many casinos.)

Once all the players are either satisfied with their hands or have busted, the dealer proceeds. Unlike the players who get to make choices, the dealer must follow set rules: drawing on any hand that is less than 17 and standing on anything 17 or higher.

Blackjack has become the game of choice for skillful players and card-counting whizzes. (A complete playing strategy and card-counting methods are outlined in Edwin O. Thorp's pioneering book, Beat the Dealer--in fact, outlined so successfully than many practitioners have been barred from playing.) Luck remains crucial, of course, but skillful players can cut the house advantage to just above 1% for certain situations. Best results come in games that deal from a single deck or a shoe with two decks. Four-deck shoes can defeat even card-counters.

When to hit or stand:
* If the dealer shows a 2, 3 or 4, hit if you have 12 or less, stand with 13 or more.

* If the dealer shows a 5 or 6, hit if you have 11 or less, and stand with 12 or more.
* If the dealer shows a 7, 8, 9, 10 or ace, hit if you have 16 or less, stand with 17 or more.

When to split pairs:
* Always split aces, though most casinos allow you take only one additional card on each ace.
* Split 8s unless the dealer shows a 9, 10 or ace.
* Split 9s unless the dealer has a 10 or an ace up.
* Never split 4s, 5s, 6s or 10s.
* Split 2s and 3s if the dealer shows a 2, 3, 4, 5, 6 or 7.
* Split 7s if the dealer's up card is 4, 5, 6 or 7.

Basic Craps:
The bets that are closest to even money are on the Pass Line, Don't Pass, Come or Don't Come. The many side bets and field bets that offer better payoffs also mean you're bucking higher odds in favor of the house.

Basic Poker Strategies:
There are no sure-fire methods of winning at poker, but here are commonsense strategies endorsed by professionals:

1. Stay away from bluffs in low-stakes games, and don't bet too high on a single hand. It will take too many pots to recoup your losses.

2. Play basic strategies, not hunches.

3. When you win a hand, don't make a big deal of it, and don't let a single bad hand get you down.

4. If you lose a big pot, don't try to make it all back on the next one. If you keep losing, pick up your money. It's not your night. Conversely, if you're winning, stick around.

OTHER HEALTH AND MONEY BOOKS

The following books are offered to our preferred customers at a special price.

BOOK   PRICE

1. Health Secrets $26.95 POSTPAID
2. Money Tips $26.95 POSTPAID
3. The Guidebook of Insiders Tips $9.95   POSTPAID
4. Proven Health Tips Encyclopedia $11.95 POSTPAID
5. Foods That Heal $19.95 POSTPAID
6. Healing & Prevention Secrets $26.95 POSTPAID
7. Most Valuable Book Ever Published $9.95   POSTPAID

Please send this entire page or write down the names of the books on another sheet of paper and mail it along with your payment .

NAME OF BOOK_____PRICE_____
NAME OF BOOK_____PRICE_____
NAME OF BOOK_____PRICE_____
NAME OF BOOK_____PRICE_____

TOTAL ENCLOSED$_____

SHIP TO:
Name_____
Address_____
City_____ST_____Zip_____

MAIL TO: AMERICAN PUBLISHING CORPORATION
BOOK DISTRIBUTION CENTER
POST OFFICE BOX 15196
MONTCLAIR, CA 91763-5196